W9-AGD-939

CASE STUDIES IN
CULTURAL ANTHROPOLOGY

GENERAL EDITORS
George and Louise Spindler
STANFORD UNIVERSITY

———————————

THE MARDU ABORIGINES

Living the Dream in Australia's Desert

Map 1: Australia. The approximate boundaries of the Western Desert are indicated by the dotted areas surrounded by the heavy black line.

THE MARDU
ABORIGINES
Living the Dream
in Australia's Desert
SECOND EDITION

ROBERT TONKINSON

University of Western Australia

Holt, Rinehart and Winston, Inc.

Fort Worth   Chicago   San Francisco   Philadelphia
Montreal   Toronto   London   Sydney   Tokyo

Publisher Ted Buchholz
Acquisitions Editor Christopher P. Klein
Senior Project Editor Charlie Dierker
Production Manager Tom Urquhart
Art & Design Supervisor John Ritland

Library of Congress Cataloging-in-Publication Data

Tonkinson, Robert.
   The Mardu aborigines : living the dream in Australia's desert /
Robert Tonkinson. — 2nd ed.
     p. cm. — (Case studies in cultural anthropology)
   Rev. ed. of: The Mardudjara aborigines. c1978.
   Includes bibliographical references and index.
   ISBN 0-03-032282-0
   1. Mardu (Australian people)—Australia—Gibson Desert (W.A.)
I. Tonkinson, Robert. Mardudjara aborigines. II. Title.
III. Series.
DU125.M3T66   1991
944.1'5—dc20   90-23145
                                                 CIP

ISBN: 0-03-032282-0

Copyright © 1991, 1978 by Holt, Rinehart and Winston, Inc.

All rights reserved. No part of this publication may be reproduced or transmitted in any form
or by any means, electronic or mechanical, including photocopy, recording or any information storage and retrieval system, without permission in writing from the publisher.

Requests for permission to make copies of any part of the work should be mailed to:
Copyrights and Permissions Department, Holt, Rinehart and Winston, Inc., Orlando, FL
32887.

Address for Editorial Correspondence
Holt, Rinehart and Winston, Inc., 301 Commerce Street, Suite 3700, Fort Worth, TX 76102

Address for Orders
Holt, Rinehart and Winston, Inc., 6277 Sea Harbor Drive, Orlando, FL 32887
1-800-782-4479, or 1-800-433-0001 (in Florida)

Printed in the United States of America

3 4   016   9 8 7 6 5 4 3 2

Holt, Rinehart and Winston, Inc.
The Dryden Press
Saunders College Publishing

Foreword

ABOUT THE SERIES

These case studies in cultural anthropology are designed to bring to students, in beginning and intermediate courses in the social sciences, insights into the richness and complexity of human life as it is lived in different ways and in different places. They are written by men and women who have lived in the societies they write about and who are professionally trained as observers and interpreters of human behavior. The authors are also teachers and, in writing their books, they have kept the students who will read them foremost in their minds. It is our belief that when an understanding of ways of life very different from one's own is gained, abstractions and generalizations about social structure, cultural values, subsistence techniques, and the other universal categories of human social behavior become meaningful.

These case studies are concerned not only with the description and analysis of distinctive cultures, but also with the ways in which they have been affected by momentous global and regional changes that have occurred particularly during the post World War II period. The case studies include attention to intercultural conflicts and adaptive processes, the struggle for survival as habitat and hegemony are destroyed, and the struggle for identity as cherished beliefs and values are challenged and often degraded by outside forces.

ABOUT THE AUTHOR

Bob Tonkinson is an Australian who received his B.A. and M.A. from the University of Western Australia and his Ph.D. in Anthropology from the University of British Columbia. He taught at the University of Oregon (1971–80) and the Australian National University (1980–1984) before becoming Professor of Anthropology at the University of Western Australia. He has done extensive field research in the Western Desert of Australia and in Vanuatu, and his publications include a monograph, *Maat Village; A Relocated Community in the New Hebrides* (1968), a book, *The Jigalong Mob* (1974), and several co-edited volumes. He is a past-president of the Association for Social Anthropology in Oceania and the Australian Anthropological Society. He was elected to the Academy of the Social Sciences in Australia in 1988 and is currently a member of the Council of the

Australian Institute of Aboriginal and Torres Strait Islander Studies. His regional interests are Aboriginal Australia and Oceania, especially Melanesia; his topical interests include religion, social organization, identity, migration, and change.

ABOUT THIS CASE STUDY

This case study is about the Mardu, a people of the great Western Desert of Australia. Some forty thousand years ago, adventurous migrants from the mainland of Asia found their way into the subcontinent. Others came later, but the largest portion probably came early. For thousands of years, these people have elaborated their culture, less disturbed by outsiders and outside influences than in any other land mass of comparable size. What they created, the adaptations they made to the different ecological circumstances afforded by Australia, with its thousands of miles of seacoast, its tropical areas, and its vast deserts and semi-arid zones, can be described with accuracy in some instances. These can be so described because some of the peoples survived the first stages of the terrible onslaught of the Western world with their cultures intact. In the case of the Mardu, the age-old adaptations appear to have continued without drastic change until quite recently, with a few groups in the remote desert region pursuing a hunting and gathering existence into the mid-sixties. Professor Tonkinson accompanied several expeditions which made contact with these remaining groups and thus had the opportunity to work with them immediately prior to their emigration to settlements.

This study is the result of both his fieldwork with surviving nomadic groups and those Mardu who had come in from the desert and settled around places where they could enjoy some of the benefits of a Western economy. Though these groups work for wages, receive health and welfare benefits, and are increasingly literate and aware of the larger world, they have tried hard to keep the "Law" given to their ancestors by the Dreaming beings who made their geography and gave them their original rituals, rules of conduct, and beliefs. It is rare in anthropological experience that one fieldworker should study the people both in their native habitat, with their traditional culture substantially intact, and under circumstances so radically changed, away from their natal territory and living under the direct influence of a powerful alien culture.

The culture of the Mardu, like all Aboriginal Australian cultures in some degree, is characterized by an extremely simple technology and material culture and an equally outstandingly complex religious and cosmological system. This fact immediately challenges everyday assumptions about the nature of civilization and its complexities. It is a beginning lesson in anthropology. It should change the reader's conception about the nature of complexities in his or her own society and challenge assumptions about the nature of human life, human thinking, and "progress."

Of particular interest to students of anthropology will be the analysis of how rituals and beliefs change in a seemingly unchanging society. Anthropological as well as lay conceptions concerning Aboriginal societies in Australia have tended toward the notion of the static, timeless culture. In contrast, the Mardu, and probably most other aboriginal cultures, welcomed change—so long as it was congruent with existing structures and behaviors. There is no notion of progress in aboriginal cultures, but there is always change. Readers with some background in anthropology will find Tonkinson's analysis of the reality of everyday life and its tensions and conflicts, in the chapter "Living the Dream," particularly interesting. For all readers, the analysis of ritual and religion, of kinship and social structure, will prove informative and challenging. This case study will stand out in the series both because it is about a most interesting people and set of circumstances and because it is written in a perceptive and engaging manner.

This new edition includes information not available when the first edition was published. Chapter 7 includes analyses of Aboriginal emigration and the frontier, the Mission Era: 1946–1969, the rise of Aboriginal self-management, mining, and outstations, and regionalism and fragmentation. Various forces are pulling Mardu society apart, but the deep concern of the older generation—that the "Law" be kept—remains a significant factor in maintenance of tradition. Though the specifics of history and relationships between the Mardu and the powerful alien and imperialistic culture of the European Australians are unique to Australia and the Mardu, the general character of these relationships is universally applicable. The implications of this case study are global.

George and Louise Spindler
Series Editors
Ethnographics, Box 38,
Calistoga, California
94515

Preface

This study reconstructs the traditional culture of some Australian Aboriginal groups living in a remote part of the interior of the continent. It begins with a brief account of the peopling of Australia in order to provide the reader with important background information about the Aborigines. This chapter also introduces the Mardu and their desert setting and concludes with some reflections about doing fieldwork with Aborigines.

Chapter 1 outlines the religious fundamentals of the Mardu worldview, for no adequate understanding of their culture is possible without an appreciation of its intellectual foundations. The aim of the second chapter is to convey a feeling for the desert habitat and daily life of these hunters and gatherers as they ingeniously cope with an extremely tough environment. Discussion of ecology and economy leads naturally to a major facet of social organization, the ways in which the Mardu structure their society. This third chapter details the complexities of kinship and various other classification systems, which contrast markedly with the desert people's uncomplicated material technology. Chapter 4 describes the life cycle of the Mardu, paying particular attention to the long and complicated male initiation process, which is the focus of great ritual elaboration. Chapter 5 provides detailed discussion of the rich and varied ceremonial life of the Mardu; it also pursues one of the major themes of the study, which contrasts the dynamism inherent in the religious life, that which allows for the excitement of novelty, with a dominant ideology that insistently proclaims that all is now as it ever was, that nothing really changes. Chapter 6 contrasts the ideal society, as laid down by the ancestral creative beings of the Dreaming, with the realities of a life which does not always accord with that ideal and in which a degree of tension and conflict is inevitable. In conclusion, Chapter 7 switches frames, from a reconstructed pre-contact past to what followed the European invasion, as it briefly recounts post-contact historical developments then sketches the outlines of the world of the Mardu in 1990. This is a crucially important chapter, one that could usefully be read first, because it tells of the dramatic transformations that have occurred in Mardu culture. Today, the Mardu are encountering unprecedented problems as they struggle to maintain their traditions in the face of rapidly mounting and powerfully erosive pressures emanating from the dominant Australian society.

ACKNOWLEDGMENTS

The writing of the first edition of this book was begun in Eugene, Oregon, and completed in Canberra, Australia. I am grateful to the Department of Anthropology, Research School of Pacific Studies, Australian National University, for allowing me to devote my entire attention to getting the manuscript finished.

This study is dedicated to the Aborigines of Jigalong, particularly Gogara, who decided in 1963 that I needed help and since then has been a true friend and teacher; my debt to him and to many other members of the Jigalong mob is profound. This book is dedicated also to my wife Myrna, whose sustained support and encouragement made the task of writing so much easier and who, in her careful reading of the draft, provided invaluable comments and insights derived from her research among the women of Jigalong. To Drs. Kirk Endicott, Richard Gould, Nicolas Peterson, and George and Louise Spindler, I offer grateful thanks for their many helpful and constructive suggestions. My thanks also go to Professor Bob Dixon for his comments on Aboriginal languages.

The fieldwork on which this study is based was financed from a variety of sources including the University of Western Australia, Australian Universities Commission, University of British Columbia, Australian National University, and the Australian Institute of Aboriginal Studies. I thank the Western Australian Native Welfare Department (now Aboriginal Affairs Planning Authority), particularly Mr. Frank Gare, who made it possible for me to participate in several desert expeditions. To Professor Ron Berndt and Dr. Catherine Berndt, who first interested me in anthropology and Aborigines and gave me a great deal of assistance and unfailing encouragement, my gratitude is immense. To my former mentors, Professor Peter Lawrence and Professor Ken Burridge, I also owe a considerable intellectual debt. Thanks are also due to Professor Roger Keesing for first suggesting that I write this book.

Besides the Aborigines, many staff members at Jigalong provided assistance, friendship, and hospitality over the years. Trevor and Peggy Levien, David and Gloria Goold, Terry and Lorraine O'Meara, and Ernie and Edie Jones all assisted in many ways. Jim and Marj Marsh have been hospitable friends, always willing to share their sensitive understandings of Mardu language and life. Joe Criddle, formerly of Walgun station, was both a colorful host and good friend.

For assistance with photographs, thanks to Ian Dunlop, Film Australia, and A.I.A.S., Canberra.

Introduction to the Revised Edition, 1990

In fully revising this monograph, I have taken the opportunity to do several things, the most important of which are to update the general introductory account of Aboriginal Australia in the light of new data and interpretations that have appeared in the last decade, most notably in the fields of archeology and ethnobotany; to take account of important new literature that has altered some of our conceptions of hunter-gatherer societies, with particular reference to the nature of traditional Aboriginal Australian societies and cultures; to add detail to certain sections in the light of recent theoretical and ethnographic concerns; to delete some of the secret-sacred detail, whose removal will not detract from my attempt to present a complex and lively religious life, yet accords with increased Mardu sensitivity to the written word (whereas previously, Mardu caveats concerning such material focused on photographic images—which is why photos of a secret-sacred nature do not appear in either edition of this book); and, in a new final chapter, to update my account of the contemporary situation of the Mardu. Their circumstances continue to be rapidly and often momentously transformed, yet core elements of the traditional past still shape important values and behaviors and are a continuing source of strength in their attempts to cope with pressing problems.

I have also taken the opportunity to bring my orthography more into line with current linguistic usage in Australia and to shorten the name I have coined for these Aborigines, from Mardudjara to Mardu. Not only is this word easier to pronounce, but it is increasingly used by the people themselves, and the language they speak is now termed *Mardu wangka* (cf. Marsh 1984).

My heartfelt thanks go to Myrna Tonkinson, who read the entire manuscript and whose many suggestions improved it immensely. For their most helpful comments on sections of the revised edition, I thank Sandra Bowdler, Alan Dench, Ken Lance, Sue O'Connor, David Trigger, Peter Veth, Fiona Walsh, Neville White, and Nancy Williams. My thanks also to Rina Fiorentino and Bill and Shirley Fockler for their help with the final preparation of the manuscript.

Robert Tonkinson
Perth, Australia
June 1990

Contents

Foreword   v

Preface   viii

Introduction / THE AUSTRALIAN ABORIGINES   1

The Original Settlers
Cultural Diversity—Common Themes
Western Desert Culture
Who Are the Mardu?
Fieldwork in the Desert

1 / THE SPIRITUAL IMPERATIVE   19

Introduction
The Dreaming
Religion and Morality
Ensuring Continuity

2 / GETTING A LIVING IN THE DESERT   26

Ecological Setting
The Desert through Explorers' Eyes
The Western Desert as a Culture Area
Living in the Desert
Conclusion

3 / THE SOCIAL IMPERATIVE   57

Kinship
Local Organization
Social Categories

4 / LIFE CYCLE AND MALE INITIATION   79

Spiritual Preexistence and Conception Totemism
Birth
Childhood

Male Initiation
Marriage, Family, and Gender Relations
Growing Old
Death and Its Aftermath

5 / THE RELIGIOUS LIFE   106

Gender and Religion
Myth, Ritual, and Songline
Sites and Paraphernalia
Magic and Sorcery
Dynamic Elements in the Religious Life
Religion, Politics, and Hierarchy

6 / LIVING THE DREAM   143

The Ideal and the Collectivity
Reality and the Collectivity
The Ideal and the Individual
The Realities of Individual Behavior
Contesting the Dream

7 / EUROPEANS AND THE MARDU RESPONSE: 1900-1990   160

Aboriginal Migration and the Frontier
The Mission Era: 1946–1969
The Rise of Aboriginal Self-Management
Mining and Outstations: Regionalism and Fragmentation
Conclusion

References Cited   183

Glossary   195

Films on Western Desert Aborigines   197

Index   199

Introduction / The Australian Aborigines

For the reader embarking on what is possibly an initial foray into the richness and complexity of the world of Australian Aboriginal cultures, the account below is meant to provide no more than a brief overview of their origins, environmental settings, diversity, and common sociocultural themes. From this continent-wide perspective, it will be easier to situate Mardu society and culture in a broader time-space framework and, thus, to comprehend it as a particular variant of a much wider set of environmental adaptations, behaviors, values, and worldviews.

THE ORIGINAL SETTLERS

There is no doubt that the full saga of the first discovery and colonization of Australia, which dates from at least forty thousand years ago, will never be accurately known.[1] Yet, as a result of the continuing efforts of archeologists, biogeographers, and other scientists, more and more is being revealed about the physical and human background to the settlement of the world's only island continent. It appears that the Australia of the Pleistocene era (Ice Age) was more arid and cooler than now and certainly much larger because of glaciation's effect in lowering sea levels. The Aborigines must have originated outside Australia, because no early forms of human or closely related non-human primates, such as monkeys, have ever been discovered there; marsupials dominated its fauna. The immigrants are most likely to have come originally from southeast Asia. Skeletal remains found in Indonesia and China appear to confirm this relationship, whereas no evidence exists to suggest that the first Aborigines came directly from more distant regions such as Africa, India, or Japan (White and Lampert 1987:8). The voyagers must have possessed seaworthy watercraft of some kind. Despite the lowered sea levels, they had to cross open ocean in several places—deep-water passages of the kind that had once formed barriers to the eastward movement of most placental mammals (except rodents) and other fauna and flora. The first settlers must have arrived somewhere on the north coast (or possibly the northwest coast, since at that time Australia and New Guinea were still a single continent,

---

[1]See Mulvaney (1975), Flood (1989), Gould (1980), and White and O'Connell (1982) for comprehensive accounts of Australian prehistory, and Mulvaney and White (1987) for recent summaries of Australian prehistory and reconstructions of Aboriginal societies at the time of first European settlement in 1788.

1

Sahul), but their motivations, the routes taken, the number of migrations, the accidental or purposeful nature of their voyaging, and the location of their first landfall can only be guessed.[2]

Like the rest of humanity in that era, the pioneers were hunters, fisherfolk, and gatherers, who possessed a toolkit of wood, stone, bone, and shell and domesticated neither plants nor animals. Yet unlike almost all the rest of humanity, the people now known as the Aborigines maintained their hunting and gathering mode of adaptation into modern times. To date, however, we have no clear knowledge, and only conflicting theories, concerning the speed and strategy of their occupation of the new homeland. With a terrain that presented few impediments, they may have adapted to inland subsistence quite early on and then spread rapidly through the interior to the far reaches of the continent.[3] Bowdler (1977) has challenged this theory, suggesting instead that the immigrants may have clung to the marine adaptation they knew best and diffused via the coastal periphery, relying mainly on seafoods and freshwater resources, supplemented by foods hunted and gathered inland, until all the marine frontages were occupied and groups eventually moved inland. Horton (1981) believes that all but the desert core was inhabited twenty-five thousand years ago, but then there was a retreat to wetter coastal areas. This movement was caused by a drying trend in the continent's climate and, perhaps, also by the disappearance of the megafauna (giant marsupials and flightless birds), although as yet there is no clear evidence implicating either the Aborigines or climatic change in megafaunal extinction. In Horton's view, reoccupation of the interior began after the end of the last glacial era, some ten thousand years ago, when climatic conditions much like those of today began.

The few known archeological sites that are older than twenty-five thousand years suggest that most of Australia was already occupied by thirty thousand years ago. People lived in the highlands of what is now the island of New Guinea as well as in the southeast and southwest, including Tasmania, whose inhabitants were eventually isolated when rising sea levels made it an island about twelve thousand years ago (R. Jones 1977). The now-arid interior was a land of lakes and streams some eighty to one hundred thousand years ago, and it remained relatively favorable until about thirty thousand years ago. Recent analyses of arid zone sites indicate that all desert habitats (with the possible exclusion of the sandy deserts) were occupied by twenty-five thousand years ago. Regional abandonment and major population adjustments appear to have occurred across much of the continent during the harsh conditions of the last glacial maximum, between twenty-five and fifteen thousand years ago. The reoccupation of the abandoned regions after climatic amelioration could have begun as early as fourteen thousand years ago.[4]

From about fifteen thousand years ago, important changes in modes of adapta-

---

[2]See, for example, papers by Birdsell and other contributors in Allen, Golson, and Jones (1977) and White and Lampert (1987). Thorne and Raymond (1989) provide a recent account of the peopling of the Pacific region.

[3]See Allen (1989) for a recent review of the evidence concerning settlement of the Australian continent. In mid-1990, scientists who had applied a recently developed dating technology (thermoluminescence) to a rock shelter in northern Australia announced an age of approximately sixty thousand years for the sedimentary environment of a collection of grindstones and stone tools.

[4]See, for example, Bowler (1987), Hallam (1987), Smith (1988), Veth (1989a, 1989b).

tion occurred in many areas of the world, perhaps as a result of significant population increases. In northern Sahul, the highlanders in what is now New Guinea embarked on processes of intensified resource exploitation that transformed them into horticulturalists who also hunted and gathered. The Aborigines, however, did not take this route; instead, they coped with population increases without changing their hunter-gatherer life-styles.[5] There were certainly limitations to this kind of economy because it enforced mobility and entailed total reliance on natural resources. Yet this also had many advantages, particularly the relaxed pace of life and the high proportion of leisure time it afforded. Also, people had to keep their material wants to a minimum; consequently, the available technology easily satisfied these modest wants—allowing the Aborigines to follow what Sahlins (1972) has characterized as "the Zen road to affluence." What the Aborigines did, as we shall see in this study, was to direct their energies into the development of a complex social and ceremonial life, which they saw as providing the ritual technology necessary for bringing about the reproduction of valued resources.

Throughout a ten-thousand-year period, up to three to five thousand years ago, there was little significant technological innovation in Australia (cf. Bowdler and O'Connor, in press); some tools were reduced in size to improve their efficiency, and there was an increased use of composite implements of wood, stone, and gum (Hallam 1987:73). During this era, however, other things were changing drastically. Sea levels were rising, at a rate up to one hundred feet per thousand years at times, and Aborigines were perhaps already having a significant impact on the environment through their systematic use of fire, though lightning may still have been a more powerful influence than humans.

The relatively late arrival from Asia of the dingo, a type of wild dog, between three and four thousand years ago, raises important questions concerning outside influences reaching Australia in more recent prehistoric times. The dingo must have been brought to Australia because it came in an era when sea levels had risen close to their present levels. The dingo's arrival seems to coincide with the disappearance of some carnivorous species, the Tasmanian tiger (*Thylacinus cynocephalus*) and the Tasmanian devil (*Sarcophilus harrisii*) from the mainland—but not Tasmania, which the dingo never reached. The last four thousand or so years also signal a marked increase in technological innovation, especially the advent of a new material technology consisting of an array of small, flaked stone tools. However, important changes such as population growth, the use of new habitats, increased trade, and more efficient resource extraction all post-date the new technology by some two to three thousand years. Current archeological opinion remains divided on the question of independent Aboriginal invention versus diffusion from Asia and on the possible linkage between the arrival of the dingo and these technological innovations. The new tools were grafted onto an earlier kit of generally larger, heavier hand-held cores and flake scrapers on the mainland. The separation of Tasmania, however, precluded the diffusion of the small tools as well as other mainland

---

[5]In Australia, large population increases may have occurred between twenty and twenty-four thousand years ago, followed by a steep decline, recovery from which occurred perhaps as recently as two thousand years ago according to evidence from both northern and southern Australia (S. O'Connor, personal communication).

artifacts such as the boomerang, spearthrower, shield, ground-stone hatchet, and skin cloak.

In the opinion of some archeologists, the past two to three thousand years have seen major technological and economic changes that went far beyond the small tool tradition. They speak of processes of "intensification" that raised productivity and probably facilitated higher population densities in many areas of the continent, and they note the systematic exploitation of semi-arid regions and eastern highlands that had been virtually empty until five thousand years ago (cf. Bowdler 1981; Lourandos 1985). However, the actual nature, degree, and social consequences of intensification remain contentious. The newer patterns entailed complex management of predictable resources, such as eels in Western Victoria, and considerable extractive technology in the case of cycads in the tropics. Aborigines also harvested seasonally superabundant resources in some areas, for example, Bogong moths in the southeastern highlands and bunya pine nuts in southern Queensland. The sheer size of these resources made possible large gatherings of people from surrounding districts and thus aided in the maintenance of society as a much larger entity than its many constituent local groups.

In addition, ceremonial exchange networks crisscrossed the continent and, while it is impossible to reconstruct their form and cultural significance from the archeological record alone, the distribution of highly valued exchange items, such as ochre or pearlshell, can be plotted to show the extent of these networks, some of which cover much of the continent (Mulvaney 1976, 1987). While most exchange transactions occurred between neighboring groups, in the interior longer journeys were sometimes undertaken; for example, the Dieri people east of Lake Eyre journeyed about five hundred miles to exchange red ochre for the narcotic plant, *pituri* (McBryde 1987, Veth and Hamm 1989).

Further excavations and research in Australian prehistory will almost certainly push the time of arrival of the first settlers beyond fifty thousand years. From what is already known, however, it is clear that the early Aborigines were subjected over millennia to significant changes in sea level that must have necessitated considerable adaptation, to climatic changes and some floral and faunal extinction, to environmental changes brought about by their extensive use of fire, and to a host of innovations and changes of greater or lesser regional significance. The culture of the early Australians could never have been static but, in most areas, stability and continuity in basic values and social structures may well have become the norm thousands of years before the European invasion shattered the old order.

The Europeans were not the first foreigners to establish cultural contacts with Aborigines and affect their lives. In northern Australia, Macassan traders from Sulawesi (Celebes), in present-day Indonesia, took advantage of the northwest monsoon to journey annually in large fleets of *praus* down to the coast of Arnhem Land where they established seasonal camps.[6] There, they gathered and processed the sea slug (trepang or beche-de-mer) until the onset of the southeast monsoon enabled them to return home with their prized harvest, which was destined for the

---

[6]On the basis of what he considers to be a conservatively estimated average annual workforce of four hundred men, Mulvaney (1989:25) suggests that over a 150-year span of contact, there would have been sixty thousand Macassan visitors to Arnhem Land alone.

Chinese market. There were conflicts with the Aborigines, but also cooperation and cohabitation, and many Aborigines visited Macassar on the *praus*. In northeastern Australia, too, Papuans made contacts with the Aborigines of Cape York via the Torres Straits islands.

These influences from the north had an unmistakable impact on mythology, language, songs, ritual paraphernalia, art forms, and material culture but surprisingly little effect on the genetic makeup of the Aborigines. Significantly, this exposure to foreign traders and horticulturalists, with their very different behaviors and technologies, failed to induce coastal Aborigines to make fundamental changes in their hunter-gatherer adaptation. Also, the effects of such culture contact, for perhaps the same reasons, were little felt in areas away from the coast. Mulvaney (1989:28) notes that the material culture, living conditions, diet and social expectations of the peasant fishermen were comparable, often inferior, to those of the Aborigines, and that relations between the two groups were egalitarian and amicable.

The drastic transformation of Aboriginal cultures began not with these northern visitors, but with the onset of permanent white settlement dating from 1788 on the southeast coast. There, most of the Aborigines soon succumbed to violence and imported diseases, while their more fortunate brethren in the tropics and the interior went about their lives unaware of what lay ahead.

CULTURAL DIVERSITY—COMMON THEMES

Physical   Aborigines, like all living peoples, belong to the taxon which is known as anatomically modern *Homo sapiens*, but when "racial" classifications were in vogue, the inability of scientists to fit them into the three major subdivisions earned them the separate status of "Australoid."

One early migration theory posited separate racial origins for the Tasmanians and mainland Aborigines, but the differences that exist are best explained by divergent cultural and physical adaptations occurring in the twelve thousand years since Tasmania became an island. The "trihybrid origin" theory of Birdsell (1967), which was based on what he considered to be significant regional variations in Aboriginal physical types, suggested that three physically different peoples entered Australia at different times in the past. Given the very long period that Aborigines have been in Australia, local differentiation in such features as skin color, hair color and form, body build, nose shape, and so forth, on which Birdsell focused, are better attributed to environmental factors, mutation, and genetic drift as selection rather than to interbreeding between two or more races migrating separately to Australia (Parsons and White 1973).

Archeological evidence indicating that there may have been two distinct types in the past comes principally from southeastern Australia. For example, skulls from Kow Swamp, although only nine to fourteen thousand years old, show "archaic" or robust characteristics (for example, large mandibles, thick cranial vaults, and prominent brow ridges), yet skulls from Lake Mungo, which are about thirty thousand years old, are "modern" or gracile in appearance. This puzzling evidence has given rise to a recent theory that there were two migrant groups: a "modern" group which came from South China and eventually mingled with an earlier "archaic" group, which had originated in Indonesia, to produce the modern Aborigines (cf. Thorne and Raymond 1989). This theory has been disputed on a number of grounds: (1) the inherent contradiction between "archaic" equalling young and "modern" equalling old; (2) biologically, there is considerable variation *within* the archaic "type"; and (3) no clear cultural traces exist of two migrations. Further evidence is needed, particularly prehistoric remains from northern Australia or New Guinea, which are currently lacking.

From intensive work on blood genetic markers, Simmons (1976) and Kirk (1983) conclude that while certain markers suggest a common ancestry between Aborigines and at least some neighboring Melanesians, the period of separation has been considerable. These authors affirm that the Aborigines are a genetically distinct group with considerable internal diversity and no close relationships outside Australia. Recent advances in molecular biology, involving the analysis of DNA to assess population genetic affinities, may in the future lead to a better understanding of the ancestry of the Aborigines. It seems clear that, biologically, both Aboriginal homogeneity and heterogeneity exist, depending on what markers are being investigated.[7]

Ecological   In a land that is as big as the continental United States (excluding Alaska), considerable variation in vegetation and climate is inevitable. The range includes monsoon savannah woodland in the north, dense tropical rainforest in the northeast, an arid interior, southern prairies of grassland and mallee (*Eucalypt*) scrub, temperate forest in the southwest and southeast corners and in Tasmania, and patches of alpine country in the latter two areas where the snow cover lasts several months. Adding to the basic difference between seacoasts, riverine areas, and the interior, each major ecological zone has a characteristic range of flora and differing patterns of seasonality. For example, in parts of the north, monsoons create distinct wet and dry seasons, while in most interior deserts rainfall is irregular and non-seasonal. In the southwest, there is a Mediterranean-type climate of hot, dry summers and mild, wet winters. Under tradewind influences, the east coast receives more uniform rainfall, and the island of Tasmania experiences a cooler maritime climate.

Such marked differences are reflected in Aboriginal population densities, extractive activities, settlement and subsistence patterns, and associated regional technologies. The more favorable areas for human exploitation, such as the north and east coasts, the southwest, and the riverine areas of the southeast, were all characterized in precontact times by much higher population densities (perhaps one to eight square miles per person, versus more than thirty-five square miles per person in parts of the desert), more complex technologies, and a more sedentary

---

[7]Cf. Parsons and White (1973:91) who conclude that Aborigines are clearly heterogeneous on the basis of allele-frequency traits, but not on morphological criteria applied to adults or to birth and growth rates of children. This is why scholars who have studied only morphological traits, such as physique or cranial form, have argued for Aboriginal physical homogeneity.

society than in the arid interior regions.[8] The amount and seasonal reliability of rainfall and rates of evaporation vary greatly throughout the continent, and most rivers and streams do not flow all year round. In combination, these factors are a major determinant of Aboriginal adaptive strategies. Nowhere is this more evident than in the Western Desert area, but over much of the continent, water—or lack of it—loomed large in the lives of the Aborigines.

Despite these regional variations, it has not been possible to establish close correlations between ecological zones and cultural differences in Australia. The continent is geologically very ancient, with the result that the forces of nature have reduced topographical contrasts and have worn the land down for so long that there are very few areas over two thousand feet in altitude. Also, while the number of plant species declines as rainfall decreases, two principal genera, *Eucalypts* ("gums") and *Acacia* ("wattles"), show remarkable persistence in all regions. In contrast to North America, for example, most ecological zones in Australia are not sharply defined. When these natural factors are considered, along with important cultural considerations (such as mobility, kinship networks, widespread cultural diffusion, and the exploitation by all Aboriginal groups of a variety of ecological areas in the course of their food quest), the lack of close fit between ecology and cultural characteristics is easily understood. Regardless of climate or richness of marine resources, for example, no Aboriginal group subsisted entirely on marine foods, however important a part these played in their diet (see Meehan 1977, 1982).[9]

Linguistic-Cultural   Prior to European settlement, there were something like two hundred different, mutually unintelligible languages spoken throughout Australia, each language having a number of distinct dialects. Aborigines looked upon linguistic differences as a major factor distinguishing themselves from their neighbors. Most Aborigines were multilingual or at least had some familiarity with one or more dialects or languages other than their own. It was often the case that a child's parents would come from different language or dialect groups, and the child would learn the languages of both parents.

All Australian languages follow a similar typological pattern. They have from four to six points of articulation for both stops and nasal consonants, but rarely have fricatives or sibilants (that is, nothing like the English *f, th,* or *s*). Nouns take case inflections, and there are generally several verbal conjugations, much as in Latin and Greek. All of the languages, excepting a group in the central north, are closely

[8]Estimates of the Aboriginal population at the time of first European settlement vary widely, from as few as 150 thousand to almost one million, occupying a continent three million square miles in area. The true number can never be known, but the most recent estimate puts it at 750 thousand people (cf. White and Mulvaney 1987).

[9]Peterson (1976b) has suggested a broad division into culture areas based on drainage basins (except for the Western Desert, which lacks coordinated drainage patterns). There are twelve such basins, but Peterson recognizes at least seventeen culture areas on the basis of differences in language and culture. His suggestion that there will be a tendency toward culture area endogamy is supported by recent genetic evidence for drainage basin subpopulations in Arnhem Land. White (1989) also argues that, in this region at least, drainage basins may have acted to concentrate populations in resource-rich stream and river systems rather than acting as barriers to interaction between groups.

related "genetically" and may have descended from a single ancestor language spoken ten thousand or more years ago. It is likely that the more divergent languages of the central north are also related, at a somewhat greater time depth, making a single large Australian family (Dixon 1980).

All attempts to relate Australian languages to linguistic families outside the continent have failed. Although there are some superficial typological similarities to the Dravidian family of southern India, for instance, it has not been possible to link them via cognates and systematic formal correspondences. Aborigines and their languages have been on the continent for so long that any sister languages they left behind in Asia would also very likely have changed out of all recognition, making it now impossible to recognize any genetic connection.

Obviously, the persistence of distinctive dialects and mutually unintelligible languages suggests that boundary-maintaining behaviors of some kind have prevented the loss of separate group identities. A major cause of this group distinctiveness, which is common throughout Australia, is the existence of very powerful bonds of sentiment that attached every social group to a particular stretch of territory. This land base furnished most of their material needs and also provided them with much of their particular identity through links of birth, descent, and totemic association. At the same time, however, Aborigines invariably perceived their society as stretching beyond the local group or region of shared dialect or language. Thus, they stressed common values and interdependence with neighboring groups and others with whom they came into periodic contact. The widespread diffusion of valued ceremonies and objects and the universal importance of ceremonial exchange are proof of the great emphasis placed on intergroup contacts.

A man, his two wives, and two of their children cross a spinifex-dotted plain en route to a new camping place.

Aborigines everywhere shared the same basic economic strategy, hunting and gathering, and, regardless of the particular resources and the technologies that were developed to exploit them, this mode of adaptation promoted many uniformities. Thus, everywhere, the band was the basic economic group, with a sexual division of labor and an emphasis on food sharing that, together, allowed more efficient resource exploitation, a varied diet of meat and vegetable foods, and an equitable distribution of food. Aborigines everywhere put fire to the same variety of important uses, cooked mostly in ashes and sand, preferred fresh food, and employed few food conservation or storage techniques.

To this partial list may be added countless shared cultural elements that relate less directly to ecological adaptation but are profoundly significant: classificatory kinship, protracted male initiation, a shared conception of a creative period, concern with the separation of body and spirit after death, totemic identity with creative beings and flora and fauna, a tendency toward the dominance of men's interests over those of women, and so on.[10]

Everywhere, there was a wealth of local elaboration and differentiation, a highlighting or a playing down of certain of these common cultural elements. In the realm of religion, for example, Berndt (1974) discerns four main groupings based largely on the nature and content of major cults or emphases in belief. Elkin (1963) makes a threefold division: a desert focus on circumcision as the primary rite, an eastern concern with sky-gods, and, across northern Australia, the dominance of complex fertility cults. Over the past decade or two, anthropological debates concerning the nature of traditional Aboriginal societies have been focused increasingly on significant regional variations in major social and cultural institutions, particularly in relation to politics, leadership, sex roles, and associated hierarchical and egalitarian tendencies.[11] Clear differences have been discerned between certain north coastal and desert groups in such aspects as boundary maintenance, control over resources, structures of leadership, and conflict orientation. Yet, with few exceptions, these regional differences are easily recognizable as variants of shared themes that proclaim a unique Aboriginal culture, unmistakable to any intelligent observer. Although certain aspects of many Aboriginal practices and beliefs have parallels in small-scale societies elsewhere in the world, even in comparison with other peoples sharing the same mode of adaptation the Aborigines stand out. This distinctiveness derives from the sheer complexity of their social organization and religion and from the total constellation of cultural traits identifying them as Australian Aboriginal.

[10]There are of course, some notable regional variations in, and distinctive combinations of, these elements. For example, the Tiwi of Bathurst and Melville Islands in northern Australia speak a language which is not closely related to those of the mainland, and they do not have elaborate male rituals or social category systems (see Chapter 3), which are common on the mainland (Goodale 1982:198). Elsewhere, Goodale (1971:338) states that ". . . the basic equality of the two sexes as unique individual members of the society is stressed in the culture"; however, she also adds that Tiwi men have greater opportunities for prestige and self-expression than Tiwi women.

[11]See, for example, Bern (1979, 1988), Chase (1984), Hamilton (1982), Hiatt (1984, 1986), Sutton and Rigsby (1982), Tonkinson (1988a, 1988b), von Sturmer (1978), and the topical reviews in Berndt and Tonkinson, eds. (1988).

WESTERN DESERT CULTURE

The major characteristics and homogeneous features of the Western Desert are discussed in Chapter 2, so the only topic to be considered at this point is the extent of variation within the region and between it and the rest of Australia.

In terms of genetic variation, Keats (1977), using a large number of blood markers from twelve Aboriginal populations, showed that the Western Desert samples clustered with those from Central Australia in contrast to groups in Eastern Arnhem Land. Closer examination of groups within the Western Desert and their immediate neighbors reveals a number of genetic clines (gradients in the frequency of a number of blood marker genes), as well as the existence of dialect "chains." White (1989:173) suggests that this is associated with a high level of boundary permeability between local groups and dialect-named units.

Little archeological research has been carried out in the Western Desert until recently. The work of Gould on the eastern side, beginning in the 1960s, suggested climatic and cultural continuities lasting at least ten thousand years. These were exemplified by the persistence of both hafted and unhafted tool types, of regularities in living-surface layout, of a similar mixed meat-vegetable diet, and of long-distance transport of valued lithic materials (Gould 1971, 1977, 1980). From his excavations at Puntutjarpa Rockshelter, Gould concludes that the lack of sharp breaks in the sequence and the absence of changes indicative of cultural transformation suggest the existence of a stable hunter-gatherer life-style in the Western Desert for virtually the entire post-Pleistocene period.[12]

In contrast, recent archeological surveys and excavation on the western side (Veth 1987, 1989a, 1989b) and in the north (Cane 1984) suggest that there have been significant changes in Aboriginal demography, technology, and economy over the last five thousand years. An era of intense aridity some fifteen to twenty-two thousand years ago would have made the Western Desert desert sandhill areas unlivable. It is probably only in the last five thousand years that such areas, including Mardu territories, were permanently colonized by groups employing a uniquely desert economy. This adaptation featured intensive seed grinding, hafted woodworking implements, and the construction of deep-shafted wells (Smith 1986; Veth 1989a).[13] Seeds, a desert staple, would have provided an abundant and reliable food source, and the deep wells would have increased the number of permanent water points, thus extending the range of Aboriginal movement and resource exploitation. Sites excavated in Mardu territory reveal a larger increase in the rate of discard of cultural material, such as stone artifacts and charcoal, during the past fifteen hundred years. Throughout the arid interior there appears to have been more intensive site occupation in the last few thousand years, which suggests population growth on a regional scale and the possibility that social intensification of some kind occurred as a result.

---

[12]However, a recent reanalysis of Puntutjarpa adzes suggests that none is older than five thousand years (Hiscock and Veth, in press), and a reanalysis of discard rates for the same rockshelter reveals a site occupation pattern identical with those elsewhere in Central Australia and the Western Desert, that is, an intensification of occupation in the last few thousand years (Veth 1989b).

[13]Such wells appear to have been common in the sandy deserts of Australia (see Hercus and Clarke 1986).

Evening camp scene. Yanindu stokes the fire; note the small brush windbreak behind her.

The physical and linguistic homogeneity that characterizes the Western Desert is consistent with archeological data from arid Australia which suggests that major population adjustments, including the temporary abandonment of the driest regions, occurred in response to dramatic climatic oscillations during the past thirty thousand years.

The ecologically unique features of uncoordinated drainage, the absence of permanent rivers or freshwater lakes, the paucity of springs, and an extreme variability in rainfall, distinguish this region. Because water is the crucial variable, Aboriginal movement is correlated most of the time with its occurrence in particular localities. However, most rain falls in summer, and certain plant staples have a seasonal cycle, so there is an element of seasonality in patterns of resource exploitation provided sufficient rain has fallen to stimulate the growth of those resources.

Population densities and average band sizes would undoubtedly have been lower here than elsewhere in Australia. Yet even in this most marginal of life spaces, the Aborigines did not exploit all available resources. Among the factors that led people to ignore edible foods are individual tastes, the availability of preferred alternative foods, food taboos (although these were few and rarely applied to all members of any given group at the same time), and other inhibiting factors such as the absence of water or because of avoidances following a recent death in that locality. A strong taboo on the skinning of kangaroos in much of the Western Desert prevented the use of skins and fur as clothing or covers (which were extensively used in cooler southern areas of Australia) or as water carriers (utilized, for example, in parts of the central desert). Gould (personal communication) notes that, in this region, no use was made of either snares or traps in hunting. The desert people practiced some drying and storage of vegetable foods at times but never developed this into a major strategy. In considering these various examples of undeveloped or ignored potential, however, it is advisable to keep in mind that considerations of mobility and portability, as well as the very low population density that was maintained, may have operated to overrule those of comfort, convenience, or maximum resource exploitation.

WHO ARE THE MARDU?

Western Desert Aborigines frequently refer to neighboring groups by selecting a word that is used by speakers of the different dialect, to which the suffix *-jarra* (having) is added; for example, Bijanjarra, from *bija* (to come), and Manyjilyjarra, from *manyjila* (to get, pick up). Groups so designated may or may not refer to themselves by the same term and may not see themselves as the unity that is suggested by such language-use labels. In the same way as the desert people, I have chosen the term Mardu (*mardu*, meaning "man, people") to refer to the linguistic groups whose home territories lie in the area surrounding Lake Disappointment on the western side of the Gibson Desert and who often use *mardu* as one of their words for "people" (see Maps 1 and 2). These groups are principally the Gardujarra, Budijarra, Gurajarra, Manyjilyjarra, and Giyajarra speakers.[14]

It is very important to remind the reader of two things at the outset of this study. First, the desert homelands of these groups were virtually abandoned by the 1960s, as more and more people migrated to settlements along the desert fringe after the coming of whites, and only in the past decade has a significant movement back to their homelands begun (see Chapter 7).[15] There are no Gurajarra speakers left and only a few Budijarra or Giyajarra. Manyjilyjarra and Gardujarra speakers are now numerically dominant and together number probably six to eight hundred. They live in several settlements, outstations, and towns in or west of the desert proper (see Map 1). Second, even though the bulk of this study is a reconstruction of the traditional culture of the Mardu, I use the ethnographic present tense. I do so because much of what is presented continues to have relevance and meaning for the Mardu of today, despite the enormous and irreversible changes that have occurred. Although the traditional local organization of these peoples has ceased to operate, and their entire economic life, for example, has been transformed as a result of their becoming sedentary, important aspects of Mardu traditional culture relating to kinship, values, and religion, retain their centrality. Most of my data are drawn from direct observations, particularly those made in the 1960s among strongly

[14]With respect to the orthography used here in writing Aboriginal words, there are seventeen consonant phonemes: *b, j, rd, d, g, m, n, ny, rn, ng, ly, rl, l, rr, r, w, y.* Four of these (*rd, rn, rl,* and *r*) are retroflexed, as in the American English *r* sound. The vowels are *a* (as in father), *i* (sheep), and *u* (boot), and the lengthened vowels, *aa, ii, uu.* The unretroflexed *rr* is trilled (the Scottish *r* sound). The *ng* sound is similar to that of the *ng* sound in "singer." The letter *k* is used only after *n* (as in the Mardu word *wanka* "alive," pronounced "one-ka") to distinguish this sound from the *ng* sound. The interdental *ly* is somewhat like the *li* in "William," but the *y* is hardly heard.

[15]Given the long history of migration, it impossible to estimate accurately the precontact populations of the groups here referred to collectively as Mardu.

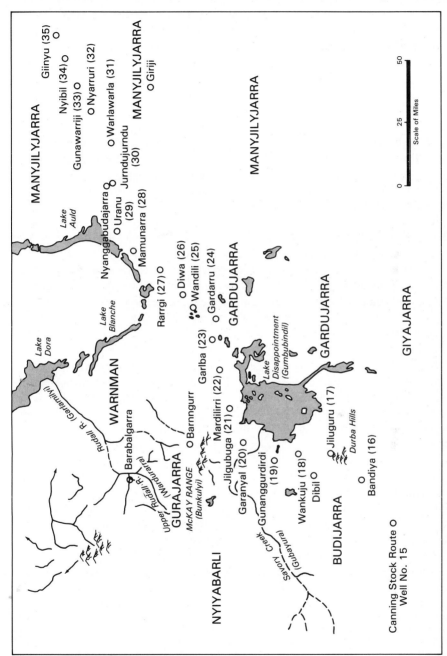

Map 2: Mardu territory.

tradition-oriented people as well as certain groups who, at that time, were among the last still living traditionally away from whites. Other data are reconstructed from statements by older Mardu about life in the desert before contact with whites.

Physical Appearance   Although the Mardu and their neighbors show much variation in stature and color of skin and hair, they share many typical Aboriginal characteristics such as dark skin pigmentation, pronounced brow ridges, broad noses, and slender arms, legs, and buttocks—as the photographs in this book illustrate. One notable Western Desert trait common among them is honey-colored skin and blond hair, which is seen most clearly among children before their hair darkens to a sandy color. Women average about 5'2" in height, men about 5'6", although some are as tall as 6'. Traditionally, obesity was rare, and the only plump people, besides babies, were some women who had borne several children. Older children, men, and women often have scars on their upper arms, and most men have prominent scar ridges (called cicatrices) across their chests. These are either self-inflicted or put on by friends to enhance personal appearance.

Unless engaged in ritual activity, people wear very little in the way of decoration. A thin hair-string belt is the only male "clothing," used mainly for holding small game so that the hunter's hands are free to use his weapons should game suddenly appear. Women sometimes wear a small pubic tassel of string or possum fur which hangs from their waist belt. Females may also wear small gum-tree nut decorations in the front of their hair. Men sometimes wear pubic pendants of pearlshell. When their hair grows long, men tie it back from their face with hair string, which doubles as decorative forehead band, or *yagirri*, worn also in most rituals. Adults frequently anoint themselves (and children) with a mixture of fat and red ochre, which they say has protective and medicinal properties. Children of both sexes go completely naked but, like their parents, they rarely complain about extremes of heat or cold. The desert people normally wear no footwear at all. Their thickly calloused soles and heels resist most prickles, splinters, and sharp stones, enabling them to traverse all kinds of rough terrain without great discomfort. However, they sometimes make throw-away sandals which protect their feet from the fierce heat of the ground if they need to make long daytime journeys in hot weather.

FIELDWORK IN THE DESERT

The exodus of Aborigines from their desert home areas was already in progress when researchers first appeared, so no one could be sure that the movements witnessed among remaining nomads were patterned in the same way, or covered the same resource areas, as before alien influences were first felt. The earlier introduction and spread of European rabbits, dogs, cats, foxes, sheep, and cattle had profound effects on the landscape and, therefore, on Aboriginal adaptations. Many desert people were using metal tools and scraps of cloth and were hunting rabbits and feral cats before they ever encountered whites.

Since 1963, I have done research among desert Aborigines in both desert and settlement situations. In more than sixteen trips, over three years were spent at Jigalong settlement. Additionally, six trips into the Western Desert itself entailed six months' work among Aborigines whose prior contacts with whites were minimal or nil. On most desert trips, I accompanied government welfare patrols and had tasks to perform as an interpreter; in every case our presence halted normal hunting and gathering activities much of the time. On a longer filmmaking trip in 1965, where the Aborigines were asked to carry out many traditional activities, our presence and the requirements of filmmaking meant that normal life was interrupted for the duration of our time with them.[16] Through this exposure to the Aborigines in their traditional environment, it was possible to learn much about many aspects of the traditional culture, though not the precise nature of Aboriginal local organization. To concede this is not to suggest that a comprehensive and reasonably accurate account of precontact culture cannot be given. With this note of caution duly proferred, let us turn now to a brief exposé of the delights and despair of fieldwork in the desert.

Anthropologists who have worked in the desert always speak highly of the warmth, humor, and patience of its Aboriginal inhabitants but curse the torments imposed by nature and by vehicles clearly out of their element. Coping with the desert is hard work, especially during the seven or eight months of the hot season. You soon develop immense admiration and respect for the Aborigines who have conquered it and made it their own. There is great beauty in the desert, in the brilliant red of the earth, the majesty of the desert oak trees, the shimmering expanses of spinifex grass (which from a distance look exactly like a prairie wheatfield ready for harvest), the vivid blue and pink hues of the sky at sunrise and sunset, and the unforgettable brilliance and clarity of the night sky—if you can ever get comfortable enough to appreciate it all.

Summer days are unspeakably hot; winter nights literally freezing; and the balmy winter afternoons can be wonderful, but only on those rare occasions when flies are absent. They teem in their indefatigable millions and easily beat out ants, scorpions, snakes, and other insects as the scourge of the desert. Unless kept at bay with nets and sprays, they can make speaking and eating almost impossible during daylight hours. When swallowed, an all-too-frequent horror, they invariably stick somewhere in your throat and refuse to move either way! Dingoes, wild or domesticated, are not vicious (with the possible exception of the one at Ayers Rock that allegedly ate a white baby some years ago), but as raiders can wreak havoc on anything left within their reach; they jump into vehicles, eat what is readily available and carry off what is not—even cans of food, into which they've been known to sink their fangs. After twice having my toilet bag stolen, ripped open, and its contents chewed up, I concluded that dingoes love toothpaste and tablets and ruefully wished the culprits sparkling white teeth and relief from diarrhea.

Even modern motor vehicles are a poor match for the desert. They bog down to their axles in sandhills. Clumps of spinifex grass jolt the vehicles and their hapless occupants unmercifully or may catch in the tailpipe and set the vehicle on fire. Scrub thickets puncture even the heaviest of tires with little provocation. Spinifex

---

[16]Information on the eleven films that resulted is provided at the end of this study.

seeds clog the radiator and force it to boil, unless, of course, the heat has already beaten them to it. Dust from bush-tracks billows into the cab, covering and choking all within; dust is no problem after a heavy rain, but then it is replaced by mud, sometimes causing vehicles to bog down for days on end. Lumbering four-wheel-drive vehicles, with their incessant thirst for fuel and water, set you thinking about the advantages of the Aboriginal life-style, with its emphasis on maintaining mobility, with the least possible material encumbrances.

Although whites and Aborigines alike personify the natural environment, their attitudes are very different in the case of the desert. To the whites, it is most often an implacable foe; to the Aborigines, it is their home and their provider, which they amiably enjoin to cooperate. For whites, the closeness of the Mardu to their natural environment is a difficult thing with which to empathize and appreciate fully. The Aborigines accept its often harsh terms and embrace it, responding with flexibility and confidence to its vagaries. Outsiders, on the other hand, cannot "see" its totemic geography and spiritual forces and have no mental maps of its water and food resources. They therefore tend to react to it with frustration and anger and, at times, fear it as a deadly opponent. With all our technology, we still fare poorly in the desert, while no doubt the spirits of countless generations of Aborigines for whom it was a familiar and beloved home mock us. Why? For seeing without ever comprehending the environment that they transformed, through their religion, into a compliant ally—at times fickle, but never an adversary, since both they and it are derived from the same ancestral life-force.

First encounters with Aborigines in their desert realm are vividly remembered: the rapid realization, as you are touched, squeezed, and discussed, that as one of the first whites they have seen, you are at least as interesting an oddity to them as they to you; their complete unselfconsciousness about nudity (and on a winter's morning you wonder how can they be so warm in their bare skins while you're freezing in every piece of clothing you have with you); the pungent smell of grease and ochre, the matted hair, the wads of tobacco that are taken from the mouth or from behind the ear and generously offered (Will refusal offend? Is *this* what our teachers meant when they said rapport must be established at all costs?); the way they constantly use their lips in indicating direction, which will soon become so habitual that you continue to do it back in "civilization," providing further proof that anthropologists are crazy (or become so, after fieldwork); and always, the rush of conflicting thoughts that beset the novice: thank God they're so good-humored . . . the flies will drive me out of my mind . . . what the hell am I doing here? . . . this sunset is stunning! . . . I'll never sort out that language—every damn sentence sounds like a single word, longer than that Welsh railway station's name . . . I could be out of this and back home in a week . . . shut up! It'll be a great experience to look back on in later years . . . maybe, but can I wait that long?

After the excitement of first contact has subsided and major logistical problems are overcome, the tasks of observing and recording and of interacting with Aborigines in the setting of a camp are, for the most part, manageable and enjoyable. Later and unavoidable bouts of culture shock produce the same kinds of depressing reaction, regardless of your personality or the foreign culture concerned. There is a growing awareness of the enormity of what you are attempting in trying to understand a system of meaning and action so very different from your own. Feelings of inadequacy alternate with frustration and anger, according to whether you are blaming yourself or them for what seems to be a lack of progress. During periods of culture shock one's ego is easily bruised and there is hypersensitivity to real or imagined slights (paranoia?). You go around mumbling complaints that invariably begin: "Why wasn't I told . . .?; they could at least have . . .; no one could care less if I left tomorrow!" On this last score, the position of the anthropologist as uninvited guest, as needing the people more than he or she is needed by them, as virtually defenseless in the event of rejection, is a nagging reality that takes a long time to reconcile. Another major long-term problem is that of coping with the realization that, no matter how far empathy, understanding, and commitment take you "inside" another culture, you will remain forever an outsider, *with* but not *of* the people, since you can no more fully transcend your cultural roots than they can. The anthropological double bind is that while our understanding requires real empathy and considerable emotional involvement, an equally pressing need for objectivity demands a degree of distance between us and the people we study.

The Aborigines generally assign resident outsiders a place in their kinship system as a matter of course, and the terrors that its complexities held in the classroom abate as constant interaction and the use of kin terms bring familiarity and eventually become second nature. Also, what appears at first encounter to be an undifferentiated mass of men, women, and children gradually separates into distinct personalities, as increasing familiarity breeds compatibility and friendship with many, indifference, or perhaps even dislike of a few. Children, especially, are open and friendly. Their company can be a real tonic on those bad days when nothing seems to go right. They can also be keen, if not always accurate, informants about everything from animal tracks to the latest allegations of adultery.

Once some sort of working relationship is firmly established, and your chief informants have chosen you, the gathering of data gets easier, provided you retain your motivation and sense of humor and are judged to have a genuine interest in learning about and respecting Aboriginal traditions. The desert people are willing and interested mentors most of the time, provided discussions are kept open-ended and they are given ample opportunity to talk about what interests them, in addition to answering all those questions on topics they may find less than engaging. Their language and temperament demand a special style in interviewing. For example, because there is no "either-or" construction in their language, a question must be phrased in affirmative or negative terms, not as a choice. The problem with presenting the question in the affirmative is that your informant could decide from your intonation that you would like an affirmation and may oblige, even though a negative answer may be a better reflection of the truth of the matter. Careful cross-checking provides a safeguard; fortunately, the desert people seem not to be in the habit of willfully misleading their ethnographers.

The Mardu I have known are not given to either philosophizing or attempting objective assessments as to their cultural origins or their complex social institutions; nor are they likely to elaborate on their motivations, symbols, and behaviors. Their usual response to the eager anthropologist who thinks out loud about deeper societal themes and possible explanations will be vague mutterings or professions of ignorance, mild agreement, noncommital shrugs, or silence if this can be managed without giving offense. The observer is certainly entitled to be carried away in flights of interpretive fancy—this is, after all, the fieldworker's task in translating the raw materials of social process into meaningful structural and symbolic abstractions—but the Mardu seem not very interested in embarking on that particular trip.

Undertaking fieldwork in a contact situation (where most of my research is done) adds new problems, such as coping with the whites, while solving some of the logistic ones that loom larger in the desert proper. The weather, flies, and dogs are much the same, but it is very difficult not to become caught up in roles such as interpreter, mediator, and people's advocate. As these activities are aimed at benefiting the Aborigines in some way, so much the better, although relations may then become strained with some of the local whites. Since minimal rapport is essential with the latter, for both practical and professional reasons, there is always a balancing act to perform.

Fieldwork is best described as the ultimate learning experience, as you begin like a child and gradually absorb knowledge—and wisdom and insight if all goes well—which matures you in the eyes of your teachers and, ideally, wins you their approval. It is also, for many Westerners working in Third- and Fourth-World contexts, their first direct confrontation with the grim realities of poverty, oppression, and death, from which their society's comforts, conventions, and rituals tend to shield them. The fieldwork experience is inseparable from a degree of frustration, anger, and grief, but in the twenty-seven years since I first arrived at the mission settlement, full of self-doubt and in fear and trembling of almost everyone (and the camp dogs, who turned out to be all bark and no bite), the good things have heavily outweighed the bad. Like most anthropologists, I thank the people I have worked with for heightening my self-consciousness and for teaching me important things about my own culture by explaining about theirs. For the Mardu, now beset by the corrosive inrush of Western culture and battling problems that have no precedents in their traditional society, the need to understand the invaders has never been greater. Yet to a large extent the survival of Australia's indigenous minority depends on *being understood*. I hope this study helps bring about a greater appreciation of Aboriginal cultural achievement and the historical reasons why things are as they are for Aborigines today.

1 / The Spiritual Imperative

INTRODUCTION

The Mardu are part of a tradition that probably represents the longest continuous hunter-gatherer adaptation in the world. The Aborigines have shown great enterprise and resourcefulness in their successful exploitation of a largely arid continent without the benefit of metal tools, domesticated animals, agriculture, written languages, and so on. Anyone bold enough to venture into the forbiddingly barren interior will attest readily to this triumph. Aboriginal societies also have many distinctive features that set them somewhat apart from most other hunter-gatherers and many other tribal peoples as well. Without doubt, their most notable characteristic is the remarkable contrast that exists between the relative simplicity of material technologies and the extraordinary richness and complexity of social and religious forms. In order to grasp the full significance of Aboriginal cultural achievements, it is necessary to understand the nature and functioning of these complex non-material forms, especially kinship and social organization, and to appreciate how religion so thoroughly permeates the social fabric that even nomadism itself can be understood as a religious act.

For many millennia, Aborigines were insulated from intrusive alien influences that would have brought new objects, ideas, and dogmas, and thus raised doubts as to the adequacy and truth of tradition. This apparently lengthy isolation must have contributed to their development of a characteristically confident and secure worldview—one which, in the desert at least, belies what outsiders would regard as the many uncertainties entailed in getting a living. Aboriginal cosmologies not only account for the origins and form of their world, but also bind them closely to one another, to the land and all living things, and to the realm of spiritual beings who are believed to control the power on which life itself depends. The Aborigines perceive the totality of these bonds as a logically unified order in which all will be well, provided they live according to the rules laid down by the spiritual beings who created their universe.

There is evidence for startling continuities in certain cultural elements, such as the ritual use of red ochre, which dates back some thirty thousand years (White and Lampert 1987). This is not to suggest that Aboriginal practices were incapable of change; no culture can remain static, regardless of how isolated, parochial, or wedded to custom its members may be. One major aim of this study is to reveal the genius involved in accommodating a major paradox: the coexistence of inevitable, constant change of some kind and a pervasive Aboriginal ideology of non-change. In Australia, prior to European contact, most changes were probably relatively small-scale and rarely traumatic (droughts and conflict aside), since even major events such as changing sea levels occurred slowly enough for Aborigines in affected areas to adapt to them.

Aboriginal existence is firmly grounded in a conception of omnipotent spiritual beings as possessors of unlimited life-giving and life-sustaining power. This power is available, more or less automatically, to all those who conform to the master plan for life originally formulated by these spiritual beings. The living are thus obliged to follow the dictates of a culture transmitted down the generations by their fore-fathers, yet attributed to spiritual, not human, actions. By denying the human innovatory component in their cultural development, and by adopting a cosmic rather than chronological notion of history, the Aborigines in effect claim primacy for religious conceptions of causation, being, and purpose.[1]

This essentially spiritual basis of life, while depriving people of the credit for independent creativity, does not deny them their individuality. Instead, among the Mardu at least, it simply removes creativity as a criterion for assessing individual social status or worth. The measure of the person becomes a continuing willingness to follow the founding design, in what Stanner (1965a) describes as a major feature of Aboriginal religion: an assent to life's terms and submission to a sacred purpose. In this way, the Aborigines reap the benefits of reciprocity, namely, the continued fertility of living things and the maintenance of a long-term ecological and social status quo.

THE DREAMING

The profoundly spiritual worldview of the Aborigines rests on a complex set of beliefs and behaviors commonly referred to as the Dreaming, or Dreamtime, which is typically described as the period of creation (see Stanner 1958). At one level of meaning, this is an indistinct era in the distant past, a time long, long ago, well before the memories of the oldest living people, when the continent was trans-formed from an empty and featureless plain by the activities of a great number of ancestral beings. For the Mardu, the ultimate origins of these beings is unimportant, as is the timing of their creative endeavors. The heroes of the Dreaming simply were, and they performed many adventurous acts. Some, the *jilganggaja* (travel-ers), ranged far and wide and engaged in a great many creative exploits throughout the vast arid interior; their *yiwarra* (tracks) are indelibly imprinted on every adult's mental map of the desert. Many others, *nguranggaja* (home-bodies), remained in one particular area or even at a specific site. The Dreaming beings were human-like, but could assume animal form at will. Much larger than life and gifted with

---

[1]Cf. Maddock (1982:119) who notes that "Aborigines claim credit only for fidelity to tradition or, as they put it, for 'following up the Dreaming.' It is the powers alone who are conceived of as creative, men being passive recipients of unmotivated gifts. As men deny the creativity which is truly theirs, they account for their culture only by positing that to create is to be other than human. To be human is to reproduce forms."

superhuman magical powers, they hunted, gathered, and behaved a lot of the time in ways similar to the people living today. In so doing, they were also creating most of the land's distinctive forms—here a winding creekbed, created by the movement of an ancestral snake; there, a gap between hills opened by a blow from the stone ax of a fighting lizard-man; in the distance, a granite outcrop made up of large oval boulders, the metamorphosed eggs of an emu ancestor. Every Aboriginal group attributes a host of physical features in its territory to the creative acts of the Dreaming beings. These events are forever imprinted on the landscape as visible signals of extrahuman powers and are immortalized in myths, songs, and rituals, which are religion's vehicles for meaning. As people engage in their daily food quest, they are surrounded constantly by what they regard as certain proof of the existence, power, and vitality of the creative beings. Their human forefathers must have sensed a need to ground metaphysical conceptions in the solid things of the landscape, as if to dramatize in an immediate and meaningful way the essential unity of the spiritual and natural realms.

The vital power, or life essence, contained in the bodies of the creators and in everything they possessed or touched remained undiminished, but not indivisible, throughout their lives on earth. Wherever they went, they inevitably shed a small part of this fund of power, which would eventually animate hosts of tiny spirit-children, ultimately to be born as human beings. This vitally important aspect of the Dreaming extends the ancestry of every person back to the creative epoch. At the same time, it underlines the uniqueness of the individual, whose coming into being is associated with a quite distinctive chain of causes, events, and interpretations. (See Chapter 4 for a discussion of Mardu conception totemism.)

The absence of any special beginning of the creative era is matched by the absence of any definite end. After their activities on earth came to an end, the Dreaming beings, worn down by their superhuman efforts and by the weight of the sacred paraphernalia they carried, ended their earthly pursuits. Their bodies disappeared or metamorphosed into stones or other natural features or into celestial bodies, never to be seen on earth again; nonetheless, their spiritual essence remained as powerful as ever. They and their associated spirits, some of which act as messengers between the spiritual and human realms, are said to take a lively and continuing interest in human affairs. Significantly, they have retained ultimate control over the reproduction of all plants, animals, and humans.

From even this brief sketch, it should now be clear that the Dreaming is a fundamental and complex conception, not only embracing the creative past and the ordering of the world, but having great relevance to present and future Aboriginal existence. For the Mardu, it still exists, as a lived reality that is at the same time "out there," a vital backdrop for the culture, and an integral part of their being; it is, as Stanner (1966) has remarked, the "everywhen." A day cannot pass without people responding in some way to its presence. The Dreaming is crucial because it is held to be the source of all power, released in response to ritual performance, but also available to individuals. There are times and circumstances of altered consciousness when Aborigines can briefly transcend their humanity and tap this reservoir, as for example during dance, dreams, and heightened emotional and ritual states.[2] Also, in the case of the Mardu, the Dreaming is credited as the source of all new knowledge, which is most commonly transmitted to humans via spirit-being intermediaries that bridge the spiritual and human realms. It is no coincidence that the word "dreaming" or "dreamtime" is now commonly used by Aborigines and whites to embrace this concept. Although the principal Mardu word for the Dreaming is *Manguny,* almost as common is the term *Jugurr,* which can also be translated as "dream." The analogy goes deeper, however, because it is during dreams that Aborigines most often encounter spiritual powers.

The Mardu see their entire culture as the legacy of the Dreaming epoch.[3] Their life-style mirrors the travels of the creative beings, and their food-getting, reciprocity, kinship behaviors, and virtually everything else within the bounds of normal activity is done in fulfillment of the life design that was ordained by the Dreaming creators. As with other hunter-gatherer societies whose adaptation demands highly symbiotic relationships with their natural environment, the Aborigines see a wholeness in their cosmic order, which comprises human society, the plant and animal world, the physical environment, and the spiritual realm (see Lawrence 1964). To maintain this unity and ensure a continual outpouring of power or life-force from the withdrawn spiritual powers, each generation of Mardu is charged with the regular and proper performance of rituals and obedience to the Law.

Although acknowledging their intimate relationship to the rest of nature, the Mardu see themselves as unique and distinct from it. Even their pet dingoes, who are in many respects very close to them, are irredeemably distanced from humans because they copulate incestuously; in other words, they lack shame and do not respect the laws of kinship. Nevertheless, the relationship between humans and nature is a close one and is expressed and affirmed in their totemic beliefs. Totemism, which in its Australian manifestation is more highly elaborated than in any other known society, posits a unity of substance or flesh between people, both as individuals and members of groups, and plant and animal species and other elements, such as minerals, that constitute the natural environment (see Stanner 1965a). The multiple totemic associations that characterize all humans and link them to the Dreaming powers are enduring and indissoluble. The existence of an intimate link between humans and animals is also reflected in the Aborigines' conceptions of the creative beings—almost all had the ability to assume either human or animal form and behavior when the occasion demanded. The Mardu may be emphatic about the essential "humanness" of Marlu the Kangaroo, for instance, yet in relating the exploits of this major creative being, a person will use the verb "hop" to describe Marlu's mode of locomotion.

[2]Despite the importance of dreams, it cannot be concluded that Aboriginal religion is either deeply mystical or preoccupied with the occult. Stanner (1965a), in summarizing the essence of Aboriginal religion, notes its essential life-mindedness, its magnification of the worth of the individual as both flesh and spirit, the preponderance of spirits who care, and the dominance of attitudes of assent to preordained terms of life.

[3]This legacy is now connoted in their use of the English word "law," the coining of which suggests that they see parallels in terms of obedience to a set of powerful dictates and of punishment for nonconformity since, in both systems, human agents are involved in the punishment process. In this study, I use the capitalized word "Law" to connote the Mardu concept, which is termed *yulubirdi,* literally "everlasting."

In addition to acknowledging the superior powers of creative beings, under whose pervasive Law everyone must live, the Mardu recognize human social hierarchy; males and the elderly are generally accorded higher status and enjoy greater rights than females and the young. Despite these inequalities, the prevailing ethos of Mardu society is egalitarian, and this is what informs the way they perceive the great transcendental powers. The "traveler" ancestral beings whose tracks crisscross the desert region are widely known because they have major rituals associated with them that are performed throughout the area. Yet these beings are not accordingly considered more powerful or senior in status than the many localized beings whose exploits are commemorated among a much smaller group of people.

The creative beings are invisible yet omnipresent; they are "here, there and everywhere, but nowhere to be seen" (Maddock 1982:106). Although unreachable in the course of everyday mundane activities, they or their spirit-being messengers are amenable to contact through rituals, dreams, and so on. The idiom for any such attempted communication is kin-based. As revered older relatives, the ancestral beings are thought to be receptive to appeals or requests on the part of their human kin. Yet the Mardu do not resort to prayer, prostration, or sacrifice in communicating with the spiritual realm. When ritual appeals are properly made, the ancestral powers, as older "relatives" who understand reciprocity, are obliged to respond positively and provide the rain, babies, flora, and fauna on which the reproduction of nature and culture depends.

RELIGION AND MORALITY

Although in Western societies there is a tendency to take for granted an intimate connection between religion and moral systems, elsewhere in the world, especially in small-scale societies, the relationship may be tenuous or virtually non-existent. In the Australian case, Stanner (1965a) has noted the absence of either an explicit or strong religious ethic or a religious creed. This he attributes to the absence of three vital preconditions: (1) a tradition of intellectual detachment; (2) a body of interpreters charged with the task of codifying basic tenets or principles; and (3) an external challenge that would have called morals and beliefs into question. Stanner has identified two complementary emphases in the doctrine of the Dreaming: the instituting of things in an enduring form and, simultaneously, the endowing of those things, including humanity, with their good and/or bad properties. He also notes that Aborigines conceived of spiritual powers as having only vaguely a moral-ethical authority. Thus, although Aborigines everywhere understood that the Law entailed an acting out of the grand design left for them by those beings, this was not a matter of unselective emulation.

In fact, many creative beings, mirroring human propensities for both good and evil, were often guilty of what would be heinous crimes in human society. Many scholars maintain that these immoral acts are there, safely locked into the world of myth, as bad examples that harmlessly accentuate the immoral in order to highlight what is moral (see R. Berndt 1970). In Western Desert myth, immoral and amoral acts are often, but not necessarily, followed by the kinds of unfortunate consequences that suggest punishment and thereby reflect a moral element. Many acts, especially homicide, have no dire consequences for their Dreaming perpetrators; often there are no clues as to motive contained in the myth, and no comment on them is offered either by the characters themselves or the human narrator. The Dreaming powers lived in a creative milieu where they sought to impose themselves indelibly on one another and on their natural environment. In Aboriginal cosmology, the ancestral creators are permitted the luxury of unpredictability and perversity.

In some respects, the lives of Dreaming beings were similar to those of humans, with the same potential for altruistic or antisocial acts. The content of Mardu mythology does suggest a moral element in much Dreaming behavior, through its concern for the instituting of a Lawful way of life and demands for adherence to the law by the living descendants. When bad things happen, especially when these go unpunished in a myth, it will end with a statement affirming that what has happened belongs only to the Dreaming. In contrast, when the event involves the instituting of a behavior or a condition that is to endure forever, it is often stated as such by one of the characters concerned. For example, one myth that ends with a fierce spear and boomerang fight between some dingo-men and a group of strangers has the men turning into dingoes and saying as they snap at one another, "We will remain dogs forever now; we are finished as men. As dogs, men will keep us. We will bite kangaroos and keep giving the meat to men. Truly, we will remain dogs, and men will always be taking us hunting."

Whatever the extent of moral ambiguity revealed by Aboriginal mythology, there is clearer evidence in rituals of the operation of moral principles. Stanner (1966) has noted structural parallels between certain myths and rituals: a steady rise to a tense crisis that has a distinct moral quality and, in the case of initiation rituals, results in a physical-moral-spiritual change in the initiates. In his view, these male initiation rituals are disciplines which both fashion the young uncompleted male and transform him into a being of higher worth (see Chapter 4).

Their Law tells Aborigines which Dreaming behaviors are to be copied and which are to be avoided. Fully aware of human imperfections, they rely on informal but effective socialization processes to inculcate notions of right and wrong. Yet, if some break the Law, as is bound to happen, it must be people and not spirits who punish the offenders. The spiritual powers do not exist to uphold the laws of society by punishing transgressors. They have long since withdrawn, leaving a detailed blueprint that guarantees normal operation of human life if faithfully followed and relying on a human sense of mutual obligation to see to it that offenders are not permitted to threaten the status quo. Even where supernatural sanctions exist, human agents are, in most cases, essential for their execution; most such sanctions are limited to specific ritual infringements (R. Berndt 1970). The great power or life-essence that is believed to reside in sacred objects and in certain songs, dances, and localities is extremely dangerous for some sections of the society. For example, if women should somehow see such objects or trespass into men's sacred areas, they will sicken and die. However, this belief is supplemented by an imperative that, because of the grave nature of their offense, such offenders should be killed if discovered.

ENSURING CONTINUITY

Every human society faces the problem of ensuring that its cultural heritage, traditions, and values are successfully transmitted through time so that each new generation comes to perceive its way of life as appropriate and satisfying. In small-scale societies which lack specialized institutions for the accumulation and transmission of knowledge, virtually the entire nonmaterial culture must be carried in people's heads. This great responsibility is borne by adults and, in the case of Aboriginal religion, it is the particular concern of initiated men, who claim to control the religious activities on which cultural survival is held ultimately to depend (cf. Bern 1979). The superstructure of Aboriginal society rests firmly on a religious foundation.

Until relatively recently, scholars have tended to focus on the limitations of hunter-gatherers' technology and economy. This has led them to see ecological imperatives as primary and, thus, to view these societies as dangerously fragile, poised constantly near the brink of starvation. Yet the reality is typically very different. For example, the Aborigines take their great skills in exploiting the environment very much for granted, as knowledge gained almost incidentally in the normal process of maturation and honed by observation and imitation. They stress instead the imperative of conformity to Dreaming laws, for what use are survival skills (which are said in any case to stem initially from the Dreaming) if people neglect the Law and cause the spiritual powers to refuse reciprocity, withholding rain and causing people and the land to become infertile? If our aim is to understand Aboriginal society primarily from within, then we begin by acknowledging that the worldview of the Aborigines accords primacy to spiritual rather than ecological imperatives as guaranteeing the good life. Also, it becomes easy to see why some scholars have reversed the maxim of Durkheim (1912), in his classic study, that Aboriginal religion is a function of society, claiming instead that Aboriginal society is more accurately viewed as existing for the sake of religion (cf. Charlesworth 1984).

Aborigines come to understand and share in the Dreaming heritage largely through the media of myths, rituals, songlines, features of the landscape, and portable objects of many kinds. All the notable marvels of the Dreaming are embodied in one or more of these elements. Creative and world-ordering acts of the first beings are narrated in myths, acted out in dance, condensed into song, and proven by a host of landforms which carry the indelible imprint of these founding dramas, as well as by portable stone objects intimately connected to the beings themselves. Landforms weld the Dreaming solidly to territory by mediating between the creative era and the human realm; song and dance provide the means by which communication with the spiritual realm is enhanced and reciprocity is guaranteed; the mythology reveals the nature of the founding design and of its creators; and totemic beliefs complete the synthesis by providing vital linkages between individuals, groups, specific sites, and ancestral beings. As will be seen in this study, the resulting unity is fundamental, not incidental, to the Aborigines' cosmic order.

2 / Getting a Living
from the Desert

A society's mode of organization can only be fully comprehended when set in the context of physical and ecological factors, and of the technologies and economic strategies that its members have developed over time. Environmental adaptation is never as straightforward as it might appear, even in hunter-gatherer societies where people's dependence on nature is so direct. This is because of the intrusion of cultural elements, which filter, distort, or reshape even the most fundamental relationships between human beings and nature. These mediating elements are visible even where ecological constraints are considerable, as in the desert, which to Western eyes is a most marginal habitat for human survival, yet to the Mardu is a land of riches. In this chapter, the desert environment and its resources are described, as a necessary backdrop for its central concern, which is the economic life of the Mardu. A glimpse of how the desert appeared to some of the early white explorers is also included to illustrate the contrast in European and Aboriginal perceptions of the same environment.

ECOLOGICAL SETTING

The homelands of the Aboriginal groups here referred to as Mardu are situated on the western side of the Gibson Desert, straddling the Tropic of Capricorn between longitudes 122°E and 125°E. The Gibson Desert, together with the Great Victoria, Great Sandy, and Little Sandy Deserts, make up the vast Western Desert, a plateau averaging one thousand feet in altitude and covering some 500 thousand square miles, almost all of which lies within the state of Western Australia (Map 1).

Owing, no doubt, to the influence of movie epics, most Westerners visualize deserts as either rugged cactus and sagebrush country or endless expanses of huge, rolling white dunes that totally lack vegetation save for an occasional palm-lined oasis, complete with camels. There are indeed camels in Australia's interior, a legacy of early explorations, but the rest of the image must be drastically reworked; the rocks and soils are bright red, the sandhills do not move, and on almost all of them some kind of plant life exists. Also, these dunes share the desert with several other kinds of landforms, so there is a patchwork of different ecological zones scattered throughout.

Gumbubindil (Lake Disappointment), a huge salt lake that covers some 650 square miles, is the most conspicuous yet least economically important landform in

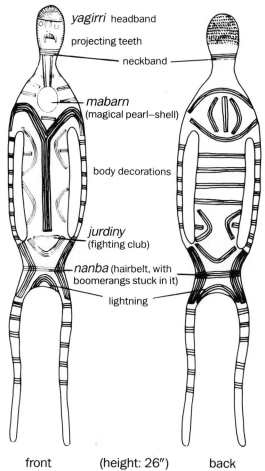

yagirri headband

projecting teeth

neckband

mabarn
(magical pearl–shell)

body decorations

jurdiny
(fighting club)

nanba (hairbelt, with
boomerangs stuck in it)

lightning

front   (height: 26″)   back

Figure 2-1. Carving depicting a Ngayunangalgu cannibal being.

Mardu country. Like the many other salt lakes found in the desert, Gumbubindil is dry most of the time and useless as a source of drinking water. Local drainage channels may fill such lakes after heavy rain, attracting a large variety of water birds which are then hunted by the Aborigines. In the case of Gumbubindil, however, no Mardu ever set foot near it, because to them it is the home of the dreaded *Ngayunangalgu* (will eat me). These cannibal beings, which dwell in their own complete world beneath the lake and emerge to attack human trespassers, are mythologically and totemically important to the Mardu. They are involved in certain curative magical activities (see Chapter 5), but a strong fear of them keeps Mardu well away from their habitat.[1]

In terms of the total area covered, the dominant landform in Mardu country is the dunefield. Averaging about fifty feet in height, lines of parallel ridges separate

---

[1]Mountford and Tonkinson (1969) provide a detailed description of these beings and associated mythology. (See Figure 2-1).

relatively flat corridors (about one- to four-hundred yards wide) of sandplain dotted with grasses, shrubs, and a few trees. Several different varieties of plant life favor the dunes, but tough and prickly spinifex grass is the most common. The different hues of green in the vegetation and the many colors of flowers that appear briefly after rain contrast vividly with the red of the ridges, rocky outcrops, and low, rugged ranges that also occur throughout much of the desert. Stands of dense scrub (*Acacia* species) sometimes surround hilly areas, as do flat, stony plains that at times resemble wheat fields when the ubiquitous spinifex is in seed. The distinctive and stately desert oak tree (*Allocasuarina decaisneana*) occurs widely, but favors sandy inter-dunal areas, and everywhere various eucalypt species dot the landscape.

Creekbeds of various dimensions, which contain water only after heavy rain and for brief periods of runoff, radiate from the hilly areas and are distinguished by the growth of large trees (*Eucalyptus* species), *Acacia* shrubs, and grasses along their banks. Claypans, shallow depressions of varying size, fill with rain via surface runoff. At such times, they become valuable water sources for both the Mardu and wildlife. Hilly areas, which rise one- to three-hundred feet above the plateau, sometimes feature rugged narrow gorges which have distinctive vegetation and sheltered pools; these are often long lasting and therefore very important when less reliable water sources dry up. Some gorges, such as Jiluguru in the Durba Hills, south of Gumbubindil, are quite spectacular. They contain huge eucalypt trees, deep pools, sheer high rock faces of brilliant red coloring, and many tropical ferns and plants that seem totally out of place in the desert interior. These gorges and the surrounding rough, stony breakaway country are the haunt of the agile rock wallaby (*Petrogale lateralis*) and its larger cousin the euro (*Macropus robustus*). They, and the larger plains kangaroo (*Macropus rufus*) which prefers open country, are hunted by the Mardu.

The range of daily and seasonal temperatures is considerable in the desert. In summer, shade temperatures range from about 80F to 130F, but the very low humidity makes conditions bearable. When clouds associated with thunderstorm activity block the heat in, or strong, hot, dust-laden winds are blowing, it is much less tolerable. Winter temperatures can range daily from below 25F at night and in the early morning to about 80F after midday, when cloudless skies allow the sun to make an impression. The air is rarely still; breezes or winds blow from varying directions most of the day and sometimes at night. Whirlwinds, called "willy-willys," are frequently seen in the desert. These thin columns of dust, ashes (of spinifex and other vegetation), and plant debris careen erratically about and wreak minor havoc when they blow through a camping area. Most of the time, the air is remarkably clear, and the quality of light is correspondingly strong and sharp, producing crisp outlines of distant landforms whose colors often undergo dramatic transformations as the day wears on. In summer, a source of frustration is the frequent appearance of mirages which beckon and shimmer with false promise of pools of blue. Sunsets feature vivid pinks and blues, and the clear dry air guarantees spectacular night skies with stars in staggering profusion; when the moon is full, its surface is revealed in incredible detail to the naked eye. The immensity of the night sky is matched by the seemingly limitless panoramas of the land that are gained from any point that is elevated above the plateau. The desert seems to stretch away

Nyungala getting water from a small rockhole.

forever in all directions and overpowers the observer, who feels reduced to near nothing. For the Mardu, however, there is security in knowing what can be seen as well as what lies beyond. There is the certainty that somewhere out there are other groups of kin and friends whose presence is frequently revealed by the telltale smoke of their campfires or the scrub they burn while hunting—smoke which is visible from distances of up to fifty miles.

By any standards, this is an extremely arid land with an average annual rainfall of somewhere between five and ten inches—a statistic that conveys little, since falls of rain are quite patchy. Some areas may receive no significant falls for several years, then a cyclonic depression or violent thunderstorm can dump several inches of rain onto the parched earth in a matter of hours, turning lowlands into one huge lake and causing short-lived but frighteningly powerful torrents in the waiting creekbeds. In most years there is a summer rainfall maximum, caused principally by thunderstorms between December and March, but between May and July winter rains may also occur, especially in the southern parts of the desert. The Mardu generally dislike winter rain, because it often takes the form of light drizzle which wets them and makes them miserably cold. August to October are the driest months.

When possible, the Mardu make use of surface waters that are abundant for short periods after heavy rains. Most of the time, however, they must rely on established and well-known sources, including sheltered rockholes, creekbed soakages (called "soaks" in Australia), wells (found in sand dune and rocky areas), a few springs, and a number of unusual sources such as the forks of large eucalypt trees and the roots of certain trees which are dug up, cut into foot-long pieces, and drained into wooden dishes.

The reliability of creekbed soaks, which have to be dug until water level is reached, varies with previous rainfall. After a heavy flood, a lot of water seeps down, and the soak will remain usable for a much longer period than after a light water flow. In sand or clay areas, the Aborigines watch for certain herbs and sedges that signal the presence of water close to the surface. True wells, which must also be dug out, often dry up; a few are far more reliable because their supply issues from deeper subterranean sources, such as where fault lines cross aquifers and allow water to move upward under pressure.

Most wells have small surface openings, and there is nothing in the surrounding vegetation to suggest their presence; therefore, the location of wells must be precisely known, not intuited from generalized knowledge. Some wells are so deep that the Mardu insert notched poles as ladders to reach the water, which may lie twenty feet or more beneath the surface. They scoop the mud out with their hands or digging dishes and use it to reinforce the walls of the the well. Small and shallow catchments are sometimes covered with sticks, stones, grass, or boughs, to block dust or debris and possibly to lessen evaporation. Grasses and sand are used to filter water, which can be extremely smelly and "full-bodied" (for example, dead marsupial mice, lizards, and birds) after prolonged drought. Such is the extreme localization of most rainfall that bone-dry wells and rockholes can be found just a few miles from full ones. Huge freshwater lakes and deep rockpools that give every indication of being permanent can disappear in the summer heat, victims of an exceptionally high evaporation rate.

Considering its aridity, the Western Desert surprisingly has one of the richest reptile faunas in the world. There is abundant plant cover and, after rain, many ephemeral plants, insects, and birds are active. Numerous mammals are also present but are often inconspicuous to the untrained observer. Besides ants and a host of different flying insects, any number of snakes, centipedes, spiders, and scorpions also threaten the unwary. In daylight hours, a few relaxed kangaroos, sunbathing lizards, or the odd skittish hopping mouse (*Notomys alexis*) may be spotted. Most animals are rarely seen, but are known to be present because of the many tracks that crisscross the sandy ground. Most noticeable, because of their movement, noise, and bright colors, are the many varieties of birds, ranging from the tiny finches that cluster noisily in shrubs close to water to large eagles and tall, flightless emus. A favorite target of hunters because of its large size, the emu frequents mulga thickets and can run at speeds of over thirty miles per hour—faster than they should travel, because they sometimes trip when distracted! Following a spectacular headlong sprawl, in a mass of ruffled feathers and red dust, they instantly regain their feet and speed, but never their dignity in the eyes of laughing human onlookers.

Each distinctive area, be it sand dune, claypan, shrub flat, or whatever, has certain plants and animals that favor it. Yet neither the flora and fauna nor the Mardu are great respecters of physiographic boundaries; all areas generally contain a mix of trees, shrubs, herbs, and grasses, and most are periodically exploited for food. In the desert, there is a relatively high degree of spatial heterogeneity in plant distribution. Walsh (1990:28) estimates that at least 148 plant species are used by the Mardu, of which 106 species are potential food sources, which variously provide seeds, roots and tubers, fruits, and gums. The Mardu categorize most foods into two major groups, *guwiyi* (meat) and *mayi* (plant food). Some other foods are separately categorized; these include edible insects or their excretions (such as sugary excretions called lerp, as well as insect galls and larvae).

The region is dominated by grasses and is rich in *Acacia* shrubs; these plants provide an abundant source of seeds which are ground into flour, made into a paste, then eaten raw or cooked in ashes. Six of the hardy bush tomato (*Solanum*) species are staples. In good years, they produce abundant fruit which ripens between winter and spring. Some fruits are eaten whole. The skins of other species are eaten raw or lightly roasted. If abundant, they may be skewered on sticks and sun-dried, then soaked in water and ground into a paste before being eaten (sometimes months later). In wooded areas, yams (*Vigna lanceolata*) may be found; the creeper is easily spotted because its bright green leaves stand out against the duller green of surrounding grass or burnt ground. Women locate the base of a plant from the mass of twining branches. Carefully, they dig, following the fine roots. Between about one-and-a-half and three feet down, these roots swell and form a tuber. When they are found, women remove the tuber cautiously so the roots can be followed further downward or to the side. The tubers are juicy and tasty; they are peeled and eaten raw or roasted in ashes. Another high-yielding tuber that is easier to dig out than yams is the bush onion (*Cyperus bulbosus*), which abounds near creekbeds and is eaten raw or roasted.[2] Sweet blackberries (*Canthium latifolium*) are gathered in the late summer months; rock figs (*Ficus platypoda*) and bush plums (*Santalum lanceolatum*) are tart but tasty fruits that bear heavily at certain times and are usually eaten raw.

Over fifty different kinds of animals, including marsupials, reptiles, birds, and introduced mammals (rabbits, feral cats, camels, and foxes) are hunted for food by the Mardu. Of these, reptiles (particularly lizards) are probably the most reliable source of meat. These, as well as small marsupials, bush turkeys, kangaroos, and emus are regularly hunted, although the presence of plains kangaroos and emus depends on favorable water and feed conditions. The Mardu know intimately where, in each habitat, they can expect to find specific food resources. The major element of uncertainty is rainfall—this, of course, is crucial because plant growth and animal survival depend on it.

THE DESERT THROUGH EXPLORERS' EYES

How did the desert interior look to the few hardy adventurers who, with horses or camels, ventured there late last century? They went in the hope of finding wealth of one kind or another—gold, inland seas, rich pastures, and so on. None was successful in this quest; several perished, and all at some time suffered terribly, counting themselves lucky indeed to escape with their lives. Those who survived

---

[2]Veth and Walsh (1988) have established that roots and tubers are a sufficiently important dietary component to be classed as staples, along with *Acacia* and grass seeds. Walsh (1990:29) suggests why: they are tasty and moist, they commonly grow near watercourse areas frequently visited by the Mardu, large quantities can be harvested in a relatively short time, and they are available in summer when other foods are limited.

A hunter poses with two major desert staples: lizards and bush tomatoes. He carries his spears and thrower in his left hand. Note the use of his hair-twine waistband as a holder for one of the lizards. Photo by Ian Dunlop.

often did so only with the help of Aborigines, but this assistance was not always voluntary. For instance, explorers sometimes captured Mardu by running them down and then keeping them chained in the hope that once the Mardu became thirsty they would lead the whites to water.[3] The explorers said little about the Aborigines, but much about the harshness of the environment. The following sections present some of "unfavorable reviews" written by the explorers who survived to tell of their desert adventures.

Colonel Peter Egerton Warburton   In 1873, Warburton led a large expedition from central Australia to the west coast, passing to the north of the Mardu. The following excerpts come from his 1875 account of his journey.

> . . . ants swarmed over everything, and over us; indeed they wanted to take away the cockatoos we had for dinner but we rescued them (p. 165).

> . . . deepened last night's well but with no better results than yesterday. Started in a north-westerly direction and sunk another . . . no water; . . . dug three more wells . . . same unsuccessful results . . . last known water already 50 miles away (p. 183).

> The heat is now very great and the camels are suffering from travelling during the day over hot sand and steep hills (p. 209).

> . . . my riding camel has completely broken down . . . and we could only get her on her legs again by lighting some spinifex under her tail (p. 211).

> . . . master bull camel has eaten poison, and is very ill (p. 213) [*It later died, as did many of the explorers' camels after eating poisonous plants.*]

> Our position is most critical in consequence of the weakness of the camels (p. 256).

> God have mercy upon us for we are brought very low. . . . Our miseries are not a little increased by the ants. We cannot get a moment's rest night or day . . . (pp. 258–259).

John Forrest   Forrest passed to the south of Mardu territory, heading east, in 1874. The excerpts below are from Forrest (1875):

> . . . most miserable country, thickets and spinifex . . . (p. 173).

> We have not seen any permanent water for the past eighty miles. . . . it is very risky going on . . . (p. 176).

> . . . the most wretched country I have ever seen; not a bit of grass, and no water . . . spinifex everywhere (p. 200).

> . . . it is a most fearful country. . . . We can only crawl along, having to lead the horses, or at least drag them (p. 202). [*All this party, too, survived*].

Ernest Giles   Giles, an intrepid adventurer, made several trips through the desert between 1872 and 1882, one of which took him and his party through the southern part of Mardu territory, heading eastward. In his later writings, Giles, who

---

[3]Frontier encounters between Aborigines and whites is a highly complex issue with repercussions that are still being felt. See Chapter 7 for further discussion.

had more than one very close brush with death, shows a propensity for the humorous turn of phrase; for example, his description of the cursed, needle-sharp spinifex as ". . . porcupine, triodia . . . Festuca irritans, and everything-else-abominable, grass" (1889, I:191). Several times in his account, he waxes most eloquent on flies:

> It was impossible to get a moment's peace from the attacks of the flies; the pests kept eating into our eyes, which were already bad enough. This seemed to be the only object for which these wretches were invented and lived, and they also seemed to be quite ready and willing to die, rather than desist a moment from their occupation. . . . they scorned to use their wings, they preferred walking to flying; one might kill them in millions, yet other, and hungrier millions would still come on, rejoicing in the death of their pre-decessors, as they now had not only men's eyes and wounds to eat, but could also batten upon the bodies of their slaughtered friends (1889,II:303).

David Carnegie   Carnegie, a Scot, made many astute and valuable observations of the Aborigines and their environment, and his book *Spinifex and Sand* (1898/1973) is a remarkable account of his Australian adventures. In 1896, he led a small party northward along the eastern edge of Mardu country:

> [*Crossing what he describes as "The Great Undulating Desert of Gravel"*] In this cheerless and waterless region we marched from August 22nd until September 17th seeing no lakes, nor creeks, or mountains; no hills prominent enough to deserve a name, excepting on three occasions. Day after day over open, treeless expanses covered only by the never-ending spinifex and strewn everywhere with pebbles and stones (p. 208).

> As for animal life—well, one forgets that life exists, until occasionally reminded of the fact by a bounding spinifex rat, frightened from his nest (p. 209).

> [*Further north*] A vast, howling wilderness of high, spinifex-clad ridges of red sand, so close together that in a day's march we crossed from sixty to eighty ridges, so steep that often the camels had to crest them on their knees . . . (p. 249).

> Words can give no conception of the ghastly desolation and hopeless dreariness of the scene which meets one's eyes from the crest of a high ridge (p. 251).

Carnegie's party spent almost a year in the interior before seeing rain fall. He attributed their survival to the capture of Aborigines to lead them to water. Carnegie and many other explorers were very well served by Aboriginal guides who, although strangers to the regions traversed, were invaluable because of their great knowledge of bird and animal habits and their superb tracking abilities.

THE WESTERN DESERT AS A CULTURE AREA

Except for the presence of higher hills in the southeastern and western parts, a similar range of landforms, vegetation, and fauna occurs in all the contiguous deserts that constitute the Western Desert; none of these areas is a well-defined or clearly demarcated region. Given the huge extent of the region, minor variations in climate are to be expected. Seasonality is more pronounced in the northwest, where most rain falls in summer, whereas in the southern areas, winter rains predominate. Taken as a whole, the Western Desert exhibits, in its climatic conditions and in the distribution of varied landforms, more homogeneity than contrast. The same is certainly true of the way of life of the hundreds of Aboriginal groups that traditionally inhabited the area. This is why anthropologists speak of a "Western Desert culture" that is distinguishable from other Australian Aboriginal subcultures.[4]

All Western Desert people speak mutually intelligible dialects of the same language.[5] Throughout the Western Desert, the Aborigines also employ an elaborate sign language. Kendon (1988:4) says of the culturally similar Warlpiri (whose repertoire exceeds fifteen hundred signs) and other central Australian groups that they possess "probably the most complex alternate sign language ever to have been developed."

Western Desert forms of social organization are basically similar, too, and in the structure and operation of the kinship systems and marriage rules, the range of variation is not great. This is true even of the northeastern region, where social categories of the subsection type are found (see Chapter 3).[6] Significantly, it is in the realm of the religious life that the most striking continuities exist throughout the desert. For many millennia, the diffusion of religious and other lore among constituent groups, sometimes even beyond the culture area, has ensured the retention of homogeneous sociocultural forms. Most of the major rituals performed by the Mardu are also part of the ritual life of groups elsewhere in the desert and show remarkable similarities in structure over time and space. Some of the Kangaroo dances captured in Spencer and Gillen's remarkable film, made in 1902 among the Aranda of central Australia, are virtually identical to those still being performed by the Mardu and their neighbors today.

The Mardu constitute, numerically and geographically, a small part of this culture area and are, in some respects, indivisible from the rest because boundaries, even dialectal ones, do almost nothing to impede the free flow of people, ideas, and objects across the face of the desert. Lacking what most peoples elsewhere would consider to be essential elements for survival, the Mardu have thrived in their desert

---

[4]There is ample evidence of this homogeneity. For instance, compare the following songs, collected at Jigalong in 1963, with those recorded twenty-two years earlier by R. and C. Berndt (1945) at Ooldea, a thousand miles to the southeast:
(a) a song sung by featherfeet killers (see Chapter 5):
    Jigalong: *baba nganana garli bambuna burnu gadi*
    Ooldea: *baba nangana gani mankuna burna gaadi* (p. 179)
(b) a chant sung over a love-magic object (see Chapter 5):
    Jigalong: *madagi na rurubungu diili lilinyba na wirubungu*
    Ooldea: *madagi na rereibunga maieli lilingba rereibunga* (p.167)
Although there are differences in the translations given for these songs, the general meanings are quite similar.
[5]For information on Western Desert languages, see Douglas (1988), Glass and Hackett (1970), Hansen and Hansen (1969), and Marsh (1969, 1984).
[6]There is some suggestion that on the eastern side of the desert relationships between people and land are more loosely structured, giving rise to extreme fluidity of local groupings, whereas in the west, marginally more favorable ecological conditions may have allowed the Mardu to maintain a closer fit between their territorial boundaries and constituent dialect-named groups (cf. Hamilton 1982, Myers 1986, Tonkinson 1988c, and Walsh 1990). It is very likely, however, that a long history of emigration from the desert, which may even predate European influences, has contributed significantly to the fluidity of social organization that has been reported for the remaining groups in the eastern region.

heartland for thousands of years. This long and clearly successful tenure prompts an important question: how have the Mardu managed effectively to exploit such a seemingly harsh and uncertain environment?

LIVING IN THE DESERT

It has been customary in discussions of human societies to characterize the Australian Aborigines in negative terms, in a sense putting them down because they lack such features as metal tools, agriculture, domesticated animals, the wheel, villages, chiefs, a market economy, and so on. A more rewarding approach would be to focus on the achievements of a remarkably resilient and resourceful people, whose dominant mode of adaptation precluded the development or adoption of many technological and organizational forms common in much of the rest of the world.

Attitudes Toward the Environment   Over countless generations, the Mardu have responded to the severe constraints imposed upon them by their arid environment by progressively modifying their technology and subsistence activities. These efforts have not resulted in any radical disengagement or alienation of the Mardu from their environment. They attribute neither superiority nor autonomy to the forces of nature, since to do so would suggest an opposition between nature and humanity. On the contrary, the Mardu see both as elements of a wider cosmic order, a totality that includes the all-powerful spiritual beings of their Dreaming. They postulate a harmony among its component parts, yet, anthropocentrically, they consider certain human actions to be essential to its maintenance and renewal.

The most visible impact made by the Mardu on the land is the burning of grassland, a continuous practice. They also dig holes, cut down trees, uproot shrubs, clear campsites, place sticks and stones in forks of trees (which warn of something sacred and/or dangerous nearby), dig out wells, and so on. Yet because they are few in number and highly mobile, their total impact on the physical and biological environment is slight. The resulting impression is one of a conservation ethos to the observer; however, this may well be an illusion—merely a product of ecological and demographic conditions. Significant alterations to the land are also ruled out by their technology and, furthermore, such activity would be inhibited by religious convictions. Creativity is the sole prerogative of the Dreaming beings, whose life design is set and immutable, leaving no room for human transformations of the landscape. The Dreaming's blueprint is clear and, as embodied in Mardu Law, it demands only assent to its terms, which include the fulfillment of ritual responsibilities.

Ecological Knowledge   Flexibility in movement and size of the exploiting group does not in itself guarantee survival. Also important is an extremely detailed and comprehensive knowledge of the environment and its economic resources, as well as how to find and use them. Children begin accumulating this fund of information and skills at a very early age. Because their lives are so closely attuned to the natural surroundings, the Mardu develop a great ability to "read" correctly the multitude of signals emanating from their surroundings. To take just one prominent example, the amount of information encoded in tracks and other markings on the ground is enormous, so knowledge of how to decipher them accurately is timesaving (such as when a mere glance tells the hunter that the marsupial he seeks is not in its burrow) and, in very bad times, could perhaps mean the difference between life and death.

For adult males, this intimate knowledge of the physical and biological world is supplemented by what they regard as an equally pragmatic and necessary ritual "technology," through which they claim to exert a measure of control over resource production and weather conditions (see Chapter 5). Through ritual acts, they communicate with and co-opt spiritual powers in order to change things to their advantage. The act of spearing an emu and the performance of a rite that will ensure the presence of thousands of emus each year are considered by the Mardu as equally productive activities. Unlike the Melanesians, for instance, who tend to surround fishing, horticulture, and pig-raising activities with a host of ritual acts aimed at protecting and promoting success, the Mardu rely mainly on occasional and brief rites to ensure continued supplies of needed plant and animal foods but devote much less ritual attention to the practical processes of resource exploitation.

Mobility and Flexibility   The Mardu have responded to the challenge of scattered food and water resources by means of a highly mobile adaptation that enables them to exploit different resource areas at different times. Their adaptation demands dispersal in small, scattered groups as the norm and the maintenance of a very low population density. The size of the basic economic group, the band (discussed in Chapter 3), varies according to local conditions and food availability, just as its movements vary in part according to the occurrence of rain. The desert people have an extensive vocabulary for cloud and rain types and weather phenomena and are experts in assessing the likelihood and possible consequences of rainfall in their territory.

The rhythm of desert life is one of alternating aggregation and dispersal of social groups, but neither these demographic changes nor the patterning of a group's movements is strictly seasonal. When considering Mardu activities, it is important to distinguish between long-term climatic variations caused by droughts and short-term variations that occur within a yearly cycle and relate to seasonal changes in climate. During droughts, germination rates decline, particularly for grasses and herbs which make up about a quarter of the food species potentially available to the Mardu (Walsh 1990). As dry periods progress, the Mardu are forced to rely increasingly on hardier perennial species and to eat "drought foods"—plants that are normally not popular. They also tend to eat more meat, particularly reptiles, and may consume stored seeds and dried fruit. All the nine kinds of seeds at times stored by the Mardu are periodically superabundant and can be collected in large quantities; some are cleaned and then stored in the boles of trees (Walsh 1990).

Manggaji harvesting seeds from woolybutt grass (Eragrostis eriopoda); *her digging stick and emu-feather headpad lie nearby as she uses a milking action to strip the grass seeds into her wooden dish.*

From her recent work among the Mardu, Walsh (1990) has identified, as short-term variations that occur in "normal years," a cyclic progression of three major seasons (determined by the positions of stars and by weather changes, specifically rainfall) that vary up to about three months in the timing on their onset:

(a) Dulbarra (analogous to spring), when rising temperatures cause reptiles to again become active, bustards and other birds are hunted, and the widest array of plant foods ripens.

(b) Yalijarra, "hot time," when most edible *Acacia* seeds ripen, plant foods are becoming more scarce, and large game and reptiles figure more prominently in the diet. The onset of summer rains is keenly awaited; then, if the rains come, there is a short period of two to three weeks which the Mardu call Bilarrgara, when termite aeletes, called *bilarrba*, disperse widely and are collected and dried.[7] After the rain, grass seeds become progressively more available for harvesting; as lizards increase their fat reserves in readiness for winter, and become less active, they are intensively hunted.

(c) Wandajarra, "cold time," when nectar-producing shrubs flower, grass and sedge seeds are abundant, and edible grubs, which are an important desert food source, are sought.[8]

---

[7]Aeletes are a winged reproductive caste of termites which do not eat and are laden with rich fat deposits.

[8]High in protein and prized for their taste, edible grubs are the larvae of the cossid moth and are dug from the rootstock of *Acacia* shrubs and the trunks of *Eucalyptus* trees. Each kind is named for the plant in which it is commonly found. Eaten alive or cooked very briefly, these fatty "witchetty grubs" (which are one to three inches long) have a pleasant nutty flavor and are quite nutritious (cf. Latz 1982, Walsh 1990).

Jambijin displays this prize haul of edible grubs before devouring them.

Figure 2-2, after Walsh (1990:33), summarizes the relationship between these seasonal cycles, resource availability and importance, and Mardu economic strategies, and provides a useful backdrop for the discussion that follows.

The explorer Carnegie must have been one of the first observers to comment that the best water sources in the desert are the least used and to recognize a basic adaptive strategy whereby small wells are used first; only when these are emptied do Aboriginal groups resort to more permanent waters. After good rains, which promote plant growth and replenish surface and rock catchments, groups of Mardu fan out rapidly toward the edges of the rain-affected area, where they use the ephemeral waters of claypans and pools. There, they hunt and gather as extensively as possible until diminishing water supplies oblige them to begin a retreat.

In comparing the subsistence behavior of the desert people with that of the Kalahari Bushmen of Africa, Gould (1969b:267) notes that, whereas the !Kung Bushmen typically occupy a camp for many weeks and eat their way out of it, the Aborigines:

> . . . eat their way into a camp by first exploiting all the food resources near the surrounding waterholes whenever possible before settling at the main waterhole. Then they consume staples between a five- and 10-mile radius of that waterhole before beginning the trek toward (but not always *directly* toward) another reliable waterhole.

The direction of subsequent movements depends on many factors, among the most important of which would be the location of known or predicted supplies of foods, the direction of recent rainfall, and the position of known chains or "lines" of water sources that will accord with the factors of rainfall and food availability (Gould 1969b). Except in extreme drought conditions, many small bands hunt and gather in the same general area of the desert year after year. For a number of ecological and cultural reasons (see Chapter 3), no band would repeat its specific round of movements exactly over time.

Ecological necessities keep people dispersed in small groups most of the time, but sociability is highly valued and, under normal circumstances, neighboring bands will make contact on seeing one another's smokes. These bands may then camp together until food or water shortages, differing travel plans, or perhaps rising tensions lead to a dispersal, and each goes its separate way. Periodically, when plentiful water is available and a relative abundance of food sources can be predicted for a given site, large numbers of people from widely separated areas assemble in response to invitations sent by the local group in whose territory these favorable conditions exist. This temporary aggregation or *jabal* (multitude) is the high point of the Aborigines' social calendar.[9] It facilitates, among many other important things, the maintenance of a shared religious life and of cultural diffusion, which desert people see as their lifelines of survival.

Despite the necessary fluidity of their nomadic life, the Aborigines are not rootless wanderers who lack territorial attachments. As individuals and group members, they maintain deeply felt and enduring bonds to certain stretches of territory and, within this home area, to sites of particular totemic and religious

---

[9]Henceforth, this will be referred to as the "big meeting," a term now commonly used by Aborigines to describe such assemblies, which remain central to their religious life (see Chapter 7).

Season	Yalijarra	Wandajarra	Dulbarra	Yalijarra
APPROXIMATING MONTHS:	--J------F------M------A------M------J------J------A------S------O------N------D------J------			
WEATHER				
Temperature	hot	cool	warm	hot
Rainfall	high intensity showers	widespread rains	occasional rains	occasional thunderstorms
WATER SOURCES				
Permanency	intermittent & ephemeral	ephemeral & semi-permanent	semi-permanent	permanent
Classification	claypans	claypans, pools	rockholes, pools	rockholes, springs, soaks
ANIMAL RESOURCES				
Mammals and birds	***	***	***	***
e.g.	emus, red kangaroos	bustards, nestlings, pups	bustards	euros
Reptiles	***	*	**	**
Insects	***	***	***	**
e.g.	termite aeletes	witchetty grubs	witchetty grubs	lerps
PLANT RESOURCES				
Seeds	*	***	***	**
Fruits	*	**	***	**
Tubers	**	***	***	**
Stores	**	*	*	***
SELECTED PLANT-GATHERING AREAS	claypans & surrounding sandplain/dune country	primary & headwater streams	sandplains & water-courses	variety of habitats
GROUP MOBILITY	high	moderate	low	relatively sedentary
GROUP SIZE	small	medium	medium to large	small
PARTS OF RANGE UTILIZED	marginal areas of range	outer favored areas of range	inner favored areas of range	dry reserve areas, probably of estate

Relative importance of food groups: *** = high   ** = moderate   * = low

Figure 2-2. The cycle of Mardu seasons, resource availability, and mobility. (After Walsh 1990.)

Camp scene: While Yanindu mends a cracked wooden dish with spinifex resin, her son Jambijin plays nearby with a docile lizard perched on his head. Although fierce in looks, the thorny lizard (Moloch horridus) *is a harmless insect eater. The smaller dish in the foreground is a temporary container made of bark.*

significance. Under normal conditions, they remain physically present within their homeland, but if separated for some reason, strong sentiments of belonging persist.

The life-style of the Mardu involves a continuing dialectic between the ecological constraints that push people apart and the cultural pressures that draw them together. Although the resulting synthesis necessitates dispersal, it must be kept in mind that the Aborigines do not see this as a bad thing, forced on them by their marginal environment, but rather as something ordained by the Dreaming; they travel in small bands because the ancestral beings did, and it is therefore the only right and proper way to live.

Subsistence Activities   Considering how arid their homeland is, it might be expected that the Mardu would have to expend a great deal of time and energy in the quest for food. This is not so and, in this respect, they are much like their fellow hunter-gatherers elsewhere in the world (cf. Sahlins 1972). Their hunting and harvesting seldom entail any real sense of urgency or battle against time and the elements. Food-collecting activities rarely occupy more than half the day—much less if there is an abundance of easily harvested fruit, tubers, or grass seeds nearby or if the men are successful in spearing large game close to camp. In summer, people hunt and gather food very early in the day, before it becomes too unbearably hot in the open; in winter, they wait until the sun is well up before leaving the warmth of their fires. Whatever the season, there is normally ample leisure time for sleeping, playing with small children, chatting idly, or for the discussion, planning, or enacting of ritual activity, which for the men, especially, is a consuming passion.

Each new day necessitates decision-making by band members as to which foods to seek and where and, eventually, about when to move camp and in which direction to travel. These decisions, which are reached informally by men and women, depend on factors such as weather conditions, the amount of leftover food in camp, the distance to available food resources, individual inclinations, and so on. The prospect of an eventual shift of camp location is ever-present because the Mardu are faced with the inevitability of steadily diminishing food returns the longer they stay in the same place; this, as Sahlins (1972:33) notes, is the major limitation of the hunter-gatherer economy, which "requires movement to maintain production on advantageous terms."

For food-getting activities, sex-role allocation remains much the same. Men and youths seek large game such as kangaroos, emus, wallabies, and bush turkeys; women and children collect plant foods and smaller game such as bandicoots, possums, small birds, lizards, and snakes, that in total make up the bulk of the diet. Women's contribution to the food supply has been variously estimated at between sixty and eighty percent of the total weight of food collected by desert Aborigines who exploit resource zones similar to those of the Mardu (Gould 1969b:258; Meggitt 1962). The vegetable foods and small game women obtain are more reliable resources than those generally exploited by men. Plant foods are either at a certain place or they are not, whereas large animals are less predictable food sources

A satisfied group after a successful day's gathering; note Manggaji's hair-twine necklet and the use of emu-feather headpad.

Ending a long and tiring dig after the rapidly burrowing rabbit-eared bandi-coot (Macrotis lagotis), *Minma finally secures his quarry.*

because they are mobile, and there is always a measure of luck in the hunt. Women and, occasionally, men hunt lizards and smaller game frequently and with greater likelihood of success; at times, lizards form a significantly large proportion of the daily diet. Both sexes can engage in hunting and gathering activities, and members of each are quite capable of sustaining themselves independently when the occasion arises, for example, if ritual matters take men away from their bands for a prolonged period, as sometimes happens.

Women usually endeavour to go as a group in search of food, because the nature of their activities allows them to be sociable and share child-minding as they work. Men are more likely to hunt alone or in pairs, since few of their hunting techniques require the cooperative efforts of a larger number. However, several men may sometimes join forces to ambush animals after they are driven into a cul-de-sac. Many desert animals are skittish and easily panicked, so hunters must be highly skilled at stalking, which requires considerable patience to move in close enough for the spear-kill. Men do not take their sons with them until the boys are mature enough to cover long distances and endure the silence and tension of stalking game without detection.

During hunting, a person's encyclopedic knowledge of the behavior of animals is tested. Kangaroos, for example, have such acute senses of smell and hearing that they can detect the presence of humans a long distance away. Should this happen, the hunter performs a perfect imitation of the response behavior appropriate to that animal, including sounds. If the animal is reassured, the hunter can continue to close in until he launches a spear. If his aim has been true, the wounded animal will not go far before collapsing.[10] After gutting the kangaroo and closing the incision with a sharp stick, the hunter sets a large fire and throws the animal in long enough to singe off its fur. Later, when the fire has died down, the carcass is tossed on its back into an earth oven and covered with hot ashes and sand. Since Mardu prefer their meat rare, it is often eaten quite bloody. Although roasting pits may be dug close to a camp, most large animals are cooked near to where they are killed rather than at the campsite. The men carry large hunks of butchered cooked meat into camp threaded on their spears like a huge shish kebab. Kangaroos are always butchered into the same cuts of meat, each of which is designated as belonging to particular kin. Meat is usually consumed within a day or so, before the rotting process is far advanced. Dogs get the inedible scraps and bones, unless they can steal something more appetizing.

For women, preparing food is usually a simple and quick task, with the notable exception of grass and *Acacia* shrub seeds, the processing of which has been described as "clearly the most strenuous aspect of traditional subsistence activities" (Cane 1989:104).[11] These are harvested into wooden dishes, then taken back to

---

[10]Dingoes are not heavily relied upon as hunting dogs, but they are useful in corraling wounded game animals to prevent their easy escape. See Gould (1980:238–47) for a detailed discussion of difficult questions concerning the economic contribution of tame dingoes as food providers.

[11]From his ethnoarcheological work in the northeast of the Western Desert, Cane (1989) estimates that the contribution of seeds to the diet ranged from between five percent (in the hot season, when few are available) to thirty to forty percent (in the cold season, in localities with abundant seed resources). Although Cane categorizes seeds as a supplementary rather than a staple food and empasizes the high energy cost of transforming them into food, he notes that seeds are uniquely valuable for two reasons— they can be stored, and some are always to be found somewhere. Both Walsh (1990) and Cane suggest that seeds were preferentially used when large quantities were available and processing could therefore be done more efficiently.

While Minma prepares a large fire to cook a plains kangaroo (marlu), *sons Nun and Jambijin play with the carcass.*

camp where they are wind winnowed and finally separated from the chaff by an ingenious and efficient panning method. The dish containing seeds and chaff is rhythmically shaken in such a way that gravity separation occurs, and the waste is easily removed. The seeds are then ground and mixed with water to make a paste which is cooked or eaten raw. Men cook large game and prepare secret ritual feasts

Manuba grinds woolybutt grass seeds into flour while daughter Nyanyawa plays by her side. (Photo © Film Australia from the film Desert People).

at times, but the bulk of food preparation and cooking is done by women. Firewood is usually readily obtained, and cooking requires a suitable quantity of hot ashes, coals, and sand, in which the food is baked. Cooked food has the sand and charcoal fragments dusted and picked off before it is eaten. Nevertheless, considerable grit is chewed and ingested with food and contributes to a wearing down of teeth in later life, although in other respects the teeth of the Mardu are excellent. Teeth are used for many tasks besides chewing; for example, men sometimes use them to flake and sharpen stone blades.

Although, as a rule, the Mardu eat only one main meal a day, in the late afternoon, everyone snacks from time to time while hunting or gathering. The most common snack foods are fruits, nectars (sucked from flowers or mixed with water to make an infusion) and tree gum, eggs, fungi (edible truffle-like varieties that grow in sandhills), lerp (a sweet, white secretion left by scale insects on leaves), and, less often, honey ants (first dig out the nest; hold the ant's head; bite off distended, honey-filled abdomen; discard head; repeat).

Children generally eat all that they hunt or gather on the spot. They frequently hunt small lizards and, at an early age, boys become skilled in throwing sticks and stones at small birds. When killed, these are roughly plucked, then thrown briefly into the ashes of a small fire prior to their rapid consumption. Lizards and native mice are cooked and eaten in the same way. Like their elders, children share food with one another, and sometimes play at distributing it. They are active and independent and often climb trees to get eggs and chicks, which are prized foods in the late-winter months. Some birds and animals may be kept as pets, but the children are so rough on them that all except dingoes usually die in a very short time. Tame dingoes are incredibly patient, allowing children to perpetrate all sorts of indignities on them without protest, just as they allow adults to abuse and kick them at times. On the positive side, they are fondled, petted, and kissed by both young and old, who also sleep with them; so it is not entirely a dog's life. Besides their status as pets, dogs are valued by the Mardu because they are believed to be excellent detectors of the presence of evil spirits or strangers with homicidal intentions (cf. Kolig 1978).

Tools   Nomadism and a lack of beasts of burden impose considerable constraints on the volume and weight of tools, weapons, and other possessions that can be carried by the desert people. Gould (1978), who adopts an activity-oriented view of Aboriginal technology, suggests a classification of the artifact inventory of the Western Desert into three kinds of tools: multipurpose, appliance, and instant.

Virtually all multipurpose tools are lightweight and portable, and most are made of wood. The essential kit of the woman is the digging stick, a wooden rod about four-feet long with fire-hardened points that are often chisel shaped. When digging out small game and tubers, it may be supplemented by small digging dishes which double as containers or scoops. The wooden dish is another major artifact of the women. This and less-durable bark containers are carved by men from large eucalypt trees, and most are two- to three-feet long, one-foot wide, and less than one-foot deep. Carried under the arm or on the head (supported by a pad made from grass, string, or feathers), they are used to transport foodstuffs, water (with grass added to lessen splashing), and, on occasion, small babies. The other essential woman's tool is a small, smooth stone which is used together with large, flat-base stones or flat rock surfaces for grinding seeds and other foods.

The inventory of men's portable artifacts is greater. Spears are mostly of the throwing type, eight- to ten-feet long, straightened shortly after cutting and stripping (from trees and roots) by heating over a fire, then manipulating by the use of hands, feet, and teeth while the wood is still supple. They are smoothed and sharpened with stone adzes and flakes. A fire-hardened tip is made at one end and a small depression which engages the tip of the spearthrower's barb at the other. Most are left smooth, but some have barbs either carved into them or attached by means of sinew taken from the legs or tail of a kangaroo. This sinew is chewed until thoroughly softened, then tightly bound around the small, sharpened wooden barb and the spear tip; the sinew contracts and tightens the joint as it dries. In the same way, the nesting barb for spears is attached to the spearthrower. A second kind of spear is the shorter, thicker stabbing variety, which is used to inflict thigh wounds in fights among adult men.

The spearthrower best exemplifies the multipurpose nature of Aboriginal artifacts. The Mardu version is two- to three-feet long, and four-inches wide, with a concave, container-like shaft (some are much flatter and usually have a geometrical snakelike design carved onto them), a barb at one end, and a stone flake set into the other with a lump of spinifex resin.[12] Besides its primary use as a spear launcher, which enables a man to throw a spear eighty to one hundred yards or hit a target with force and accuracy within about forty yards, it has many other uses: as a tray in which to mix native tobacco and ashes or ochres used in body decorations;[13] as a fire-making tool; as a scraper and knife for woodworking and preparing and butchering game; as a percussion instrument, when tapped in accompaniment to singing; and as a hook for obtaining fruits, berries, or other objects that are out of reach.

The returning boomerang is about two-feet long, cut from suitably bent mulga trees and then carved; it is used for fighting and as a musical instrument, but not for hunting. Its sharp edges and susceptibility to wind gusts make it a vicious and unpredictable weapon, which is thrown so that it bounces short of an opponent and ricochets up into the body, unless deflected with a parrying shield. Shields are two- to three-feet long and six-inches wide; they are used with marvelous dexterity by men to deflect incoming missiles, and they double as clubs in fighting at close quarters. Boomerangs, shields, and wooden fighting clubs (two or more feet long and cut from heavy wood or roots) are not usually carried during hunting activities.

The selection of suitable trees from whose trunks or roots tools will be manufactured requires considerable skill, for a man has to visualize what the finished shape will be. After "seeing" the completed tool in a tree or shrub of the right shape, he may either cut the part immediately or memorize the spot in case he decides to return at some future time when the need for that particular tool arises.

Men carry a limited assortment of small flake knives which are used for a variety of cutting and scraping tasks. Most are hand-held in use, but favorite blades may have a small resin handle attached. The use of large hand-held axes has ceased since the acquisition of metal tools and since the Mardu have had access to metal objects that can be made into tools. Many desert people began using metal tools long before they first encountered whites. These highly valued items were acquired from frontier settlements and diffused via exchange networks throughout the interior.

Appliances, Gould's second category of artifact, are left at a site and reused on subsequent visits. The large base-stones used in grinding food and ochre are quite heavy and so are left at camping grounds and places close to seed-producing areas. Hand-held stone pounders, used for mashing bones to extract marrow, and, formerly, hand axes (which weighed four to eight pounds) are sometimes left on hard antbeds that provide a solid working surface or on granite outcrops where flat rock

[12]Resin is found in tiny globules at the base of the stalks of spinifex species which prefer wetter areas. To collect resin, clumps of spinifex are beaten, causing the globules to fall off; these are then winnowed to separate them from sand. Fire is used to fuse the resin into a ball which is soft when heated but becomes rock-hard once cool. It is used to mend holes in dishes and for hafting.

[13]Wild tobacco (*Nicotiana* species) is probably as prized by the Mardu as nectars and other sweet foods. It is often called by the same generic term, *wama,* which today is also used to refer to alcoholic beverages. The tobacco leaves are stripped from the plant, dried, and crumbled, then mixed with ash (made by burning leaves of an *Acacia* or *Grevillea* shrub or the bark of the coolibah tree (*Eucalyptus microtheca*) and then chewed as a wad. In hot weather, especially, it keeps the mouth moist (Gould 1969a:9). It also stains the teeth and the roof of the mouth.

surfaces occur. A supply of stone suitable for flaking may also be carried to camping sites to form a reserve for future visits.

Instant tools, the third category, are implements fashioned from raw materials available close at hand. They are used when a particular need arises, then discarded. Stone axes, pounders, and flakes are often made in this way. Similarly, grass circlets made by women to cushion dishes carried on the head, and some of the objects used in fire making, are used then thrown away. The side of a spearthrower forms part of the main fire-making toolset. A mixture of tinder-dry grass and powdered kangaroo dung is rammed into a split piece of dead wood. The thrower is sawed rapidly across the open crack and ignites the mixture. It usually takes only one or two minutes of hard sawing to produce fire.

Another instant tool is the spindle, a thin stick about eighteen-inches long with two small crosspieces at right angles to each other threaded several inches down the shaft. Most twine used by the Mardu is made from human hair; strips of possum fur and bark may also be used. Hair is spun by men or women, who roll the spindle up and down the thigh to produce the spinning motion that twines the hair, which has been mixed beforehand with fat and red ochre to bind it and help retain its suppleness. A ball of string is formed around the crosspieces and, when the task is completed, the sticks are removed and discarded.

Shelters and Camp Layout   Shelters are of simple construction and require little effort to make. The Mardu sweep or scrape a suitable site clear and burn the surrounding area to discourage unwelcome animals. If there are no handy tree forks at the campsite, simple storage platforms are made by wedging grass into nearby shrubs; leftover meat and other food can then be kept beyond the reach of dogs. The summer camp (*buri,* meaning "shade") is a semicircle of leafy shrubbery or branches stuck upright in the ground, with grass sometimes added to thicken the shade. The simple winter shelter is really only a windbreak of uprooted grass or shrubbery, with a slight depression dug out in a row on the leeward side for each family member. Small fires are set between every depression, with a length of wood placed parallel to the sleepers. The wood can then be pushed into the fire throughout the night so as to keep the coals warm. In the uncommon event of winter rain, and if Mardu are far from suitable caves in which to take shelter, more elaborate wet weather camps may be constructed.

Each family group camps separately and has its own cooking fire. Boys and young men sleep apart in bachelor shelters but usually eat with their respective families. The distance between camps varies between about ten and fifty yards, depending on the nature of friendship and kinship ties, current amity or tension, and the need for privacy. When different bands gather, they orient their camps so that each group is situated closest to the direction of its home territory. All campsites are located some distance from a water source, rarely closer than one hundred yards, so as to allow game undisturbed access to water. Also, if a site is sacred and therefore dangerous to all but initiated men, bands will camp further away. In sandhill country and when winds are not too strong, the tops of high dunes are preferred as campsites because they provide a good vista. In fact, in most cases, the Mardu choose campsites that afford a clear view in all directions. Their dislike of camping in hilly country or any partly enclosed areas relates to fears of attack by revenge expeditions (see Chapter 5).

Environmental Management   Research conducted in recent decades has shown that earlier views of hunter-gatherers as passive food collectors must be revised, since it is now clear that "hunter-gatherers *actively manage* their resources, whether through strategic ecological or economic courses of action via social controls and political maneuver, or by virtue of the power of symbol and ritual" (Hunn and Williams 1982:1). Hunter-gatherers are now seen as purposefully engaged in the preservation, manipulation, and management of their natural resources. This takes place not only through the use of mundane techniques, for example, the propagation of seeds, but also more broadly, as in the use by Aborigines of ritual as a "technology" of production (see Chapter 5). However, the present discussion is focused on more direct forms of resource management.

The most obvious evidence of Aboriginal "management" is provided by the use of fire, which is a major practice throughout the continent.[14] Aborigines use it to "clean up" the land by burning away dead growth while at the same time promoting plant regrowth. Whenever they shift camp, the Mardu carry firesticks and, while traveling and hunting, they set fire to the vegetation en route. Firesticks carried close to the body provide a surprising amount of warmth, and burning spinifex gives out intense but short-lived heat. The abundant smoke that results indicates not only a group's presence but also its direction of travel, making the chances of meeting up with like groups much greater, although there is no message inherent in the pattern of smoke. The firing of vegetation facilitates tracking by clearing and exposing the sand and also flushes out small game such as marsupial mice, snakes, and lizards. Although the time of firing is not seasonally determined, the Mardu do not burn vegetation indiscriminately. Sandplains and sand dunes may be burnt as soon as there is enough vegetation to carry a fire. Watercourse areas are fired less frequently in order to protect certain important plants, and ranges and uplands rarely burn because they do not often have enough fuel (Walsh 1990). Mardu burning activities provide the most telling evidence of their modifications to the landscape. The ground is cleared by a fire; then, when rain falls, new plants grow on the burnt patch. For example, the Mardu burn spinifex to "bring up" grasses, herbs, and bush tomatoes that are more useful as food resources, since spinifex seeds are unreliable and laborious to harvest. Many of these early colonizer species provide bushfood for Mardu and fresh growth for game (Latz 1982, Walsh 1990). As the burnt patch ages, other plants replace the early species. The small fires lit by Mardu as they travel thus result in a mosaic of plant communities, which are an important feature of desert ecosystems.

In harvesting tubers, the Mardu generally leave the older "mother tubers" intact and try to avoid damaging others that are left in the ground. By fragmenting roots and tubers during their digging activities, the Mardu may contribute to the reproduction and dispersal of these important resources (Walsh 1990:34, Veth and Walsh

[14]For accounts of the significance of fire in Aboriginal culture, see Jones (1969), Kimber (1983), Latz (1982), and Lewis (1982, 1989). For the use of fire in the Western Desert, see Gould (1971) and Walsh (1990).

A hunter fires spinifex grass as he travels.

1988). Seeds of the bush tomato are frequently scattered on burnt areas near campsites. The spread of *Solanum* species to areas beyond their normal range could result from the exchange of seeds and fruits during big meetings (Walsh 1990:35).

More generally, Mardu strategies tend be aimed at avoiding the total depletion of food resources anywhere, though obviously those areas surrounding favored camping spots near major water sources would be susceptible to intensive exploitation at times. Mardu patterns of movement from campsite to campsite tend to follow watercourses, the bases of hills, and sandplain areas where spinifex has been recently burnt because, in these areas, plant communities are more resource rich, water sources are more common, and walking is easier than in poorer, hilly areas.

Reciprocity and "Trade" Anthropologists use the term "generalized reciprocity" to describe the kind of sharing that habitually occurs among people who live together and/or are closely related. Among hunter-gatherers, it is the dominant form of exchange and for very good reasons. Regardless of differences in skill and stamina that inevitably occur among hunters, there is an unstated conviction that everyone eventually gets as much as they give, so that things even out in the long run. In any case, the fulfillment of kinship obligations is a primary responsibility in Aboriginal culture, and a willingness to give is one of the most significant indicators of individual social worth. Large game is always shared with other families in the band and the hunter allots himself one of the poorer cuts. Most sharing of vegetable foods, on the other hand, takes place within the family or "hearth group"—a term used to underline the importance of the cooking fire as the focal point of each family's activities. The Mardu sometimes share vegetable foods, especially when daughters, daughters-in-law, and other younger female relatives give them to older women whose gathering activities have been curtailed by infirmity. In this way, band members ensure that the elderly are adequately nourished.

Most material goods needed for subsistence can be obtained within the home territory of every local group, but a few scarce and valued resources necessitate exchanges of some kind. These transactions enhance sociality at the same time as making highly desired items available to people in areas that lack them. The small amount of trade that exists among the Mardu takes place within three main contexts: ritual activities during big meetings, gift exchange between friendly kin when small bands meet, and as part of obligations owed to certain close kin and affines. The more scarce resources, such as red ochre, stones prized for toolmaking, and pearlshells (from the northwest coast) diffuse through countless such exchanges, but there are no markets and no set standards of value for such items. Trade, as usually understood and in the case of nonsacred material objects, is a peripheral element in desert culture. In gift exchange, the most commonly swapped objects are foodstuffs; for example, a man gives meat to his parents-in-law and receives vegetable foods from them. The significance of exchange lies far less in the nature or value of the items than in the act of reciprocity itself, which affirms and reinforces a continuing bond. The alliances that are forged in this way help to promote a level of harmony, between individuals and groups, that is essential in the harsh desert environment. The maintenance of friendly relations through reciprocity enables people to extend their food-getting activities into the territories of other groups—an absolutely vital adaptation for coping with prolonged periods of drought.

Nutrition and Health   No detailed nutritional studies have been made among Western Desert Aborigines, but several medical surveys have been carried out among people who have had little prior contact with whites (for example, Elphinstone 1971). Such studies have concluded that the desert people seem adequately nourished and that their diet is well balanced, with no vitamin or protein deficiency detectable. In addition to game animals, particularly lizards which are the most reliable source of animal protein and edible grubs that are very high in protein, many of the grass and shrub seeds that are desert staples have protein contents in excess of twenty percent and are also good sources of fatty acids and energy. When ripe, most bush tomatoes (*Solanum* species), which are important staples, are very high in vitamin C (Peterson 1977). Desert fruits supply essential vitamins, minerals, and dietary fiber; roots and tubers are good sources of moisture and energy as well as other nutrients (Veth and Walsh 1988). Mardu are emphatic that it is essential to eat a mix of different sorts of food and, in so doing, they are probably consuming the full range of nutrients required to stay healthy.

Their nomadic, small-group life-style, as well as the dry desert air, must contribute to the physical health of the Mardu, who suffer few serious ailments and, from my observations, would perhaps have a life expectancy in excess of fifty years. Trachoma, an eye disease that can cause blindness, is probably the most widespread serious affliction, especially among old people, some of whom become completely blind. Boils are common, as are periodic intestinal upsets brought on most often by eating large quantities of fatty meat, such as emu. Many people receive burns when they thrust an arm or leg, or they roll entirely, into the fires that burn close beside them while they sleep during winter nights. If burn sores develop, they are treated with mudpacks. If children survive the first year or two, they will probably continue to be healthy. Many children have distended bellies, but this appears not to be symptomatic of malnutrition or parasitic infestation, and children lose their potbellies as their stomach muscles develop in adolescence.

Head lice are endemic and their removal is a frequent grooming activity of adults and children alike. A novel treatment for this condition is to catch a snake lizard (*Lerista* species; a four-inch, pink, two-legged creature) and put it on one's head, where it proceeds to feast on the lice.[15] People sometimes suffer from headache, which they treat most often by binding hair-string very tightly around the head. This kind of hair-string, called *yulyja,* is soaked in a mixture of fat and red ochre and is frequently used to alleviate all kinds of aches and pains.

Illness that lingers or is considered serious is treated by a diviner-curer (see Chapter 5). The few herbal medicines used by the Mardu are applied to the body or are drunk as infusions. Liniments include cooked and pounded quandong nut kernels, used for muscular aches and pains, and a very strong menthol-smelling grass that is chopped finely or pounded and mixed with water to treat chills and

---

[15]See Trigger (1981) for a fascinating account of the cultural significance of head lice among Aborigines in northwestern Queensland.

fevers. Skin irritations and infections are treated by similar means, and a root is sometimes held between the teeth and gums to relieve toothache (Walsh 1990). Sickness caused by eating toxic substances or plants is rare because the Mardu know and avoid these, but they do make some use of poisonous plants, such as a *Duboisia* species, in hunting emus.[16]

Given that the Mardu live in one of the world's toughest environments, it might be assumed that, in terms of mental health, they would be a tense and morose people wracked by anxieties caused by the constant threat of drought. In fact, nothing could be further from the truth; the Mardu display the same confident outlook that has been reported for many other hunter-gatherers and is "the reasonable human attribute of a generally successful economy" (Sahlins 1972:29). As will be seen, in the Mardu case, this outlook is based essentially on religious confidence. Since personality factors will be discussed later (Chapter 6), all that needs to be said here is that the Mardu seem to be very well-adjusted individuals. As one would expect, they are every bit as complex and given to behavioral idiosyncrasies as any other peoples, with the same capacity for exultation or despair. Despite outbursts of anger and violence, daily life is most often characterized by relaxed and harmonious interaction, sharing, and considerable humor, so the impression conveyed to outsiders tends to be abidingly positive.

CONCLUSION

This brief overview of the habitat and subsistence activities of the Mardu has not attempted to offer a comprehensive account of economic life, since quantification of the kind typical of formal economics is absent (no such measurements were ever made). There is also no attempt here to discuss the political dimensions inherent in getting a living—except to hint strongly at one the the major themes of this study: the permeability of boundaries and the stress on cooperation and harmony as overriding considerations in an ecologically marginal environment.[17] The relationship of economic life to politics, including gender relations, and the religious life is discussed later (Chapter 5). All that remains to be noted here is that, although the desert may test the Mardu severely in times of prolonged drought, it almost never tries them beyond the limits of their considerable ingenuity and endurance. Having fully mastered the necessary subsistence skills, they cope with an irregular rhythm of life by imposing their will intellectually rather than physically on the desert (their extensive use of fire notwithstanding). The chapter that follows describes the vital

---

[16]Choosing a site with more than one water source, the men block all but one waterhole with sticks and other materials, then put crushed leaves of the poison shrub into the uncovered pool. Upon drinking the water, emus (or other animals) quickly become drugged and unsteady, making them an easy target for the hunters who watch from a nearby blind. The guts of any animals thus poisoned are not eaten, and the water is not drunk until a long time after; a pile of stones or similar signal is left as a marker to warn other Mardu.

[17]For a detailed overview of Australian Aboriginal economies, see Anderson (1988) and for a full account of an Arnhem Land economy, see Altman (1987). For other accounts of various Aboriginal economic adaptations, see Part 2 of Mulvaney and White (1988).

part played by certain manifestations of the intellectual edifice that comprises Mardu culture: multiple systems of classification that impose order, predictability, and pattern on social life. Mardu lives unfold within a seemingly disordered and unpredictable habitat which affects their social organization in many different ways, yet their complex classificatory systems cannot be explained by reference solely or even predominantly to ecological imperatives.

3 / The Social Imperative

The denial by Mardu of human creativity in favor of the world-creative acts of spiritual powers leads them to regard their kinship system, marriage rules, social categories, and so on as givens, part of the master plan bequeathed them by the creative beings of the Dreaming—and also as imperatives, because the Law demands conformity to them. Since Mardu culture produces neither revolutionaries nor skeptics, this suggests a close fit between environmental adaptation, the forms and practices of social organization, and religious ideology.

This chapter examines several major kinds of classifying systems that give form and substance to Mardu social relationships. The intimate connection between the Mardu economy and these elements of social organization will be obvious, since systems of production throughout Aboriginal Australia are structured in accordance with kinship principles.[1]

KINSHIP

Kinship is a system of social relationships that are expressed in a biological idiom, using terms like "mother," "son," and so on. It is best visualized as a mass of networks of relatedness, no two of which are identical, that radiate from each individual. Kinship is *the* basic organizing principle in small-scale societies like those of the Aborigines and provides a model for interpersonal behavior. In familistic societies of this kind, sex and age are the two major determinants of an individual's status, but neither is sufficient to regulate behavior, so kinship assumes a central role. Thus there is virtually no relationship of dominance, deference, obligation, or equality that is divorced from considerations of kinship. Quite unlike the situation in industrialized societies, where a person has daily dealings with many people other than kin, the moral universe of the Mardu is populated solely with relatives. All people with whom a person comes into contact are classified and

---

[1]See Wolf (1982) for a clear account of such "kin-ordered" modes of production, which embed social labor in particular relations of kinship between individuals. In his view, this particularization of relationships limits the scope of tensions and conflicts and thus inhibits the rise of larger-scaled oppositions akin to classes.

known by a particular kin term, and adult social interaction is modeled on a set of behaviors that ideally characterize the kin relationship involved.[2]

A basic feature of all Aboriginal kinship systems is that they are classificatory; that is, the kinship terms used between people who are consanguines (blood relatives) are also applied to more distantly related, and unrelated, people. Classificatory kinship is based on two major principles. First, in reckoning kin relationships, siblings of the same sex are classed as equivalent, so that my father's brothers are classed together with my father and are all called by the same term, which in Mardu is *mama;* similarly, my mother's sisters are called *yagurdi* (mother). Therefore, my parallel cousins on both sides of my family (MZChn and FBChn) I classify as "brother" and "sister" because they are children of people I call "mother" and "father."[3] In turn, I call the children of my male parallel cousins "son" and "daughter," since any woman my "brother" calls "wife" I will also call "wife." Secondly, the classifying principle can be expanded to embrace a theoretically infinite number of people; the web of kinship thus extends far beyond consanguineal and local group limits to include the most distant of kin and former strangers.

The social universe of the Mardu includes "kin," "strangers" (who are sufficiently like them to be incorporated into the category of "kin"), and "distant people," those who are never encountered and who are thought to possess many less-than-human characteristics and behaviors such as long teeth, cannibalistic habits, huge sexual organs, and assorted depravities. When strangers are encountered, they need only to establish their kin relationship with one member of the group for all of its other members to be able to categorize them correctly in kin terms. If not even this much is known, their social category is used to help designate them adequately. Since all normal interaction occurs among "kin," the Mardu make constant use of kin terms of address and reference. Kinship as a framework for action is particularly useful when people who are not well known to each other come together. It provides them with a ready-made, mutually understood, interactional code and thus eliminates the need for any tentative period of negotiation of suitable behavior. A kin term is simultaneously a status term, so it encodes a great deal of information that is useful for framing interaction between individuals. Regardless of whether some other person is loved or hated, admired or envied, patterned kin behavior allows both actors a measure of predictability in their encounters.

Within the limits set by these ideal patterns of behavior, there is always scope for variation. In other words, the Aborigines are not so rigidly imprisoned by their kinship system that the free expression of feelings and emotions is stifled. Enmeshed they certainly are, by the fact of birth and the impossibility of opting out of

---

[2]R. and C. Berndt (1988:90), outlining the centrality of kinship in Aboriginal life, note that it is "in effect a shorthand statement about the network of interpersonal relations within [a group]. . . . It does not reflect, except in ideal terms, the actuality of that situation; but it does provide a code of action which those members cannot ignore if they are to live in relative harmony with one another."

[3]In this study, letters are used frequently as shorthand for kinship terms: for example, "MZS" is "mother's sister's son." "E" and "Y" are "elder" and "younger;" "W" is "wife." Also, to avoid confusion, "Z" is used for "sister" and "S" for "son." Quotation marks indicate classificatory as distinct from consanguineal relationships.

the system, but the Mardu appreciate individual differences and their kinship system makes some allowance for differing preferences and sentiments.

Many factors account for variations within the broad limits imposed by kin categorization. For one thing, no terminological distinction is made between close blood relatives and distant kin; while, for example, a person generally behaves toward all those women termed "mother" in a similar way, the emotional component in the behavior will be very different for one's physiological mother (genetrix), and for those other "mothers" who were part of one's early socialization, than for distant "mothers."[4] The kin terminology, then, gives no clues to the intensity of feelings that exist within a given relationship. Except for terms that distinguish older from younger siblings, the classificatory system ignores relative age, so that in every category there will be a range of individuals from infants to very old; for example, some of one's "mothers" will be infants and young girls and some of one's "sons" will be middle-aged and old men and so on. Frequently, then, the relative ages of the two people concerned will modify the nature of their interaction. Close friendship, especially if it dates from childhood, often leads adults whose relationship ideally entails restraint to relax the rules a little.

People possess a fund of information concerning the personality and behavior of their relatives, which provides a reliable guide to the expected actions and reactions of these kin in given situations. People's personal likes and dislikes of others are obviously important in motivating decisions to seek or avoid contacts. The physical setting, a person's emotional state, general disposition, and felt needs can also influence conduct. Knowing only the kin categories involved, an outsider should be able to predict with some success the kinds of interpersonal behavior that will obtain. Unless the system demands extreme restraint or outright avoidance, which operate regardless of personality factors or sentiment, these other factors must also be taken into account to understand just what is going on.

The relatively restricted and patterned behavioral field that is created by kinship has advantages for interaction among Aborigines. Besides providing some measure of predictability in behavior, it enhances each individual's sense of self and of belonging. Strong feelings of security and well-being stem from being enveloped in a cocoon of kin, with all of whom some feeling of mutual obligation and responsibility ideally exists. I have not heard Mardu express resentment or frustration at the restrictions that their kinship system places on them, though undoubtedly there are many younger, sexually active people who may privately wish that many more kin of the opposite sex belonged to the "spouse" category. Instead, people talk with satisfaction about the good feelings that come from being surrounded by so many others who are "one family," "one country," and "one people" with them and from whom nurturance and support can be sought.

The Mardu, realistically, do not expect children—especially small ones—to conform to the kinship system. Children's lives in the desert are remarkably free from restraints, and very little pressure is put on them in their socialization.

---

[4]Should the need arise, the term *walyja* (own) is used to distinguish consanguineal from classificatory kin, but this is not an infallible guide, because people sometimes use the term in reference to other relatives with whom some special bond is felt but no close blood tie exists.

Nevertheless, they are born into a world of kinship statuses and hear kin terms in constant use, so as soon as they are considered capable of assimilating knowledge they are taught the shoulds and should-nots of behavior toward various kin. They observe the system in action and thus learn both the ideal and actual patterning of social relationships as part of growing up. People of the grandparent generation, in particular, teach them songs and dances, tell them stories, and instruct them about the proper behaviors and obligations associated with kinship; sometimes they also jokingly scold them for "improper" behavior. Children begin conforming to the rules of kinship behavior in early adolescence, as very powerful feelings of shame and embarrassment develop, causing them to become increasingly self-conscious.

The several groups that constitute the Mardu share basically the same kinship system, and there is no kin category that is found in one and not the others.[5] There are some differences in vocabulary, however. Although the terms given below are those of the Gardujarra speakers, many of them occur widely throughout the Western Desert, though not necessarily in reference to the same category.

Table 3-1 lists the terms of address, from both male and female perspectives, and the kin categories to which each refers, as well as the reciprocals of each term. From this table it can be seen that males and females share most terms, and each sex uses 17 different terms of address. (*Wumari* is not an address term because men and women so related completely avoid one another, the rare exceptions occurring during certain rituals and in the event of a serious dispute.) The system groups several different categories of kin under a single term in many cases; for example, all one's relatives in the grandparent and grandchild generations are merged under two very similar terms, differing only for the sex of the person addressed. Whenever identical reciprocal terms are used, as between spouses or most same-generation members and their grandparents, the relevant expected behavior is predominantly symmetrical or egalitarian. On the other hand, when two people address each other using different reciprocals (for example, "father"-"son"), a status difference and asymmetrical behavioral norms are suggested; that is, one person will defer to the other, as in most relationships between adjacent generations, but also between older and younger siblings.

Besides the many address terms listed in Table 3-1, the Mardu make extensive use of reference terms which derive partly from the single terms, but are usually used in the dual case when a person refers to two different relatives, one of whom is being addressed, or to many relatives standing in the same relationship. This large set of dual terms adds considerable complexity to the system of kin terms—to say nothing of the headaches it causes for the struggling anthropologist! But for the Mardu who are continually using them in reference, the dual terms simplify the identification of people they are talking about. Also in common use are birth-order terms: *murrgangunya* (first-born), *malyurda* (middle), and *nyirdi* (last-born), which as address and reference terms may persist long past a person's childhood (as in our society when a young adult is referred to as the "baby" of the family).

The kinship system of the Mardu is bilateral insofar as it accords about equal

---

[5]The Mardu kinship system contains elements of two key Australian types: Kariera and Aluridja (see Elkin 1954; Tonkinson 1974).

TABLE 3-1   KINSHIP TERMS

Male Ego		
English	*Mardu*	*Reciprocal*
SPOUSE	mardungu	same
EB; FBS; MZS	gurda	marlangu
EZ; FBD; MZD	jurdu	marlangu
F; FB; WMB	mama	gaja
M; MZ; WFZ	yagurdi	gaja
S; ZDH; BS	gaja	mama
DH; ZS	gaja	gaga
D; ZSW; BD	yurndal	mama
FZ; MBW	gurndili	gaja
MB; WF; MMBS	gaga	gaja
WM (some FZ; MBW)	wumari	(same)
WB; ZH; MBS; FZS	yungguri	(same)
some MBS; FZS	wajirra	(same)
some MBD; FZD	yinkarni	(same)
ZD; SW	ngunyarri; yurndal	gaga
FF; MF; DS; ZDS; FMB; MMB	nyamu	(same)
FM; MM; SD; DD; ZDD; FMZ; MFZ	nyami	(same)
some MBDS; FZDS; MBDD; FZDD	bunyayi	(same)

Female Ego		
English	*Mardu*	*Reciprocal*
SPOUSE	mardungu	(same)
EB; FBS; MZS	gurda	marlangu
EZ; FBD; MZD	jurdu	marlangu
F; FB	mama	yurndal
M; MZ	yagurdi	yurndal
S; ZS	gaja	yagurdi
BS	gaja	gurndili
D; ZD	yurndal	yagurdi
FZ	gurndili	yurndal
HM; HF	ngunyarri	(same)
MB	gaga	yurndal; ngunyarri
DH	wumari	(same)
BW; HZ; MBD; FZD	juwari	(same)
some MBD; FZD	wajirra	(same)
some MBS; FZS	yinkarni	(same)
FF; MF; SS; DS; BDS; FMB; MMB	nyamu	nyami
FM; MM; SD; DD; BDD; FMZ; FMZ	nyami	(same)
some MMBS; MMBD; MFZS; MFZD	bunyayi	(same)

stress to male and female descent principles. The bilaterality of kinship is well illustrated in cases where a person is confronted with a choice in reckoning relationship to the children in a single family; in many cases, the person calculates through the father in allotting terms to some of these children and through the mother for others. This kind of flexibility shows the egocentric nature of kinship reckoning, which makes it possible even for full siblings to use different terms for the same person; for example:

> A man Rali calls Nyinga "mother" but her husband Jiin happens to be related to Rali as "son." He follows Jiin ("S") in calling two of their three children "grandchild," ("SS") but in reckoning his relationship to their older daughter he follows Nyinga ("M") and thus calls the girl "sister."[6]

Once a choice is made in situations such as this, it usually remains fixed, because there is a strong emphasis on keeping kinship alignments stable, both in the terminology used and in maintaining the relevant patterned behavior. Yet some changes can and do occur, resulting in modifications in behavior between certain people. This is best seen in connection with ritual operations (see Chapter 4) when new relationships are activated between a novice (and some of his close relatives) and the men who perform the operation on him, such that restraint and avoidance become the new norms.

Although the Mardu themselves do not describe kinship behaviors in terms of a continuum, it may be helpful to consider the different gradations of expected behaviors as falling between two extremes: complete avoidance and uninhibited joking. Table 3-2 shows the approximate range of behavior exhibited between a male Ego and people in other kin categories to give some idea of what kinds of behavior are expected between which categories of kin and to show the range of variation involved. The two extremes are usually easy to detect. Avoidance relationships, typified by the "WM"-"DH" affinal link, demand that one or both parties take rapid evasive action if either seems likely to come within twenty or thirty yards of the other. Joking relationships, which are more common among same-sex than opposite-sex pairs, involve rowdy exchanges of sexually explicit epithets and mock abuse, with much body contact, which amuse onlookers at least as much as the joking pair.

Whenever there is an element of restraint in the relationship, it suggests the presence of *gurnda* (shame/embarrassment) between individuals so related. Restraint signals also an asymmetry of status that calls for a measure of deference, respect, obedience, authority, and so forth. Restraint relationships entail restrictions on behaviors such as touching, joking, passing objects directly hand to hand, sitting together, visiting the camp of, calling by name, looking directly at while talking, and arguing with or physically assaulting any members of certain kin categories. This system is regulated principally by the pervasive inhibitor of shame or embarrassment rather than by threats of punishment.

The Mardu are mindful of the status differences that exist between members of adjacent generations and are restrained in their interaction unless extreme anger or

---

[6]Throughout this study, fictitious names are used in the case examples.

sexual attraction motivates them temporarily to ignore the norms—in which case they will be upbraided as *gurndabarni* (having no shame). With fairly unrestrained relationships, on the other hand, it is up to the pairs concerned to decide how familiar and physically close they want to be, depending on personality and individual inclinations.

In general, women enjoy a greater number of relatively unrestrained relationships with one another than do men and can talk and interact freely with most other female kin. This freedom may relate to the much greater time they normally spend together in groups than do male hunters. As Table 3-2 indicates, Mardu men interact freely with some categories of male relatives and with certain individuals in others, but a man's behavior toward most close consanguineal adult kin is marked by various degrees of restraint. As might be expected, spouses ideally enjoy a relaxed relationship, but men generally interact in a restrained manner with their parents, siblings of both sexes, and adult offspring.

TABLE 3-2   KIN BEHAVIORAL PATTERNS (MALE EGO)

Avoidance	Restraint	Moderation	Lack of Restraint	Joking
wumari (WM; "WM")				
	gurda (EB)			
	jurdu (EZ)			
	yinkarni (cross-cousin "Z")			
	yurndal (D; "D")			
	yagurdi (M; "M")			
	gurndili (FZ; "FZ")			
	yungguri (WB)			
	← mama (F; "F") ——————→*			
	← gaja (S; "S"; ZS) ————→			
		gurda ("EB")		
		marlangu ("YB"; "YZ")		
		jurdu ("EZ")		
		gaga (MB; WF)		
		ngunyarri ("ZD"; "SW")		
		wajirra (some MBS; FZS; "MBS"; "FZS")		
		bunyayi (female; see Table 3-1)		
		←——— yungguri ("WB") ———→		
			mardungu (W; "W")	
		←——— gaja ("ZS") →		
		←——— gaja gaga ("MB") →		
			nyamu (FF; "FF"; SS; "SS"; etc.)	
			nyami (MM; "MM"; DD; "DD"; etc.)	
				bunyayi (male)
				wajirra
				(cross-cousin "B")

*Arrows indicate approximate range of behavioral variation occurring within these categories. Note the difference between consanguineal and classificatory kin in some categories (for example, B, Z, and MB) and sex differences in others (for example, cross-cousin "sibling" and *bunyayi*) (see Table 3-1).

The terminological distinction made between older and younger siblings indicates a status difference based on relative age. Older siblings share an obligation to discipline younger ones who make trouble, but they should also speak for them and defend them against unwarranted verbal and physical attack. The mechanics of wife selection are such that brothers rarely compete for the same women, so sexual jealousy is not usually a factor in their relationships. However, the ambivalence inherent in the chastiser-defender roles that older brothers must play no doubt leaves a residue of resentment among some younger siblings, which must be controlled because open conflict is untenable between brothers.

Marriage Rules   The prescribed form of marriage among the Mardu is between cross-cousins; that is, a person marries a classificatory cross-cousin ("MBD" or "FZD" for a male; "MBS" or "FZS" for a female) who is called by the term "spouse." However, some cross-cousins are classed as if they are siblings and therefore not marriageable.[7] A person enjoys a very relaxed familiarity with same-sex relatives in this category, but shows the same restraint toward a relative of the opposite sex as if he or she were a sibling. Also, most consanguineally related cross-cousins call each other "spouse," but marriage between them is uncommon because a spouse comes ideally from groups that are both genealogically and geographically distant.

There are some differences in the interpretation of marriage rules among different Mardu subgroups. With Manyjilyjarra and Warnman speakers, marriage sometimes occurs between actual cross-cousins, particularly between a male and his MBD, and a man ideally marries any daughter of a woman he refers to as *wumari* ("WM"), but never the daughter of any *gurndili* ("FZ"), who is regarded as similar to "mother" and whose daughter is therefore *yinkarni*, cross-cousin "sister," not "spouse." Among the Gardujarra and other southern groups, however, the mother of a man's spouse is most often *wumari* but is sometimes related to him as *gurndili* (here, a distant "FZ"). In this case, there is an important behavioral difference: a man does not have to avoid his *gurndili*, although the pair should show mutual restraint.

Sister exchange, in which the kin groups of two men from different groups who classify each other as "B" exchange their sisters in marriage, is possible within the Mardu system, but in fact is quite rare.[8]

Instead, they prefer long-term reciprocity. There is an expectation that the sons or sons' sons of a family which gives one of its females in marriage will eventually receive a wife from the recipients when circumstances permit. The bestowal of infants or little girls is closely linked to male initiation, specifically circumcision;

---

[7]No single factor accounts fully for this selectivity, and male Mardu sometimes explain it by statements to the effect that "you shouldn't have too many wives." The deliberate classification of potential spouses as "sisters" does indeed lessen the range of choice and therefore seems counterintuitive. However, the loss of marriageable women and associated unrestrained relationships in one generation is compensated for in the next. Whereas a man acts with restraint toward "daughters," this is replaced in the case of daughters of cross-cousin "sisters" with a *bunyayi* relationship, which is mutually warm, open, and unrestrained—an exception to the general tenor of relationships between members of adjacent generations.

[8]For a clear discussion of the non-symmetry of a structurally symmetrical Western Desert kinship system and its relationship to alliance theory, see Sackett (1976).

the distant "MB" or "FZH" who is chosen to remove the youth's foreskin, thus symbolically "killing" him, must bestow a daughter upon him as compensation for this drastic act. Circumcision marks the beginning of a prolonged series of gift exchanges between the families of initiator and novice and establishes relationships of strong restraint and avoidance. This inconvenience is offset, however, by advantages derived from such close alliances with distant families whose territory could be a welcome refuge in times of food or water shortages in a family's home area.

Wrong Marriages   Unlike the conventions of some groups to the northeast of them, which favor marriage between second cousins (that is, between pairs whose parents are related as cross-cousins), the Mardu prescribe marriage with both first and second classificatory cross-cousins, thus allowing the individual a wider selection of spouses. This is perhaps one reason why there is such a low incidence of "wrong" marriage; that is, a union between two people who are not related as "spouse" (see Sackett 1975). For such couples to cohabit would, in almost all cases, be considered incestuous, regardless of genealogical distance; a "sister" is a sister, whether consanguineal or classificatory, and should therefore be treated with a restraint that is devoid of sexual overtones.

The only non-"spouse" sexual relationship that is not considered incestuous is that between a man and his "ZD," which is favored by a few people as a "lover" relationship. It seems, however, that marriages between such *nyagaji* (wrong) pairs are rare; on the basis of my genealogical data, going back several generations, they would have constituted less than three percent of all marriages. (I recorded no cases involving "incestuous" unions.) If children are born of *nyagaji* partners, other people generally follow the mother in reckoning their kin relationship to the offspring, ignoring the father's affiliations and thus "straightening" the system of kin reckoning and section membership.

LOCAL ORGANIZATION

The social and spatial arrangement of Mardu groups involves two closely related elements—kinship and territoriality—which in turn entail both economic and religious concerns. Not surprisingly, considering the great uncertainties of rainfall in their homelands, Mardu local organization is notable for its flexibility and fluidity and a lack of stress on boundaries and exclusiveness of group membership.[9]

[9]Major references concerning Aboriginal social organization include: Barker (1976), Bern (1979), R. Berndt (1959), Berndt and Berndt (1988), Birdsell (1970), Gould (1969a, 1969b, 1980), Hamilton (1980), Hiatt (1962, 1966, 1984, 1986), Keen (1988), Meggitt (1962), Myers (1986), Peterson (1972, 1975, 1976, 1986), Shapiro (1979), Stanner (1965b), Tindale (1974), Turner (1980), and Williams (1986). This topic has long been contentious, for a number of reasons: the effects of European influences; variable Aboriginal conceptions of "belonging" with respect to geographical and social boundaries; and the difficulty of isolating groups larger than bands, such that the existence of "tribes" in Australia is open to serious question. In the Western Desert case, certainly, there is no evidence of the kind of corporateness of economic, political, and boundary-maintaining activity that would justify its use as a label (R. Berndt 1959).

The difficulties of drawing boundaries around local groups, especially in the desert, underline a fact of great importance: with the exception of secret-sacred facets of the religious life, most of which in any case is structured to cut across spatial and social groupings, any strong development of sentiments and behaviors supporting exclusiveness and extreme parochialism would be ultimately self-destructive in such a drought-prone environment.

To clarify the nature of Aboriginal local organization, Stanner (1965b) has proposed a useful distinction between what he terms the *estate* and the *range*. The estate is the traditional heartland of what is most often some kind of patrilineal descent group. It consists of a limited number of important waterholes and sacred sites to which the members of the group are intimately related through strongly felt bonds of attachment and belonging. Whereas the tie to the estate is primarily a religious one, the relationship of social groups to their range is principally economic. A range is the large area exploited by bands during the food quest, and it normally includes within it an estate which a majority of members of the bands concerned think of as their home area (termed *manda* by the Mardu.). Although severe drought may sometimes force bands to move far away from their estate, a powerful longing for "home" and, among men, strong religious obligations draw them back to the heartland as often as ecological and social circumstances permit. In the desert, the ranges of neighboring estate groups invariably overlap; it is also possible for individuals to develop strong allegiances to more than one estate in the course of their lives, which further adds to the openness of local organization.

The following account begins with a description of the broadest named collectivity among the Mardu and ends with the smallest, fundamental unit, the family.

The Dialect-Named Unit   As noted earlier, the unity implied by the term "Mardu" was traditionally not recognized by the people so designated, for they belonged to several different dialect-named units (see Map 2). This term refers to all those who identify with a stretch of territory named for a particular dialect, regardless of which dialects are actually spoken.[10] As Rumsey (1989) observes, language and country are *directly* linked, and the *mediated* link is between language and people. To paraphrase Rumsey (1989:75), Gardujarra people are not Gardujarra because they speak this dialect, but because they are otherwise linked (by descent, totemic connection, or other affiliatory criteria) to *places* to which the Gardujarra dialect is also linked. I refrain from calling them "groups" for several reasons. Individual members of the Gardujarra, Giyajarra, or other dialect-named units often use the dialect label when identifying others, but in self-reference it is generally too broad so they more often use the name of a major and mythologically prominent waterhole in their estate. In other words, Mardu identity inheres in sets of associations and affiliations that are pitched at more specific levels of geographic and social

---

[10]In earlier works, I have followed Berndt (1959) in calling this the "linguistic unit." Although preferable to "tribe," this label is also problematic because multilingualism was universal in Aboriginal Australia, thus ruling out any simple one-to-one correspondence between language and territory (cf. Dixon 1976, Sutton 1978, and Trigger 1987).

reference than the dialect-named unit. The Mardu can identify territorial boundary zones between themselves and neighboring units, but instead of seeing their territories as enclosed or bounded tracts, their dominant conception of them is as clusters of points in space and as tracks, both ancestral and contemporary, that link many such points together in a regional web (cf. O'Connell 1976, Peterson 1986:56). Therefore, boundaries in some areas are vague, especially between water sources and where prominent landforms are absent.

While most members of the same group speak the dialect associated with their particular territory, some (for example, recently inmarrying women or men) may not; generally, however, a Mardu whose parents are from two different territories will speak both dialects, as well as those of other neighboring areas. Members of a dialect-named unit never congregate as an exclusive group or act as a corporate body. In fact, social and cultural life entails the frequent cross-cutting of such units, and the largest assemblies of people (*jabal*, meaning "multitude"), which gather once or twice a year to engage in ritual and other activities, never coincide in personnel with a single dialect-named unit. This "big meeting" invariably includes members of several different dialect-named units, and no two such gatherings will have even a nearly identical membership. Between one meeting and the next, differing circumstances will prevent some groups from attending, while allowing others who missed the previous gathering to attend.

Normally, member groups of the same dialect-named unit would be bound to interact more often and have closer kinship and friendship ties to one another than to distant groups, but they have no reason to make linguistic boundaries coincide with exclusive, on-the-ground assemblies. Such a condition would be quite impossible. Given the nature of marriage arrangements, kin networks, the mixing of dialects by groups whose estates lie near boundaries with other dialect-named units, and the many other cultural factors that stress wider cooperation and a shared regional identity, it is clear that the Mardu view of "society" encompasses a huge and unknowable but "related" totality embracing the entire Western Desert bloc (cf. Tonkinson 1987).

The Estate Group   Each dialect-named unit comprises a number of estate groups whose members are normally dispersed in bands throughout, and perhaps beyond, its territory. The Manyjilyjarra, who occupy the largest area, traditionally would have had more estate groups than, say, the Gurajarra, whose homeland is much smaller (though ecologically more favorable) and probably contained only three or four such groups. It is impossible to estimate with any certainty the size, population range, or number of estates in each unit, partly because of dislocations and migrations resulting from European influences, but also because estate-group boundaries tend not to be clearly defined. Like the larger dialect-named unit, the entity here referred to as "the estate group" has no reality as an exclusive, on-the-ground collectivity, so it can be difficult to identify. There are no unilineal descent groups such as lineages or clans in the Western Desert region, but certain cultural principles operate to ensure that the estate group has a core of patrilineally related men and women. Nevertheless, membership criteria are not rigorously defined, and most people are able to maintain a primary allegiance to one group and secondary allegiances to a number of others. Possible affiliative criteria are many, and individuals can exercise choices in their estate group memberships.

The following reconstruction of a Manyjilyjarra estate group whose "main place" is Giinyu (now Well No. 35 on the Canning Stock Route; see Map 2) is included to illustrate the likely significance of such Mardu groups. Manyjilyjarra speakers are almost all "descended" from the Dingari, a generic term for the many different groups of Dreaming beings who left the Manyjilyjarra behind on their eastward travels.[11] Prominent among them were the Possum and Native Cat people and the Minyiburru women along with their pursuer Nyirru, a man with a huge penis and an insatiable, rapacious, sexual appetite. After many adventures en route eastward, the women finally decided to flee into the sky. Nyirru tried to climb up after them, but the Minyiburru pushed the ladder down, and he has remained beneath them ever since—visible as three stars that represent his knees and penis, in an intercourse position facing the Pleiades, which are the Minyiburru. According to the Dreaming myth, when the Minyiburru were camped at Giinyu, they spotted Nyirru in the distance, headed in their direction. The women fled in panic, leaving behind two of their number (whom Nyirru caught and raped to death) and a big hairless dingo bitch called Giinyu. The bitch later gave birth to hundreds of pups of all kinds and colors, which dug themselves nests all around their home area, thus creating the holes that are a distinctive feature of the site (pitted, sedimentary rock patches in sandhill country). The dingoes remained there forever and composed the Yinirarri ritual so that people would know of their exploits. The group of people who identify themselves as Giinyumardaji (*mardaji* meaning "belonging to that place") are known to others as the "dingo mob." Many of them have dingo as their *jugurr* (ancestral totem—that is, they believe that they sprang from the life essence left behind by the Dreaming dingo beings), but some identify Minyiburru or Nyirru as their *jugurr,* and a few have other Dreaming beings associated in some way with the Giinyu estate.[12] This use of a major totem as a convenient label regardless of individual totemic associations is common in other parts of Australia; for example, Strehlow (1965:140) notes that, among the Aranda, men of the same estate group may call themselves "honey-ant" people, yet for many this group of Dreaming beings is not a personal totem.

Most men who head families that constitute the several bands whose estate locus is Giinyu are related in the male line. This situation comes about because of a strong preference for children to be born somewhere in or near the estate of their father so that both will share the same ancestral totem. When adverse conditions force bands away from the Giinyu estate for long periods, some children may be born elsewhere. In this case, the father may try to arrange a birthplace that is associated with one of the Dingari mobs, but again, this may not be possible.

Birth on the estate is thus not the only criterion for membership; a person can be a member by virtue of having been conceived there or because of his or her father's membership of the estate group (and through the mother to her natal estate, though

[11]For accounts of the Dingari beings and the significance of the associated ritual complex, see R. Berndt (1970) and Myers (1976).

[12]The conception totem is the plant, animal, or mineral form that the spirit-child (left by the ancestral beings in the form of life essence) assumed at some later time (see Chapter 4).

this linkage is less often stressed). For males, there are other important avenues which exist through the religious life. The estate in which a youth is circumcised becomes "his" (to the extent that, when asked for his ancestral totem, he may give the name of his circumcision site rather than that of a Dreaming being), and he is thereby entitled eventually to learn all the secrets of the estate group elders, provided he returns periodically for ritual activities there. Obviously, the more of these criteria that coincide, the stronger the primary attachment, but because full congruence is rare, every individual is entitled to membership in more than one estate group through bonds of shared spirit and substance (discussed in Chapter 4).

Many of the sisters of Giinyu men live elsewhere, in accordance with Mardu residence preferences which clearly favor patri-virilocality; that is, a woman should join the band of her husband sometime after marriage, and their children should grow up in the country of the father. Yet women's strong attachment to their natal estate group and its territory, in this case the Giinyu area, draws them back from time to time. If ceremonies are planned, they will be expected to play an appropriate role, for they share with their male kin a responsibility to "look after" sites and ceremonies associated with their natal estate group. During these visits, their husbands use the opportunity to hunt meat for their in-laws in continued fulfillment of affinal obligations. This is one reason men are periodically absent from their estate, but they also leave their families from time to time when religious business takes them elsewhere.

The consanguineal, or "blood," ties that link families in the same estate group are generally less important as bonds to the estate than are religious links, which are of course shared with others who may not be blood relatives. The tracing of blood ties does not extend back great distances in time (the genealogical depth of recognized ties is rarely more than three or four generations) and, because of a strong taboo on uttering names of the dead, ancestors are eventually forgotten. Like most other hunter-gatherers the world over, the Mardu have little interest in maintaining long genealogies and enshrining them in ritual. This is partly because wealth and status are not acquired through inheritance, and there are no human ancestor cults of any kind (spirits of the dead are not enjoined to assist their living kin in worldly affairs), so it is pointless to trace family trees into the distant past. However, a more important reason for this "genealogical amnesia" is that the key connections with the past are those linking the Mardu totemically to their Dreaming ancestors and to the spiritual realm, the source of all power.

Although all estate group members are landowners in their shared responsibility for protection and ritual nurturance of its territory, the women are typically scattered by marriage among different estates in the region, and children are, of course, not considered ready to perform such adult roles. So, it is the men of the Giinyu estate group who assume the heaviest religious responsibilities as guardians of its sacred sites, objects, and rituals. They collectively "own" the Yinirarri ritual left for them by the human-animal dingo beings, and, periodically, they must organize its performance at or close to Giinyu. For this event, they invite men of neighboring groups; because most visitors will have long since been initiated into the Yinirarri, they will participate fully, with the Giinyu leaders acting as planners and directors of the various ritual activities. On every occasion, there are novices present, so they must be initiated into the ritual and will receive instruction from the Giinyu men who, as dingo people, are best qualified for this task.

Performance of the Yinirarri is believed to stimulate the supply of dingoes throughout the desert. In addition, each year the Giinyu estate men must perform increase rites (see Chapter 5) at Giinyu and Girrbin to the east to ensure that plenty of pups will be born and at two other sites within the estate area, one for mulga seeds and the other for one variety of bush tomato, both of which are important Mardu food staples. The older men most closely associated with these sites carry out the simple increase rites there, assisted by others whose bands happen to be somewhere in the vicinity at the time.

Perhaps the greatest responsibility of the Giinyu men rests with the care of the cache of sacred objects associated with the Yinirarri and other rituals and kept carefully hidden in "men's country" close to the waterhole. Besides being regularly checked and anointed with protective fat and red ochre, these sacred objects are revealed to novices—from Giinyu as well as those who are brought specially from other areas—when they undergo the very important initiation stage of Mirdayidi, a ritual of great regional importance in ensuring the permeability of boundaries among the Mardu and between them and their neighbors (see Chapter 4). The Mirdayidi entitles initiates not only to full access to the territory and resources of the Giinyu estate group, but also to a role in any religious activities that take place there. The bond to Giinyu and its people that is forged through the Mirdayidi is as strong as that resulting from having been circumcised there.

Because of the existence of multiple criteria of attachment to estate, no two Giinyu people name exactly the same set of sites when asked to identify their home country. Every individual imbues some places with special meanings and significances that are not shared by many others.[13] The tie to the land is extremely strong for everyone, because one's home territory is the locus of social identity and of "belonging" in a spiritual as well as emotional sense. When, through choice or necessity, Giinyu people move beyond their normal range area, their travels are facilitated by these various individual attachments that extend far from Giinyu itself, as well as by a multiplicity of kinship and marriage ties, and the bonds of shared language, religion, and values. Boundaries are easily crossed; it is not necessary for people to obtain permission to hunt and gather there because the males have already ritually "paid for" rights of entry (see Chapter 4). Besides, how self-defeating it would be for any group to refuse others access to resources and thus invite later retaliation when, as would inevitably happen at some future time, drought forced it into the territory of other groups.

The Band   As the on-the-ground, land-exploiting unit, the band is the most visible expression of Aboriginal local organization. Among the Mardu, it is composed of one or more families whose male heads are more often than not patrilineal-

---

[13]Myers (1976, 1986), writing about the Pintupi, whose territory lies to the east of the Manyjily-jarra, concludes that their social organization is the outcome of individual decisions and affiliations, thus giving rise to considerable overlap in membership of estate groups, which are therefore unbounded. He suggests that these are not unilineal descent groups, but are best viewed as bilateral kindreds—something that Shapiro (1979) has also posited as a feature of Aboriginal social organization.

ly related. The size of the band varies from perhaps as few as six or eight people to thirty or more, depending on a number of factors both ecological and social. A variety of visitors will come and go, including, for example, visiting in-laws who come to spend time with their daughters or sisters and their children, intending sons-in-law who spend varying periods hunting meat for their future wife's parents while at the same time giving the girl concerned the opportunity to become accustomed to them prior to marriage, patrikin of the males, and young men and their guardians who are retracing the path of ancestral beings in fulfillment of initiation requirements. If times become bad, in that water or food shortages occur, a band may be forced to disperse into single-family groups. At other times, when conditions are favorable, bands may disappear for a time through the fusion of two or more neighboring groups. The Mardu word for the band is *gabudurr* (small group), which is named most often for a site or sites in its heartland, followed by a suffix indicating "belonging to that place."

Although it is flexible in size, movement, and membership, the band is prevented from becoming a free-floating amorphous mass by its attachment to an estate, with kinship and "descent" as important factors. Residence preferences, combined with the ritual responsibilities of the male landholders of the estate group, provide territorial attachment and ensure the presence of patrilineally related men in the several bands that habitually exploit an estate and surrounding range. Taking the Mardu region as a whole, the ranges of the bands that occupy it overlap considerably, but strong sentiments and responsibilities focusing on the heartland maintain the integrity of the different estate groups no matter where their constituent bands happen to be at any time.

The Family   The family, or hearth group, which consists of a husband and wife or wives and their children, is the smallest identifiable group in Aboriginal society. It is the group in which much nurture and socialization of the very young takes place, and the closest emotional ties are evinced.[14] Although it is the fundamental domestic unit, the family is never socially isolated in ways that make it an exclusive agency of either socialization or emotional support. Each family typically camps, cooks, and eats alone, but within sight of other families. There is very frequent visiting among families in the same band and, in most cases, interaction is not inhibited by kinship relationships of avoidance or extreme restraint. Food is never denied those (most often the young men and older boys, who sleep together in the *girriji* or "single persons" camp) who may wander across to the campfire at mealtimes. When Mardu talk about being "one family," for example, they are invariably including kin beyond the nuclear family, like uncles, aunts, and cousins, and also those who are or have been closely associated with them in some significant way.

If the male head of the family is middle-aged or older, it is typically polygynous; that is, the man has at the same time two or more wives, one of whom may be an older former widow. Few Mardu have more than three wives at any given time, and

---

[14]For detailed ethnographic description of the family and the importance of both intra- and extra-familial relationships in two contrasting Australian environments, see Hamilton (1981) and Meggitt (1962).

many, especially younger men, have only one. The family loses the services of its daughters when, at the age of about twelve, they are given in marriage. Yet the loss of the considerable productive capacity of these girls as food gatherers is offset by their father's acquisition of wives from other groups.

SOCIAL CATEGORIES

As with many other societies, Aboriginal social organization is replete with duality—the categorization of objects, animals, people, or whatever into two opposing but complementary groups. Among the Aborigines, dualism is most clearly seen in varying combinations and permutations of social categories or "classes" whose degree of elaboration is unparalleled anywhere in the world. An unconscious urge to oppose the uncertainties of a hunting and gathering life with intellectual constructs that impose order, system, and predictability may well underlie such dualism. Dual organization of some kind is so universal that it has been attributed to some characteristic of the functioning of the human brain (see Lévi-Strauss 1962). For the Australian case, Burridge (1973) offers an alternative suggestion. He links this duality to the polarity of life, the rhythm of dispersal alternating with aggregation. In this sense Aboriginal life does swing between two extremes: the predominant condition of peaceful, perhaps monotonous, and low-keyed life in the small band contrasting with large gatherings, which are brief but always highly charged, tense, exciting, and eventful interludes.[15] The Mardu, however, do not describe the two phases of this oscillation as a dualistic opposition, but see them simply as behavior to be emulated because it was ordained in the Dreaming.

Almost all Aboriginal societies are divided into two, four, or eight categories, but this is not to say that the few exceptions are somehow deficient in their functioning. Where four-category (section) and eight-category (subsection) systems exist, they are based on dual organization, whether or not this is explicitly recognized or exemplified in named subgroupings. The distribution of these various category systems is geographically uneven and is not correlated with ecological differences.[16] Whereas moieties (division into two categories) may or may not be named sociocentrically, sections and subsections always are.

All these social categories have certain common characteristics. Because membership is ascribed by birth, it is impossible for individuals to change categories. Moieties indicate intermarrying divisions and, by the same token, divisions into which marriage is forbidden, but they do not regulate marriage, because this follows prescriptions that are expressed in terms of specific kin relationships. So, although the categories are exogamous, they are not "marriage classes." Nor do they exist individually as actual on-the-ground gatherings of people, which is why they are not "groups," although at certain times and for specific purposes members

[15]Durkheim (1915) was one of the first scholars to discuss this polarity and its implications for Aboriginal society and religion.

[16]Service (1960) attempted to derive such a correlation, without conspicuous success; see R. and C. Berndt (1988) for a critique.

of paired categories may assemble in discrete groups. In both section and subsection systems, a child's category is always different from those of its parents. These categories crosscut estate groups and the kinship system and are of a different order from kinship, which is an egocentrically defined network of relationships whereas categories are sociocentrically ordered. Social categories are very much less important than kinship in everyday life, but there is a significant correspondence between the two. The categories, by lumping together sets of kinship terms within each, do provide individuals with rough guides to the kind of patterned behavior expected of them.

Meggitt (1962) has observed that, as a mode of classification or a guide to specific action, social categories are too broad and ambiguous a referent. In a society like the Mardu, which possesses a four-section system, section labels are in constant use as terms of address and reference. The Mardu sometimes use personal names, but these are such an intrinsic and inseparable part of the self that they should not be bandied about indiscriminately. Rare is the adult who will say his or her own name or will reveal the names of any members of kin categories toward whom restraint must be shown. Adults sometimes resort to teknonymy (the practice of referring to other adults by the name of one of their children, of either sex), but more commonly use section terms to label others. Since there are only four such terms, and the same term is used for male and female members of each section, their use is imprecise and sometimes confusing to the outsider, as the following typical exchange shows:

> Mardu: That Banaga (section name) saw a big snake-spirit yesterday.
> Anthropologist: Which one?
> M: I don't know . . . it could have come from Linbul (a waterhole associated with two ancestral snake-men.)
> A: No, I mean who saw it?
> M: That old one (*jirlbi* can refer to an old person of either sex).
> A: Woman?
> M: No! Old man! That one, over there—see!
> A: Which one? Three old Banaga men are sitting in that camp.
> M: The one with the beard.
> A: Two of them have beards; do you mean Buyu or Wadagaba?
> M: Yes, him (Mardu has no equivalent of "or").

Of course, the anthropologist soon learns quicker ways of arriving at the needed information, but the Mardu show no such confusion in their use of section names, because the conversational context generally conveys the sex and identity of the person to whom they are alluding.

Although the kinship system is dominant in regulating behavior, reference to sections provides a useful general guide. Once a stranger's section is known, people can immediately reduce the possible kinship relationship to a finite number. However, no interaction will occur until others present have ascertained the stranger's kinship connection and then formally introduced him or her to the other local people present. This necessity to know the kinship link prior to interaction is a major reason why incoming strangers always remain at some distance from a camp. Even if known to all, however, etiquette requires that they always await a signal

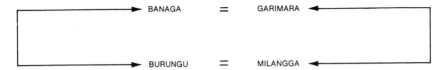

Figure 3-1. Mardu sections.

from an older male to join the group. This is especially important should avoidance relationships obtain between certain individuals.

The shown diagrams are of Mardu section names and their arrangement and are intended to help the reader better understand the working of the system of social categories. In Figure 3-1 the symbol = indicates intermarrying pairs of sections. The double-ended arrows connect the sections of a mother and her children (siblings are *always* members of the same section).

The system works this way. Taking, for example, a Garimarra female as Ego, or starting point, she will marry a man of the Banaga section whom she calls by the term for "spouse." She cannot marry just *any* Banaga man because his section also contains her real and classificatory mother's fathers, son's sons, and certain cross-cousins who are classed as "brothers," all of whom are nonmarriageable relatives (see Figure 3-3). This is why the section system considered alone does not regulate marriage. The sons and daughters of this Garimarra woman will be in the Milangga section and will eventually marry Burungu spouses. Her daughter's children will belong to Garimarra, her own section, but her son's children will be born into Banaga section, eventually to take their spouses from among the Garimarra.

Continuing with the same Ego, it is possible to derive the sections to which all one's relatives belong. From Figure 3-3, it can be seen that the section system

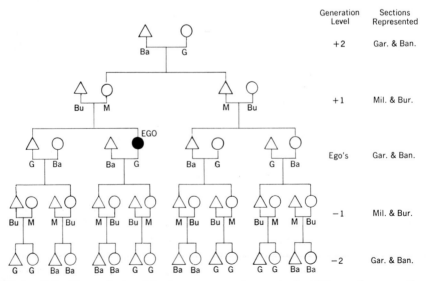

Figure 3-2. The relationship between section membership and generation levels.

groups together certain categories of relatives into each of the four divisions. (Remember that "Z" symbolizes "sister" and "S" is "son.") Many of the relatives listed in Figure 3-3 are grouped together and are called by the same kinship term, so the system is not as complicated as it looks.

Figure 3-4 shows the three possible forms of dual organization that are inherent in the section system: mother-child pairs of sections, called matrimoieties (Banaga-Burungu and Garimarra-Milangga); father-child pairs, or patrimoieties (Banaga-Milangga and Garimarra-Burungu); and what are called merged alternate generation levels (Banaga-Garimarra and Burungu-Milangga), which are the intermarrying pairs of sections.

Nowhere in the Western Desert are matrimoieties found, and there are neither corporate groups nor social entities based on this kind of dual division. At large gatherings, the Mardu group their camps into two patrimoiety "sides," also used in the seating arrangements for certain men's rituals and seen in intergroup gift exchange. The most important division is the merged alternate generation levels which figure prominently in many religious activities. Patrimoieties and, particularly, merged alternate generation levels are useful because both separate into opposite groups some kin categories between whose members restraint or avoidance relationships exist.

Neither division is named sociocentrically, that is, has a single name that all members of society can use to label it. Individuals identify them only egocentrically, as *marndiyarra* (my patrimoiety), *yarigirra* (other patrimoiety), and *marirra* (my generational side) or *yinara* (other side). The choice of terms used thus depends on the division to which the speaker belongs. Figures 3-2 and 3-3 indicate why this third dual division is termed "merged alternate generation levels." One's "own side" comprises not only all members of the same generation, but all grandparents and grandchildren on both sides of the family. This merging of own, +2 and −2 levels into one has parallels in the merging of some of the kin terminology, for example, the use of only two terms for all +2 and −2 members. From an individual's perspective, the "other side" consists of all +1 and −1 members (parents, children, MB "uncles," FZ "aunts," ZS, ZD, and so on).

As noted earlier, a person's "own side" (own generation plus +2 and −2 levels)

BANAGA	GARIMARRA
H; ZH; HB; HZ; BW; MF; FM; MBS; MBD; FZS; FZD; ZSD; ZSS; SD; SS; and so on	Ego; Z; B; FF; MM; FFZ; MMB; HMF; HFM; DS; DD; ZDS; ZDD; BSS; BSD; and so on
BURUNGU	MILANGGA
F; FZ; HM; BS; BD; DH; SW; MMBS; MMBD; FZDS; FZDD; and so on	S; D; ZS; ZD; M; MB; HF; FMBS; FMBD; FZSS; FZSD; and so on

Figure 3-3. The relationship between sections and kin categories, from the perspective of a female Garimarra Ego.

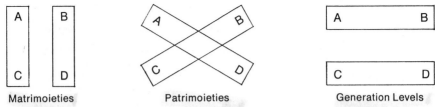

Figure 3-4. Dual grouping possibilities inherent in section systems.

has a majority of kin with whom relatively unrestrained interaction is possible, whereas the "other side" (+1 and −1 levels) is composed mainly of people with whom one interacts asymmetrically; that is, either owing or receiving respect and deference, generally in a somewhat restrained manner. In most ceremonial activities involving division into "sides," the two groups sit a short distance apart, and throughout the proceedings their members joust verbally with each other in loud and light-hearted fashion. Such exchanges, which engender great amusement on the part of all present, take place between members of the same or opposite sex, most often people of kin categories that are related as wife-bestower/wife-receiver. Their targets, which relate mostly to reciprocal obligations and marriage arrangements, involve joking offers of, or demands for, gifts of meat or vegetable foods—or for women as wives—and accusations of stinginess in the provision of wives or of other failures to reciprocate.

These expressions of good-natured ritual opposition enliven an already exciting and happy atmosphere, characteristic of religious activities that unite members of different groups in a shared experience. At times when the two sides are most actively opposed, good-humored banter is directed en masse at the opposition group or at all "other side" members of the one sex. Comments dwell on shortcomings such as poor hunting ability, laziness, lack of generosity, and failure to live up to promises. But interpersonal opposition, which in some rituals involves mild forms of physical aggression (for example, in rainmaking rituals, the throwing and spitting of water), is directed only at "other side" members who stand in specific kin relationship(s) to Ego, and most *milyura* (poking fun) is targeted at members of these kin categories.

The *garnku-jinjanungu* division is another kind of dualism that is very important as an organizing principle in some religious activities, particularly male initiation and those rituals associated with death and burial, and is quite similar to the generational division. Members of the *jinjanungu* group are predominantly Ego's "own side" group, but with the exclusion of all close consanguineal kin—"B" and "Z," some "cross-cousins," and any other kin who, as members of the same or neighboring bands, feel an emotional bond to that person—all of whom side with the opposing group. The *jinjanungu* group is active in the mechanics of actually organizing and carrying out the appropriate ritual tasks. Members of the large *garnku* group, which consists of "other side" members plus those listed above, minus Ego's "S" and "D" who join the *jinjanungu*, make most of the preliminary plans and are consulted regarding the conduct of activities; however, the *garnku*

Division	Type	How Defined	Mardu Term	Major Cultural Referents
1.	Patrimoiety (A+D; B+C)	egocentrically	marndiyarra ("own"); yarigirra ("other")	some camping arrangements; some rituals; some gift exchange
2.	Merged Alternate Generation Level (A+B; C+D)	egocentrically	marirra ("own"); yinara ("other")	many rituals
3.	Activist–Mourner (modified A+B; C+D)	egocentric basis, but sociocentrically named	jinjanungu ("Activist"); garnku ("Mourner")	initiation rituals; activities and rituals following a death

Figure 3-5. Dual social categories among the Mardu.

group plays no active role during the proceedings because its members are too "sorry" for the initiate or deceased to do anything more than express grief through crying and wailing.[17]

The Activist-Mourner groups may be involved in complementary or ritually opposed behaviors and activities. Certainly, there are occasions when ritual protests associated with the seizure of a youth for his initiation erupt into hostile accusations of unseemly haste and insufficient prior consultation with the close Mourner relatives concerned or when relatives who arrive after a death aggressively accuse the deceased's close kin of callous neglect. These confrontations, although expected and typically short-lived, usually necessitate intervention by others to prevent injury. Yet, they are highly ritualized and controlled because of an overriding emphasis in the religious life on harmony, a state that typically transcends whatever divisions exist in the organization and execution of group activities.

Apart from the use of section terms in address and reference, the categories and divisions just described have little relevance to the mundane hunting and gathering activities of the Mardu band. In this arena, kinship provides the principal guide to most interpersonal behavior. But whenever larger gatherings occur, and when any kind of ritual performance is envisioned, social category and dual-group membership inevitably become relevant to some of the resulting activity. These different but interrelated idioms, kin and category, are both clearly important, since each ". . . enables Aborigines to make statements to which exact expression cannot be given in the other" (Maddock 1982:95). Yet, a puzzling question remains: why, in imposing order on their world, did the Aborigines evolve so many unique and complex classificatory systems? Munn (1973) points insightfully to a significant transformational aspect of social categories, which are of a higher sociocultural order than the egocentrically based system of kin reckoning: sections and subsections provide a generalized sociocentric grid onto which kin relationships are

---

[17]For convenience, members of this dual division are henceforth termed "Activists" (jinjanungu) and "Mourners" (garnku).

projected and thus locked into the wider social structure. But what does the imposition of a seemingly unwarranted level of complexity mean to the individual who must live with all this? As already noted, if a burden exists, it is not felt by the Aborigines, who see sections as a useful idiom and labeling device as well as an essential preliminary guide in establishing relationships with strangers. Burridge (1973) has provided the most plausible explanation to date, by suggesting that the elaboration of different sets of rules and conventions is connected to two major themes in Aboriginal social organization. First, these many classificatory schemes crosscut one another so thoroughly that

> No category which groups people together for particular purposes contains persons exclusively of that group and no other; and each category groups together those who, in other situations, will be differently grouped. Rivalry is balanced by cooperation, opposition by complementarity. There is no group of persons whose relations with the features of the natural environment are precisely the same, [and] each category contains those whose particular relationships with, and responsibilities for, particular features of the environment are different (p. 133).

Secondly, these schemes operate to separate out and individualize people. Through them, the Aborigines ensure that each individual emerges as unique in relation to the sum of the many different categorizations. This uniqueness is embedded within a broader cultural framework that stresses cooperation and unity.

A tension between individualism and conformity is of course characteristic of all human societies, which must arrive at a satisfactory balance between egotism and the need for shared, predictable behaviors lest they fall into extremes of anarchy or totalitarian control. Among the Mardu, the ritual functioning of merged alternate generation level groupings (described above) provides a good illustration of the kind of tension that exists between these individualizing versus unifying pressures that are simultaneously exerted in the desert culture. This dichotomy is exemplified in the religious life (Chapter 5) and, particularly, in the activities and rituals that surround male initiation, which is described in some detail in the following chapter.

4 / Life Cycle and Male Initiation

Like many other peoples, the Mardu have myths that explain the beginnings of human mortality, following an earlier state wherein everyone lived forever. One such myth:

A Dreaming man died . . . no one knows why . . . and Wirlarra the Moon-man, who was traveling with his large pack of dingoes, found the body and decided to try to save the man. He dragged him along by the hand but the body was rotting and pieces of it began dropping off, whereupon the Moon-man, being a clever magician, would stick them back on again. Some people saw him doing this and burst into laughter, ridiculing him for dragging a smelly corpse around. He was very angered by this, and embarrassed, so he scattered the pieces of the body far and wide, saying to the people, "From now on you will die and stay forever dead." Had these people not ridiculed the Moon-man in the Dreaming, human beings would never have to die.[1]

However, this kind of death is physical only. Just as the creative beings of the Dreaming grew tired and eventually died, yet endure in spiritual form, so does every Aborigine live on after bodily death. Life is cyclical, beginning and ending with a spirit which is indestructible because it is of the same essence as the Dreaming powers. The Mardu have no beliefs in reincarnation; the spirit returns to the place from which it originally came and dwells forever there with other spirits of the dead.

SPIRITUAL PREEXISTENCE AND CONCEPTION TOTEMISM

The Mardu have no one word for power or life essence, yet it is evident from their conceptions of the Dreaming that all creative beings are limitless reservoirs of power, which is immanent in everything they have touched, possessed, transformed—or have, themselves, been transformed into. Besides depositing spirit reservoirs of particular plant and animal species at certain sites along their routes, the Dreaming beings left behind similar homes for *jijigarrgaly* (spirit-children) in various locations.

Despite individual variations in beliefs, the Mardu are generally agreed that spirit-children are very small and human-like—except for webbed feet and a very

---

[1]No doubt because of its regular cycle of "death" and "rebirth," the moon is frequently associated with death in Aboriginal culture (see R. Berndt 1974).

hairy body—and very clever, as well as dangerous to anyone trespassing close to their favorite haunts (usually caves, rocky hills, large sand dunes, and big trees). A stranger who comes too close to the home of a spirit-child may be attacked magically, and women who trespass may become instantly pregnant. Spirit-children, who wander far in search of nectar from flowers and dew for their sustenance, take on the form of a particular animal, plant, or mineral before first encountering their human mother; this manifestation is later identified as the baby's *jarrin* or *nyuga* (conception totem). The spirit-child magically enters its mother through her stomach, mouth, or loins or under the nail of her thumb or big toe. Once inside, it is usually quite protective of her, but sometimes it may cause her to behave in uncharacteristic and excessive ways. A spirit-child is generally thought to have its own food and to be self-sustaining in the womb, so, in this sense, the mother plays no part in its prenatal nurturance (see Montagu 1974, Mountford 1981).

A woman's husband sometimes participates in the spirit-child's finding of its mother, either by seeing its approach in a dream or by hunting and catching it in animal form. In most cases, however, he plays no role at all because the spirit-child is so clever that it has no need to be guided to its mother. On rare occasions, it chooses not to enter its "proper" mother, but goes into the womb of one of her "sisters" instead. The example that follows illustrates the autonomy of the spirit-child.

> A middle-aged Mardu woman, whose only child, a son, is now an adult, periodically cares for a small girl, the physiological daughter of a younger "sister" who agrees that the child is actually the older woman's "own." In spirit-child form the girl was a kangaroo, hunted down and clubbed to death by the older woman's husband. When buried in hot ashes, the animal would not cook through properly, and when the younger "sister" ate some of the meat she later vomited—both signs that it was probably a spirit-child in kangaroo form. When the baby was born, she carried marks on her head and chest which corresponded to the parts of the kangaroo's body that were injured, thus "proving" her to be the older couple's child, who, for reasons known only to the spirit-child, had been born from the wrong mother.[2]

In discussing the topic of maternity and paternity, the Mardu talk only in terms of spiritual powers, never physiology. When questioned, they deny the relevance of semen or intercourse to procreation. A child's "real" father is the husband of its mother. Given the prominence of the social father role in everyday life, and the markedly spiritual Mardu perception of the cosmic order and its creative and life-ordering processes, the idea of the male as responsible for the creation of life, or even as a catalyst, is contradictory and superfluous. Spiritual explanations are paramount and fundamental, and belief in spirit-children provides every person with a life-sustaining and virtually direct link to the great powers of the Dreaming.

---

[2]This example of the independence of the spirit-child has important implications for the long debate that has raged about whether Australian Aborigines are ignorant of, or deny, physiological paternity and maternity. See Tonkinson (1978b), where other examples of "wrong" mothers are given.

In identifying conception totems, people view any unusual characteristic or behavior of objects in the natural world as suggestive of the presence of spirit-children. Three typical examples follow:

> Marnagal, a young man; ancestral totem, Two Men; conception totem, wallaby.[3] His father, Jadurda, was hunting one day when a wallaby suddenly appeared from nowhere and, instead of fleeing, hopped toward him and allowed itself to be easily speared. When, a short time after, his wife Minu realized she was pregnant, he knew that the wallaby was really a spirit-child, and when Marnagal was born, on his shoulder was the mark of his father's spear. Jadurda's elder brother, Gagubanya, told him that Two Men had been hunting at that place in the Dreaming and one had thrown a club at a kangaroo and lost it. It later became a spirit-child which turned into the wallaby that entered Marnagal's mother after Jadurda had killed it.

> Mulila, a little girl; ancestral totem, Minyiburru women; conception totem, yam. Her mother, Nibala, was digging for yams with several other women of the same band near a Dreaming campsite of the Minyiburru. She found a huge tuber of unusual shape which, when roasted, would not cook through. She vomited after eating it and later found out that she was pregnant. When Mulila was born, her left leg bore the mark of her mother's digging stick where it entered the tuber.

> Rabuji, a man in his sixties; ancestral totem, Ngayunangalgu; conception totem, snake. A Ngayunangalgu Dreaming being left a beard hair in the bed of Savory Creek (Map 2) where a large mob of them were camped. The beard hair became a snake, which Rabuji's mother speared with her digging stick. She vomited after eating some of it and later realized that it was really a spirit-child, not an ordinary snake. The carved wooden figure shown in Figure 2-1 was crafted by Rabuji to show me what Ngayunangalgu cannibal beings look like. His crayon drawing of the Lake Disappointment area and associated mythology, shown in Figure 5-2, includes himself in beard hair-become-snake form.

When identifying their conception totem, many Mardu will point to a birthmark or blemish in telling the story of how they found their parents. Although everyone has a conception totem and is frequently named after it, the Mardu do not necessarily feel a special bond with the species or object that was chosen by the spirit-child in finding its parents. If it is an edible food, only a few say they would never eat it. The medium itself seems less important than the message of a personalized link between each individual and a spirit-child that was left behind by some Dreaming being. This message also explains why people who share the same conception totem feel no emotional or spiritual oneness on this basis.[4] In contrast, in areas of Australia that have totemic clans, shared descent is claimed from a common male or female ancestor and is symbolized in terms of spiritual sameness or "shared flesh," so the clan totem is not eaten by clan members (Elkin 1954).

---

[3]I have termed this ancestral, not cult, totemism because Mardu who share the same substance—that is, were left by the same being(s)—do not form "cult lodges," which are common in some other parts of the continent. No corporate groups are organized on this basis or carry out exclusive and secret rituals centering on the exploits of the shared totem (see Elkin 1954).

[4]Nor does the conception site itself assume great importance by entitling an individual to active membership in a "conception clan," as occurs among the Aranda (Spencer and Gillen 1899; Strehlow 1965).

BIRTH

When a woman feels that she is about to give birth, she removes herself to a secluded spot away from camp and is attended by one or two "own side" female relatives (such as a "sister" or "grandmother") who act as midwives and massage her if labor is prolonged. She crouches over a small depression in soft sand, perhaps near a tree to support herself as she bears down during the birth. A midwife severs the umbilical cord with a sharp stone or her teeth, covers the afterbirth, and cleans off the baby with sand or ashes. Some of the cord may be made into a necklet to be worn by the baby as protection against sickness. The mother and baby remain in seclusion for four or five days, warmed by a constantly burning fire.

If the baby is deformed or otherwise visibly abnormal, or if the mother is in a weakened condition, the baby may be killed at birth by smothering it in the sand.[5] Women say that infanticide is only practiced when considered necessary, is uncommon, and must be done at the moment of birth lest the mother see the child's face or hear its cries and thus become so overwhelmed by compassion that she will not allow its death. It is impossible to assess with any accuracy the incidence of infanticide among the Mardu traditionally, but the indications are that it was a rare and extreme measure.[6]

It is customary for "grandmothers" of the baby to come and scold it, saying, "Bad! Bad!," probably to dissuade malevolent spirit-beings from taking an interest in it. It will not be given a name until quite some time after its birth; grandparents or other relatives usually name it. The most common criteria for naming are place of birth or conception totem; whichever is chosen, the name obviously reinforces the link that is implied. During the postnatal seclusion period, the father and all other close consanguineal relatives keep their distance. The married couple resume sexual intercourse a month or two later. Birth is not celebrated ritually, and there is no elaboration of either postpartum taboos or magical measures to protect the newborn from harm.

CHILDHOOD

The Mardu use many labels, based on physiological maturation stages, to cover the childhood phase of life; for example, there is a separate term for newborn, unable to sit up, able to crawl, walking but only just, walking properly, no longer breast-fed, no longer carried. Then follows a long period known simply as *ngulyi* (child), until girls' breasts begin to grow and, as *durndurn,* they are considered ready for marriage; boys remain *murdilya* until they are seized prior to circumci-

---

[5]Individuals who are, or who become, partly crippled, blind, or senile or who are later found to be deaf-mute or mentally deficient, are neither ostracized nor shunned. Mardu say that only unmanageable, homicidally deranged persons would be put to death but add that no such maniacs have ever existed among them.

[6]Other researchers report similar findings for Aboriginal Australia, and it appears that abortion or infanticide was never in widespread use as a means of population control (cf. Cowlishaw 1978, and Hamilton 1981).

sion. These labels, like kin and section terms, are frequently used in address and reference as substitutes for personal names.

Once in the camp, the infant becomes the center of attention in the family and the band, surrounded almost continuously by its parents, siblings, and older relatives who shower it with affection. Adults show extreme indulgence toward children of all ages, and a crying child can be sure of a quick response from its mother and others nearby, who pacify it by acceding to its demands. Parents who allow their small children to cry for long periods risk criticism from others for not looking after them properly. Small children are breast-fed on demand, which usually pacifies them. They continue to suckle for several years, even after the birth of a younger sibling or when the mother is no longer producing milk. Most children wean themselves eventually, since mothers see no point in deliberately or traumatically ending the practice.[7]

Given the nature of their shifting outdoor life, it is not surprising that toilet training of small children is casual. Small children are encouraged, and occasionally scolded, to leave the immediate vicinity of the camp to defecate and later to cover their feces. The onus for this and other early training lies with the mother and other adult females of the same band, who may act as wet-nurses on occasions. In toilet training, older siblings and other children of the group sometimes contribute by lighthearted scolding or ridicule, but they are careful not to offend the little one too much, lest it begin screaming.

Temper tantrums are tolerated with great patience and resignation by adults— and less so by older siblings. The offended child is rarely disciplined unless it is jealously threatening violence against a younger sibling or one of its parents at a time when they feel unwell. If the adult loses patience, the child is slapped—a self-defeating act, though, because it then continues the tantrum with renewed vigor. Screaming, writhing on the ground, hurling whatever it can lay hands on at the offending adult, the child, if able to talk, also lacerates the alleged oppressor with foul language drawn from a large supply of obscenities and blasphemy that children master very early in their speaking careers. Mardu society is child-centered in the sense that children almost always prevail, except when they seek to accompany their father (or their mother if she is similarly involved) when he is leaving camp to discuss or perform rituals with other adult males of the group, or when the child wants to go in a direction that would lead it anywhere near "men's country."[8]

Children are free to do very much as they like most of the time and are given very few explicit instructions by adults. Elderly people, particularly those who are too old or infirm to participate actively in daily hunting and gathering activities,

---

[7]What appear to be naturally low fertility rates among Aboriginal women in traditional society may be attributable partly to the inhibitory effect on ovulation of constant lactation; see Hamilton (1981:126–129).

[8]This term is used here to denote any site or locality which, through mythological significance, ritual use, or the presence of sacred objects, is considered sacred and dangerous to all but fully initiated men and is therefore taboo to all others. Most areas so designated owe their sacredness to Dreaming events and are therefore permanently taboo. Some, however, may be only temporarily sacred; they revert to open areas when the sacred objects are removed and the sticks, stones (stuck into tree forks), and broken branches which indicated their boundaries are removed.

Minma, with son Jambijin watching, shapes a new spearthrower with his metal ax. (Photo © Film Australia from the film series People of the Australian Western Desert.*)*

spend much of their time in the camp as guardians and entertainers of the small children. As tellers of stories and singers of songs, and as "grandparents," they normally enjoy a relaxed and affectionate relationship with the children. From these elders, children acquire much of the lore of their people; a great deal is also learned from their observation and emulation of peers and older members of the band.

The children play at many different kinds of games, few of which are competitive (though they also sometimes fight), and their toys are simple and easily gleaned from the local environment. Much of their play emulates aspects of the lives of adults: boys or their older male relatives make toy spears, shields, clubs, and bark boomerangs with which they "hunt" and "fight," whereas girls prefer to play *milbindi*, in which they draw lines in the sand to represent hearth groups and make up stories about family life and people's various exploits. For the first half-dozen or so years of their lives, the children usually play in mixed-sex groups and their games sometimes include "making camp" and "mothers and fathers." This at times includes attempts at sexual intercourse and the staging of adultery, elopement, and so on. This amuses adults, although an older relative may mildly scold them if the couple concerned stands in an "incestuous" relationship, as a reminder about the correct behaviors they will have to observe as adulthood approaches.

Children learn about sexual intercourse when they are quite young and still sleep in the same camp as their parents, and, since it is not a forbidden topic of conversation, by hearing about it. Sex is never separate from concerns about kin

Jambijin launches his toy spear by hand; he holds a toy thrower in the other hand.

relationships, and this is the arena where, for adults, considerations of morality are always involved. The desire of married couples for privacy or lack of interruption in their conjugal sex life is no doubt a factor in the separation of band families into spaced camps. It may also influence growing children in their decision to sleep somewhere else.

Any time from about the age of seven or eight onward, boys go to join their peers and older unmarried males in the *girriji* (single persons) camp, and girls begin sleeping at the camp of grandparents or other old female relatives who share a *girriji* camp. This is about the time that the sexual dichotomy of play groups becomes more pronounced. Boys are increasingly likely to go off in their own groups, playing and getting food away from the women and younger children. They are not yet old enough to go out with the men, but their growing realization of the separateness of men's and women's activities no doubt encourages them to disengage themselves somewhat from the females and from identification with the roles of women. By now, they have learned the skills of gathering and of tracking and hunting small animals and lizards; much of the time, they use these skills to obtain food for snacks. In this respect, there is an important difference between the older boys and girls: boys are not expected to contribute to the food consumed by the family as a group, whereas girls are increasingly regarded as providers. For girls, the transition from their family of orientation into an early marriage is one of essential continuity in daily activities. A girl's change of status to wife and then mother goes largely unheralded, in marked contrast to a boy's long path to full social adulthood.

Sometime around the age of eleven or twelve, the fortunes of boys and girls begin to diverge markedly. A girl will soon be given to her husband. Considering her tender age and attachment to her natal group, her husband might remain with his in-laws for some time after being given his new wife, especially if he is young and she is his first wife. This arrangement allows her to adjust to the status of wife in the security of her own people and territory. At the same time, the husband is discharging important obligations to her parents by hunting meat for them and forging close ties to his brothers-in-law. Whereas the girl will ultimately move to the band of her husband, her brothers remain in their father's group until they are seized as a preliminary to circumcision. For them, marriage will not be possible until ten to fifteen years after the beginning of their adolescence, when their initiation into full manhood is complete.

MALE INITIATION

For boys, initiation is a momentous event which entails a vital transition from child to man via symbolic death and rebirth. This is accomplished largely through the youth acting passively as the recipient and not the instigator of activities that will accomplish the transition. What is required of the initiate is unquestioning acceptance, silent endurance of physical pain, and an absolute commitment to obey his elders, guard the secrets of the men, and hunt meat for the elders in exchange for the powerful knowledge he is gaining.

Growing boys have mixed feelings about their coming initiation. They are frightened of the ordeals they suspect lie ahead, yet they are also aware that others before them have survived. When their time approaches, they become understandably anxious to be inducted into the secret world of the men, to attain adulthood, and eventually to earn the right to marry. Although the Mardu keep no track of actual ages, they decide when a boy is ready largely by his physiological maturation. Precocious behavior or troublemaking may precipitate one of two decisions: seizure and induction ahead of the planned time, to put a stop to his excesses, or a deliberate delay of a year or two, leaving him to suffer the embarrassment of seeing his peers begin the road to manhood while he remains a *murdilya* (uncircumcised). Usually, several boys are inducted at the same big meeting, so there is often an age difference of two or three years among them. The shared experience of being initiated in the same year sets up among the youths a ritual relationship, *yarlbu* (age-mate). This bond of lifelong friendship and mutual support provides each youth with a network of reliable friends in several different territories.

Tooth Evulsion   This rite, called *yirraburda* (tooth-hit), is not practiced by the Mardu but is common among their southern neighbors, so some Mardu boys have it performed on them when their bands come into contact with southerners. They are aged between ten and twelve when they are seized without warning and taken into the bush away from camp. There, to the accompaniment of songs concerning Marlu and Walbaju, two Dreaming Kangaroo-men who first performed the rite on each other, several boys have a front incisor knocked out with stones used as hammers and sharpened sticks as chisels.

Nose Piercing   The first initiation rite for most Mardu boys is *nyiirnka,* the piercing of the nasal septum, performed when they are young adolescents called *mulyajudu* (nose-closed). The ritual is timed so that there are distantly related people of the boy's "own side" generation level grouping available to perform it; there is a ritual division of labor between Activists and Mourners (see Figure 3-5, p. 77, for an explanation of these dual divisions).

Nujaga is about fourteen, tall for his age, with sandy-colored straight hair, a big smile, and several small cicatrices on his shoulders, put there by his "B" and friend Dabuni. His potbelly is gone, and he has the beginnings of a moustache. He is camped at Barnngurr rockhole (in the McKay Ranges, west of Lake Disappointment) with about forty people currently traveling in three bands. He and four or five boys are at the rockhole, killing finches with stones and eating them, so he has not noticed that a group of his relatives (Mourners) have just placed a quantity of vegetable food (quandong fruits, bush tomatoes, and seedcakes) on the ground not far from his family's camp. With a high-pitched, attention-getting cry followed by hand signs, the boys are called back to camp. Nujaga barely has a chance to notice the food before he is seized by two distantly related men, a "WB," Wibudun, and "grandfather," Libana. The Mourners, who sit by the food, bow their heads and wail softly as Nujaga is brought over and surrounded by members of the Activist group. The younger children have stopped playing and are watching from what they judge to be a safe distance.

Nujaga is held and comforted by Libana and another "grandfather" while Wibudun pushes a sharpened spear point into his septum and another "WB," Giya, braces a *mulyayidi* (nose-bone) against the other side of his septum. The bone is from an eaglehawk's wing, chosen because Warlawuru, the Eaglehawk-man, is the Dreaming creator of this rite. Nujaga winces in obvious pain but makes no sound and holds still as the spear point is twirled to enlarge the hole and Giya pushes the nose-bone through. His "grandfathers" loudly announce to the Mourners that it is all over, and there is no bleeding; still wailing, they return to their camps. Nujaga and the Activists then sit down and eat the feast. His "grandfather" Libana feeds him, because he is not permitted to talk or feed himself until some days later, after some Activist relatives have taken him hunting. They tell him to move the bone frequently so as to keep the hole open. Later he will not wear the nose-bone constantly, but will sometimes use the hole as a convenient place to carry a spare hook for his spearthrower, in case the other breaks or is lost (see Gould 1969a).

Circumcision   Despite the fact that it occurs early in the long road to manhood, circumcision is the initiation stage surrounded by the greatest elaboration of activities, both public and secret-sacred. Because it ultimately concerns so many people and so much organization, this stage entails considerable planning and discussion on the part of a boy's male relatives. Headed by his consanguineal and classificatory elder brothers, they must seek the permission of his father and other close patrikin before any action can be taken. The dual Activist-Mourner division pervades all activities, and both groups are indispensable. The major burden of the care, comforting, and instruction of the youth lies with the smaller Activist group. His "grandfathers," in particular, stay close by at all times and are a great source of reassurance. His "EB" are members of the Activist group, but are described as "a little bit *garnku*," so on certain occasions they side with the Mourners. Two other named groups are important: the *jilganggaja* (travelers), the Activist men who accompany the youth on his precircumcision travels after he has been seized, and the *manggalyi,* the distantly related "mother's brothers" and "wife's brothers" who are selected to perform the actual operation; of these, one of the two "MB" will bestow a wife upon the young novice.

Since this initiation stage embraces a time period of several months and a host of different activities, the following account provides only highlights of the sequence of major events. No two sequences are ever exactly the same because particular circumstances favor the inclusion or deletion of minor activities; even when two or more youths are cut at the same meeting, there must be changes in the personnel involved. For each individual, the membership of the two major groupings differs— not only because the groups are egocentrically based, but also because in each case some people decide for themselves whether their feelings for the novice will cause them to side with the *garnku* and play the more passive Mourner role.

(a) *Seizure*. Ritual activity surrounding circumcision begins with the seizing of the novice. From the moment he is seized until his circumcision, a novice is termed *marlurlu* (because it was Marlu, the Kangaroo-man, who first took a novice on a long precircumcision Dreaming trip through the Western Desert). From this time until six to eight weeks after the operation, when he returns from seclusion to the life of the band, he will not speak, and no one will utter his name—exactly as if he were dead. This accords with the idea of circumcision as a symbolic enactment of death. There are many parallels between the two kinds of transition, and the terminology surrounding this stage reflects them; for example, after circumcision, the novice is termed *bugurdi* (*bugu* meaning "dead"), and the act of return is called *yudirrini* (being born).

Yagarr, aged about sixteen, is a thick-set youth of quiet disposition. His band has met up with two others, one of which is Manyjilyjarra like his own, the other Warnman, at a soak called Nyanggabudajarra, in limestone country northeast of Lake Disappointment (see Map 2). It is mid-afternoon, and he is relaxing after a long but successful lizard hunt with his father. He is taken completely by surprise as two distantly related Warnman Activists approach quietly and grab him. One, Laljan, his "S," places a thick hairbelt around his waist and thus becomes his *warlungga,* a ritual term that connotes a subsequent avoidance relationship between the pair. On seeing this, Mourners of both sexes burst into loud and prolonged wailing, and Yagarr's mother and several other women seize digging sticks and stones and gash their scalps as Activist women rush to restrain them. Yagarr is taken from camp by a group of Activists who dance to a site about four-hundred yards downwind, safely out of earshot of camp. After dusk, they are joined by the Mourner men for an all-night session of singing and dancing of the Nyurnguny ritual.[9] The Activists and Mourners sit in two circles, their faces lit eerily by small fires. They alternate slow sonorous rhythms with very rapid, exciting bursts of singing when the vigorous banging of wooden sticks on the ground sends up billowing clouds of choking red dust. The songs they sing highlight some of Kangaroo's exploits with other Dreaming beings. Yagarr lies just outside the Activist circle, head down, as Minuji, a "grandfather," lightly covers his ears during the singing and spreads his fingers across the youth's eyes during dances so that the dangerous powers of these secret-sacred sights and sounds will be lessened.

Nothing is explained to him, but the Activist men keep telling him that this is *yulubirdi,* "the Law," the truth, something powerful and dangerous never to be divulged to the uninitiated. Whenever one of the short dances is performed, the men identify the ancestor being depicted. Yagarr, exhilarated but tense and tired, is prodded every time he appears to doze. Just before dawn, the Mourner men leave the rest and return to camp to assemble the women. Yagarr is told to stand, and, led by the arm by one of his "grandfathers," he is taken back to camp surrounded by the dancing Activists. There, the Mourner men and women lie facing away from Yagarr, wailing softly and watched by the Activist women who sit nearby, silent. Two strongly built Activist men seize Yagarr by his head and feet and tell him to hold himself rigid as they lay him at right angles across the backs of the Mourner men and the sides of the Mourner women; then, the entire assembly wails as he is led away a short distance. Later, when the four or five Activist men who will accompany him are ready, Janu, an old "spouse," and Malyudina, an old "grandmother," walk over and present Yagarr with a firestick and a club. In kind but firm tones, they tell him to bring back many people from afar, and say, "Don't get homesick for your family or worry about them; they will be waiting when you get back." Yagarr's guardians anoint themselves and him with red ochre and fat, and don hair-string head and arm bands as well as thick hair-belts, so that they will be readily identified as *jilganggaja* (travelers).

(b) *The Journey.* The purpose of the journey is twofold: to contact as many distant groups as possible and issue them formal invitations, symbolized by bullroarers and carved "message" sticks whose power is such that it impels people

---

[9]Nyurnguny, the most widespread Western Desert ritual, is closely linked with both circumcision and subincision. Since it follows the path of Kangaroo and associated Dreaming beings through thousands of miles of the desert, it comprises several hundred songs, so in one session only a segment of the total would be sung.

to acceptance;[10] and secondly, to acquaint the novice with the totemic geography of distant, hitherto unknown, territories through instruction and the performance of rituals with bands encountered there. Whenever the travelers see smokes, they send one or two messengers ahead to make contact and announce the coming of the *marlurlu*.

Yagarr is kept at a distance until the locals have summoned other nearby bands and ensured that the Mourners in these groups have had time to amass some food for the travelers. After the locals have assembled, the travelers chant and dance into the area around the wailing Mourners, then place Yagarr on the latter's backs and sides. The same night, after the travelers have been fed, all the men take Yagarr to a suitable spot for a long session of dancing and singing. The travelers may stay for several days and the Kangaroo and other rituals will be held day and night.

The travelers continue, heading southwest then south past Lake Disappointment until they locate the Giyajarra bands from which Yagarr's *manggalyi* ("surgeons") will be drawn. These Giyajarra people, and other bands encountered during the return journey, join the travelers and swell their ranks as they head north through Gardujarra country en route to Giriji rockhole (six or eight days' travel east of Nyanggabudajarra) in his father's estate where the big meeting is to be held. Messengers go ahead from the approaching bands to give the bands in the Giriji area time to assemble and make the necessary preparations, which include preparation of the *warluburgu* (circumcision ground) by Activist men.

(c) *The Arrival and Circumcision Preliminaries.* The incoming group makes camp at Junyba, a soak a short distance from Giriji, where it will await the arrival of people from other areas. When smokes have ceased to appear on the horizon, and it is assumed that no more groups will be arriving, preparations for the actual welcome begin among both the host groups and the visitors. Seedcakes are sent to the visitors, who eat a meal about mid-afternoon before they begin decorating their bodies.

Mourner women of both visitor and host groups put on red ochre, and Activist females of both groups don white ochre. Host men decorate with a charcoal and white Kangaroo design; the visitors in this case have chosen a Nyarnayi design (see Chapter 5). All the men supplement their body design with arm, neck, and forehead bands of hair twine or possum fur, feather-bundle headdresses, whittled wood "pompoms" stuck in their forehead bands, and pearlshell neck and pubic pendants. They carry boomerangs painted with white ochre stripes. The children are decorated with white ochre patterns by their mothers and older siblings; they and the women carry leaf-bundles which they shake in time with their stamping dance steps. Each group, hidden from the other by an Acacia thicket, practices its massed dances in readiness for the ceremonial welcome.

Figure 4-1 shows how the host people arrange themselves in readiness for the entry of the visitors. Led by the arm by two young Activist boys, Yagarr is completely surrounded by the dancing, chanting crowd of over a hundred men, women, and children as they approach the assembly at Giriji. In front of the visitors are the Activist men, who feint a boomerang attack as they approach the line of crouching host Activist men who are ready to "defend" their people against the "invaders." After completing a noisy circuit

---

[10]Other messengers go in small groups to contact bands elsewhere in the area. They carry with them a special hair-belt, *gajabuga,* which is a symbolic substitute for the novice himself.

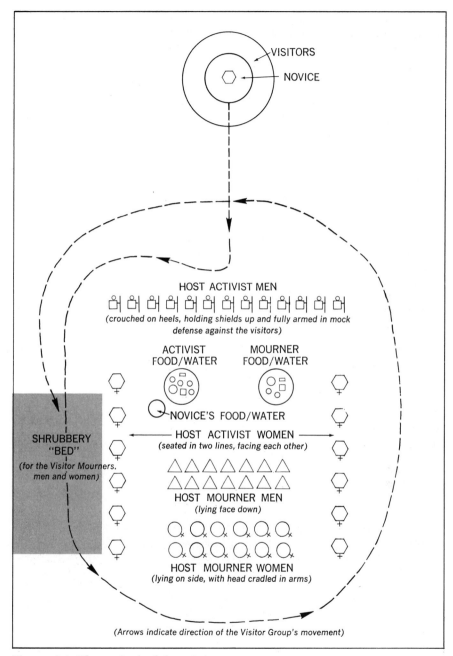

Figure 4-1. The arrival of the novice.

around the hosts, the visitor Mourners lie on the shrubbery bed and join the host Mourners in wailing while the Activists and Yagarr continue to circle. Two "WB" visitors seize him and place him crosswise on top of the host Mourner men and women, then on the visiting Mourners, then they seat him close to and facing each of the host and visitor Activists. This done, two Activists lead him to a spot close to the circumcision ground, well away from the camping area, and wait with him there. Meanwhile, both groups complete their welcome dances and spend the next two hours until dusk airing disputes, the early settlement of which is essential if the ritual activities are to be carried through in an atmosphere of peace and goodwill—a precondition for their success.

Before the women and children arrive at the ground, some visitor Activist men decide to perform the tossing rite on Yagarr. They throw him high into the air, while one of them hits him with two long leafy branches, then catch him. They do this in emulation of Kangaroo, who tossed his Dreaming *marlurlu* high into the sky to release his spirit and make his penis "light" so that it would not bleed or cause great pain during the subsequent cutting. With his spirit thus released, Yagarr will not die during the operation.

Everyone assembles close to the ground (a rectangle measuring some thirty by twenty yards), which has a large shrubbery windbreak erected at one end. Host Mourner men enter it first, light a large fire, then dance in rapid sidesteps up and down before sitting in a circle near the windbreak end. This activity is repeated by the host Activist males who follow, then sit a short distance away in a separate circle. The women of both groups and "sides" enter and sit inside the windbreak; the visitor females are preceded by their Mourner males, who enter and dance before joining their host counterparts. The visitor Activists are the last to enter and dance, then they and the host Activist men commence singing some Kangaroo ritual songs that can safely be heard by women and children, who by this stage are all present at the ground. Some of the Activist women stand and dance *nyanbi,* a distinctive shuffling step, done with feet close together, that leaves a double furrowed track as they propel themselves along, their arms swinging in time with the men's singing and beating of sticks on the ground. Meanwhile, the Mourners sit quietly, except for some gentle sobbing and wailing. Then, after quietly informing the host Mourner men that they have chosen suitable "surgeons," and having received the Mourners' permission to proceed, four Activist males walk across and suddenly seize the four men selected from the ranks of the visitors to be *manggalyi* (surgeons) : two "MB" will do the actual cutting, and two "WB" will assist.

Yagarr is now led onto the ground and told to lie down close to the circle of singing Activist men. The "surgeons" line up on one side of a small fire, then the host female Mourners file past on the other side to identify them. These women then lead all the rest and the children back to camp, after being loudly ordered from the ground by the Activist men. The host Mourner men then view the "surgeons" and return to camp, because they are too "sorry" to remain for what follows. By now it is early evening; the wind has dropped, and an almost full moon is helping illuminate the scene.

(d) *The Operation.* The novice is circumcised on a human "table" formed by six to eight Activists, while several "grandfathers" (both "MF" and "FF") look on and comfort him, the rest of the Activists quietly sing, and the Mourners softly wail.

Yagarr neither utters a sound nor struggles in any way, but he bites very hard on the boomerang that has been placed in his mouth. He lies inert, as if self-anesthetized, betraying his suffering with little more than an occasional grimace. Beneath him, the men forming the table joke with one another, complaining of the discomfort and Yagarr's weight, and urge the "surgeons" to hurry up. The hovering "grandfathers" keep up a chorus of reassurances, for the benefit of Yagarr and the Mourners, saying repeatedly that all is well. Afterward, he is led away by an "EB" and told to kneel over a smoke fire. The "surgeons" collect several hair-belts and weapons that they had left near the ground earlier and then file past him. Yagarr's supporting "EB" raises his arm in a gesture of acceptance of these gifts. After a final ritualized showing of themselves to the assembly, the "surgeons" leave the ground; a short distance away, they throw firesticks high into the air and make a high-pitched "baubaubau" sound, thus signalling the completion of the circumcision. This causes a loud outbreak of wailing in the camp. After Yagarr's "grandfathers" make a ritual presentation and explanation to him of his first sacred objects, a pair of bullroarers which he will use to signal his need for food, everyone returns to the main camp except for several "EB" and "grandfathers" who will camp with Yagarr in men's country for the duration of his seclusion.

(e) *The Seclusion.* The novice is joined within a few days by other youths who are circumcised after him; they camp nearby and can communicate only by sign language, since talking is forbidden among those deemed to be ritually "dead." In the camping area, ceremonial gift exchanges take place between the initiate's close Mourner relatives and the "surgeons." This short rite is called *yulburru* ("dust," because it involves the sprinkling of dust on the ground by both groups), and appears to be a symbolic peacemaking between the "bereaved" and the "killers." This rite clears the way for the latter to reenter society and for members of the two groups to interact in daily life, although direct contact between the novice's family and the "surgeons" will henceforth be minimal and highly restrained. At the same time, *yulburru* is a manifestation of the very strong bond that now exists between the families concerned.

Many nights during the seclusion period, the men organize rituals that can be performed in the camp area and attended by the entire assembly. Meanwhile, at secret dancing grounds out of sight of camp, the men hold periodic performances of the Nyurnguny ritual. The initiates in attendance are now permitted to see some of the dances through the protective screen of the fingers of their "grandfathers" which partly cover their eyes. The youth cannot yet see most of the sacred objects used in the dances, however, since these are too dangerous at this early stage of initiation. Later, the Kangaroo ritual is supplanted by the Walawalangu ritual, which centers on the creative exploits of Two Men (Wadi Gujarra) who traveled extensively within and beyond Mardu country. Walawalangu is always held at night at a special ground in men's country, because its songs and dances are secret-sacred to initiated men. The men sit in two circles, divided in most instances on a patrimoiety basis.

Yagarr and three other novices lie on their backs in the center of the opposite moiety circle, with a mother's brother supporting each novice's head and periodically hitting him lightly on his chest with a bullroarer as the songs are sung to a hand-clapping accompaniment. (Later, the novices will learn that this is done to make them strong and as a magical protection for their upper body against spear wounds.) The men wear no decorations, and there are few dances, but there is an important instructional element in that many of the well-known Dreaming beings associated with this ritual turned into heavenly bodies (principally stars, constellations, and starless areas of particular shape), which are pointed out to the novices as the appropriate song is sung. No detailed information is given, but the names and locations of the various beings are announced and pointed out, together with impassioned comments on the great power of this Law and the absolute necessity of upholding it.

(f) *The Return*. By the time the novices' penises are considered well-enough healed, the main business of the big meeting is over, and many groups have already departed for the return journey to their home areas. The families of the novices, and some other groups, have remained to help celebrate the return of the youths to society at large. After informing the camp that the novices are healed, Activist guardians take them hunting to get meat as repayment for the ritual knowledge revealed to them.

Yagarr and the others arrive back in men's country about dusk, carrying the lizards and small game they have hunted and cooked. They and all the men assemble at the Walawalangu ground in their two circles, with a simple charcoal V-pattern decorating their chests. The novices are given some seedcake and water, their first sustenance for the day, while the men feast on the meat and other seedcakes prepared earlier by the women. It is a clear moonless night, specially chosen so that the stars and other heavenly bodies will be sharply visible when they are pointed out during the singing, which will continue throughout the night. The two circles sing simultaneously much of the time but each follows a different track of the Two Men—one covering areas to the north of Mardu country and the other those to the south, until the tracks converge in the Durba Hills south of Lake Disappointment, where the Mardu say the Two Men finally departed from the earth (see Chapter 5). Several dances are featured during the night, but the climax of the ritual comes just before dawn. Yagarr and the other novices, who have been kept awake all night, are fully anointed with blood by Activist men, to the accompaniment of a song telling of a similar rite performed by the Two Men shortly before they left the earth.

As this occurs, one man goes back to the camping area and rouses all the women and children. The close relatives of Yagarr and the other youths don red ochre and sit together between the dancing ground and the camp, while all the young boys stand facing the direction of the (unseen) ground, holding a supply of bark boomerangs at the ready, to prevent the entry of the malevolent spirits which can be heard crying out angrily as the returning novices approach. The sound is actually produced by the bullroarers being swung by Activist men. While still out of sight of the waiting women and children, a "mother's brother" puts a large hair-belt and a possum-fur pubic tassel on each novice. The women cry out as they hear the increasingly loud noise of the bullroarers. The noise suddenly ceases just before the men appear in a headlong dash toward the camp, where they are met with a hail of boomerangs flung over their heads by the young boys. Yagarr and the others are led to a group of their close female relatives who sit with legs apart facing small piles of leafy bushes onto which the novices fall. Their mothers and the other female kin clasp at the youths and wail very loudly for several minutes.

Although the Mardu say that the anointing is to make the youth strong, the return to the life of the society by the blood-covered novice, who lies on a leafy "nest" between his mother's loins, is clearly symbolic of birth.[11] The return is not yet complete, however, for the novice must camp with the boys for a short time before he can move into the single-men's camp.

Several older, uncircumcised boys come and take the novices to camps they have set up for them a short distance away from the main camping area. Exhausted and covered in dry blood, they sit with heads down in embarrassment, looking much the worse for wear as the smaller boys crowd around to gaze at them and probably ponder a similar future

---

[11]In some parts of Australia, the novice is said to die when swallowed by a giant rainbow python which later regurgitates him, proof of which is his forlorn and blood-covered state. The theme of swallowing and regurgitation recurs throughout the continent (cf. Hiatt 1975).

fate. Yagarr eats; he is alive, but he is not the youth who left them several months before; never again will he revert fully to the behaviors of childhood. He has seen and heard new things, has withstood trauma and pain, and, through wondrous revelations, has gained wisdom—dead is the boy, newborn is the man-in-the-making.

(g) *Betrothal.* In return for having ritually "killed" the initiate, one of the two "MB" who removed his foreskin bestows a small daughter on him. This brief ceremony takes place shortly after his return to society, in public and as part of the *yulburru* rite described above.

A little girl, Banginya, is carried by one of her older brothers to where Yagarr sits, surrounded by his family and other close kin, while her parents witness the ceremony from a short distance away. He is given a spearthrower which he gently lays on her head or across her back; as he does so, those present tell him that from now on, whenever he encounters her and her family, he must hunt meat for them.

Subincision   Novices remain in the status of *bugurdi,* wearing their hair in a bun, until sometime within the following year when another big meeting is held and some suitably distant relatives are available to act as surgeons. Subincision, practiced by all Western Desert Aborigines, entails the slitting of the underside of the penis, thus exposing the urethra, which does not heal closed. Its physiological effects are to make urinating splashy and ejaculation less forceful, although it does not affect male fertility. The sole reason offered by Mardu men as to why they practice subincision is that it is the Law, done in emulation of Dreaming beings who subincised one another as badges of full manhood and proof of their right to participate in the sacred life. Men point to the emu, particularly, in providing a Dreaming validation for the practice, since this large flightless bird has a distinct penile groove not unlike that of a subincised man. The particular songs and dances that accompany subincision pertain to Garlaya, the Dreaming emu-people, though, as in the case of circumcision, the ritual is the Kangaroo line and the dances performed in the days following the operation involve Kangaroo and other ancestral beings. The operation itself is surrounded by less ritual than circumcision and affects the community at large far less, but the subincised penis has great symbolic significance as the physical manifestation of manhood.

After being subincised, Yagarr remains in seclusion for about a week, during which time the Nyurnguny ritual is performed daily. On the first day, he is placed in his "own side" singing circle, taught how to beat time with the wooden stick, and encouraged to begin singing the songs. Another day he is "dressed"; that is, an Activist relative decorates him with a forehead band, thick hair-belt, and a *jininy,* a carved wooden ornament worn on the back of the head during dancing. (The *jininy* is similar in size and shape to a bullroarer, but can be seen by women and children.) Another day, he dances for the first time, and more and more dances and associated sacred objects are shown to him.

Food and gift exchanges have already taken place between Yagarr's family and the two distantly related "WB" and "MB" who performed the operation, but a further *yulburru* takes place between the two groups after his return to camp, as a gesture of reconciliation and an acknowledgment of their new relationship. Yagarr now is a *girriji* (bachelor), and he will remain so until he is considered qualified to marry. From now on,

Yagarr's progression through further initiation stages depends in part on his reputation among the older men as a good provider of meat, a willing participant in all activities, and as a "quiet man" who does not cause trouble through inappropriate sexual activity. The following decade or so involves the gradual revelation of more and more secret-sacred knowledge and his assumption of greater responsibilities in ritual activities.

Intermediate Stages   The brief descriptions that follow cover the most important of the initiatory stages between subincision and marriage:

(a) *Bungarna*. A year or two after subincision, the young man is presented with a small pearlshell pubic pendant, or *bungarna,* which he will wear on appropriate ritual occasions thereafter. The presentation is made by "EB" in the camp area. Elderly Activist women instruct him to look after the shell, obey the Law, and keep away from trouble over women.

(b) *Mirdayidi*. As noted in Chapter 3, this major initiatory stage takes place at a mythologically important site where an estate group has a storehouse of sacred objects. Periodically, a novice or, more commonly, a small group of novices who have reached the appropriate stage of initiation will be shown these objects for the first time and will eat a Mirdayidi ritual feast.

All available initiated males assemble somewhere close to the camping area. The novice is then seized, and the Mourner women wail for him. The men sit in a circle into which the novice is led and then made to lie face down on the stomachs of all present. "Own side" relatives tie several hair-belts around his waist, and he is sent away, accompanied by several young men, to hunt a large quantity of meat in payment for all that he will soon be privileged to witness and learn. He and his companions will spend two or three days hunting. Meanwhile, the old men who are guardians of the storehouse go to the site to clean the sacred boards and prepare the nearby ceremonial ground. Some of the older men and women who hold the high ritual status of Mirdayidi food preparers work at a spot not far from the camping area; the women grind and mix the grass seeds into paste, while the men do the actual cooking of the large seedcakes.

When the hunters return, the novice, laden with cooked game and weak with hunger and thirst (he has not been permitted to eat or drink while out hunting), must run the last quarter mile or so past men who leap out from hiding and pursue him, hitting him on the back with the small sacred boards they are carrying. The severity of the beating depends on the novice's secular conduct, and the worst hidings are meted out to those who have a reputation as egotists or womanizers. More senior men stand behind large boards and form two lines close to the storehouse.

The novice runs between them, throws down the meat, then collapses at the feet of the singing men. In the ritual that follows, he is brought into physical contact with the sacred boards and their great power and is fed a piece of seedcake that has been rubbed along a board to pick up some of its coating of animal fat and red ochre. He and his fellow hunters then eat the Mirdayidi seedcake feast amid more ritual. The insertion of the food breaks the ban of silence on the novice, but more significantly, the ingestion of the spiritual essence of "country" confers on the young man privileges and responsibilities associated with the estate group concerned. Each type of sacred board is named and identified to him, together with a brief explanation of the mythological and territorial associations of the designs carved on it. Men will make much of any boards that have been carved by the novice's close relatives in the patriline, impressing upon him their labors on behalf of the Law and the importance of continuity, for he must do the same.

Throughout the revelations and instruction, Activists hold center stage and exhort the novice to be a good Law carrier, and he may be loudly and severely chastised by his many "EB" for past misconduct. The atmosphere bristles with a tension so palpable that the novice cannot help but be profoundly moved. His susceptibility to indelible messages about power and responsibility is at a maximum in this situation of total control and dominance on the part of the elders, who personify the Law of the Dreaming in all its omnipotence. Calm is restored to conclude the ritual, as the rest of the men eat the Mirdayidi seedcakes and meat before the boards are carefully put back in their hiding place, and everyone returns to camp.

Having eaten his first Mirdayidi, during which he has been dramatically confronted with what are, in a sense, the sacred roots of his own being, a young man must soon be taken on journeys to be ritually inducted into the estates of many other Mardu groups. These vital steps must be taken before marriage can be contemplated, because it is only through the Mirdayidi that he gains full rights of access to other territories. Through gifts of secrets and food, these other groups share their ancestral substance with him: he has eaten off the boards and ingested their power in a shared sacrament. He is thus committing part of himself to these estates and their Dreaming beings, becoming a kinsman in spirit as well as flesh. Later, he and his family will be free to hunt, gather, cut trees, and camp in these territories, and he will know much of their totemic geography, including sites to avoid. The imperative that young men travel widely to broaden their geographical and religious horizons is of great pragmatic as well as spiritual significance in Mardu society.

(c) *Board Carving*. After he has eaten Mirdayidi in several different areas, a young man's qualities are discussed by the men of his own and closely allied bands, who decide if he is ready to progress to the next stage, which involves the carving of sacred boards.

The young man is seized and is taken to the storehouse of his estate group, usually in the company of a few others of the same status, perhaps when several bands are camping together or during a big meeting. After being shown the remaining very large sacred boards in a ritual similar to that of the Mirdayidi revelation, each novice is presented with a small wooden board that has been shaped and outlined with a geometric design but is uncarved. Several diviner-curers magically remove carving chisels from the bodies of older men whose carving is of high standard and insert these into the young men's torsos, arms (to steady their hands), and heads (to allow them to see clearly while carving). Activist relatives then present the novices with *jimirliri* (chisels) of sharp stone or animal teeth hafted with spinifex resin to a short wooden handle. The Activists instruct them in the use of the chisel, since the carving of the fine, parallel grooves is an exacting task requiring great skill and patience. The "elder brother" or "grandfather" who traced the design outline briefly explains its mythological significance and territorial associations. The pattern will be a variant of the three or four commonly used by the Mardu. The novices remain in seclusion, fed and supervised by Activists, for about a month until they have finished carving their first board. They must then hunt large quantities of meat to repay their elders before returning to their families. Later, a young man will be given more small boards to carve, but will outline them himself, advised by an older estate-group relative regarding the appropriate designs and themes for his estate and its Dreaming beings.

(d) *Board Cutting*. Some time after he has successfully carved several sacred boards, the young man, along with others of the same status, will be seized by Activist men who send the novices out to hunt and bring back plenty of meat for the old people.

> On their return, each initiate is given an ax. After the food has been eaten, a large group of men accompanies the novices to a suitable stand of trees where they are instructed in the selection and cutting of wood that will be made into sacred boards. Each cuts and shapes a small sacred board and presents it to his Activist elders for one of them to carve. When this is done, the boards are presented to the novices in a ceremony at the estate group's storehouse. The men exhort them to continue cutting and carving boards throughout their lives, since each will become a repository of life essence, exactly like the boards carried by the Dreaming beings wherever they traveled and deposited in storehouses throughout the land.

With the completion of this step, the young men are now termed *garndamari* and are eligible to claim their *bilyurr* (promised spouse) in marriage.

MARRIAGE, FAMILY, AND GENDER RELATIONS

A marriage takes place when the parents of a man's betrothed send her to his camp; the couple then cohabits on a permanent basis. There is no marriage ceremony among the desert people.

A large number of marriages—of girls to much older men—occur as the result not of a circumcision betrothal, but of arrangements made between a suitor and the girl's parents. There may not be an outright request, lest a refusal cause embarrassment, but intermediaries take meat and other gifts to the girl's parents to initiate the relationship, and such gift giving continues over a period of years whenever circumstances permit it. The Mardu say that if a couple has a daughter not yet betrothed, they think about who has been generous to them and decide to promise her to a man who has supported them. A formal betrothal may then take place, or the girl will be encouraged by her parents to visit the suitor's camp and take gifts of vegetable foods to him. Since marriage is never solely the concern of the couple, but brings two family groups into closer alliance, the attendant reciprocity helps guarantee that every effort will be made to ensure that the girl will eventually remain with her spouse as promised. In many cases, a girl is very much younger than her husband, and she enters marriage as a co-wife, whose food-gathering skills may be of greater value to the family unit than her reproductive potential, especially in the first few years when she is unlikely to conceive.

On the other hand, a man's first wife may be a much older woman, a widow whose abilities as a provider are proven and who is usually considered much less likely than a young wife to pursue the kinds of adulterous liaisons, even elopement, that lead to conflicts. People view marriages of this kind favorably, for not only will the older woman be a reliable and steadying influence, she may also become a companion, co-worker, and chaperone to one or more younger wives. Many men rely on their older wives to keep an eye on the others, which accords with the status difference that exists among them; the younger are expected to defer to the older.

Sexual jealousy may at times cause discord between co-wives—especially if the age difference between them is small—since many men favor the younger, newer woman as a sexual partner. However, the prevailing state in most polygynous families is one of comparative harmony. If an older wife no longer has young children of her own, she shares fully in the rearing of her co-wife's children and is as much a mother to them as their genetrix. Because social parenthood is stressed, most children grow up with at least two "real" mothers with whom they have close emotional ties, as well as many other "mothers" toward whom they feel varying degrees of attachment. Most older women welcome the addition of a young, strong girl to their family unit because she will contribute much to the daily labor of gathering and preparing food and, it is hoped, will bear children upon whom they can lavish much love and attention.

There are no rules restricting the number of wives a man can have, but practical considerations such as the availability of eligible women and a man's ability to control and retain them limit most to between one and three wives at any given time. The number of male and female births is about the same, and there is no evidence that infanticide (which is rare in any case) is practiced differentially with regard to an infant's sex.[12] Polygyny is made possible by a cultural practice: delaying the age of marriage for men while ensuring that females are married very young.

This does not mean that young men are denied sexual access to women, apart from periodic demands for abstinence occasioned by ritual activities (some of which entail celibacy for married men as well as bachelors). Mardu admit the inevitability and even the necessity of sexual activities, but premarital and extramarital affairs or liaisons are subject to certain norms. They should not be "incestuous," and they should be conducted as discreetly as possible, although secrecy is virtually impossible to maintain for long, since even a small child can read tracks and draw accurate conclusions. Also, such affairs should not cause a woman to neglect her wifely or maternal responsibilities and, above all, they should not be such as to pose an overt threat to an existing marriage.

Any move by a pair of lovers which brings public attention to their relationship is seen as tantamount to a declaration of intention to elope. Elopement is strongly condemned because it threatens the continued functioning of at least one family unit and, equally seriously, it threatens affinal alliances whose rupture would badly affect relationships between two or more kin groups. Little wonder that eloping couples, if and when eventually caught, will be severely punished—or even killed—if a wronged husband and his kin are sufficiently affronted, and the guilty couple's kin relationship is "incestuous."

Elopement certainly occurs from time to time among the Mardu, despite the risks of punishment entailed and the inevitable disturbance of the social status quo. The very few who suffer ostracism and severe punishment to remain together are still not considered married, however, until the woman's former husband or betrothed has publicly relinquished his claim to her. People acknowledge the possibility of personality clashes and incompatibility of temperament between spouses but do not consider these to be sufficient grounds for divorce. The family is very rarely

---

[12]My impression is that male conflicts resulting in death were similarly uncommon traditionally.

a socially isolated unit. The continual presence of close kin and the sex-based division of labor mean that husbands and wives spend less time alone together than with other band members or others of their own sex. The marriage bond, while often close, is not exclusive since the partners' interaction so often includes other adult members of the band. In the life of the camp, other families are always within sight and earshot, and the level of contact among them is high.

Men are more fortunate than women in having a socially acceptable reason to remove themselves from domestic annoyances or tensions. Part of the considerable time they spend in "men's country" is inevitably taken up with idle chatter and siestas, yet the men's preoccupation with religious matters is so great that their frequent absence from camp, other than to hunt, is rarely a pretext; much serious discussion, planning, and performance of ritual and other religious activities takes place. Mardu women, on the other hand, have much greater responsibilities for child-care and food preparation than men, so they have less freedom to absent themselves from the domestic hearth. Women's secret-sacred ritual activity is much less frequent than that of the men.

Most couples settle easily into the roles of spouse and parent. A great deal of mutual concern and regard exists between most spouses, despite an absence of public displays of affection or of protestations of love and devotion. The stability and durability of most marriages would seem to reflect this; divorce is uncommon among the Mardu. Given the volatility of many people, however, domestic tranquility can be quickly disturbed by real or alleged neglect, laziness, infidelity, dereliction of duty, and so on, resulting in conflict. In such cases, women may be more than a match for their husbands verbally, but in physical exchanges they usually fare less well (see Chapter 6).

Many Mardu will say that most men beat their wives only if they wantonly neglect their domestic responsibilities or are excessively active extramaritally. It follows, then, that wives who are beaten may not receive the sympathy or support of other band members, male or female, if they are held to be culpable. Women have far fewer marital rights than men. A man who has committed some kind of serious offense may offer his wife or wives for intercourse with those he has wronged, as a gesture of atonement. His spouses should comply without complaint. Also, he may offer them as temporary partners to "B" who are visiting, as a demonstration of hospitality and friendship. Again, the women concerned should raise no objections, whether or not they are consulted prior to the "lending." However, neither wife-offering nor wife-lending is a frequent or long-lasting occurrence.

From the foregoing, it should be clear that status differences exist between Mardu men and women, and definitely favor the former, as in other Aboriginal societies.[13] Both hierarchical and egalitarian tendencies are present in virtually all human societies, but hunters and gatherers are notable for the prominence of the latter, and in some there appears to be genuine equality between the sexes (cf. Endicott 1981). It is true that Australian Aborigines are often singled out as atypical

---

[13]For some time, this topic has been a matter for discussion and debate among scholars of Aboriginal Australia. Merlan (1988) provides an excellent overview and detailed bibliography. In relation specifically to the Mardu, see Tonkinson (1988a, 1988b, 1990).

of hunter-gatherers, for a variety of reasons, including the extent of sexual inequality and gerontocratic control over women and the labor of young men (Woodburn 1980, 1982; Bern 1979; Hiatt 1986). Significant regional variations exist, however, and, in parts of northern Australia, these inequalities are far more marked than among the Mardu. In fact, in mundane daily life, free of crises, the Mardu exhibit a strongly egalitarian ethos; the only obvious inequalities are manifest in the content of certain kin behaviors, where a certain deference and respect are offered or received on the part of both men and women. Although children are exempt from their strictures, and factors like age and friendship modify them, these status inequalities are intrinsic to all Aboriginal kinship systems. However, their ego-centered networks are such that there is in most cases an overall balance between deference owed to a person by certain others and shown by that person to different others (Tonkinson 1988c:151–154).

In Mardu society, where a strong egalitarian ethos co-exists with Lawfully ordained status inequalities, the question is not one of ascertaining *if* such inequalities exist, but of *when,* to what extent, and for how long they become manifest. The greater strength of male interests is demonstrated in two main contexts: when disruptions serious enough to invoke sanctions occur and in matters relating to the religious life, particularly whenever collective activity is being planned or undertaken. At these times, clear status inequalities emerge. When hierarchy is invoked in mundane social contexts, as when a man asserts his right of dominance over his wife or wives, it arises out of some kind of disruption. Between spouses, a man's aggressive assertion of his superior rights is not characteristic of normal family relationships and usually lasts only a short time.

The ideology of mature Mardu men, especially when expressed in all-male company, contains ample attestations of superior male status, knowledge, responsibility, and power. Yet only in the major arena of the religious life is there significant potential for generating and maintaining status inequality and hierarchy, and the outcome entails differentiation within as well as between the sexes (see Chapter 5).

GROWING OLD

By middle age, Mardu men have very detailed knowledge of the secret-sacred life and assume increasing responsibility for the organization and performance of religious activities. Some will eventually attain the status of a leader for the rituals with which they are most closely associated. For married women, too, prestige and authority in matters connected with their own as well as certain male rituals increase with age. Provided they remain alert and responsive, older men and women derive considerable stature from their accumulated wisdom. The elderly become less active in subsistence tasks and rituals, but assume greater responsibility for the caretaking and management of the religious life.

In keeping with this changing role, older people can expect material assistance in the form of foodstuffs from younger relatives who must repay the nurturance they have received by feeding and caring for their aged kin. The norms of classificatory kinship assure older, less-active hunters and gatherers that there will always be relatives to support them. Also, a number of choice and easily chewed foodstuffs are reserved for the elderly via food taboos, for example, the flesh of the porcupine-like echidna. In religious life, too, reciprocal obligations ensure that younger men will supply meat to their elders.

The elderly are generally well treated and cared for; should they become senile, however, they will no longer be venerated or sought after for advice, and their social importance will decline. They continue to be fed, but unlike infants with whom there are some parallels of helplessness, they become marginal, not central, in the life of the band. The ability to remain mobile is essential. Every effort is made to spare the elderly and infirm from too frequent or arduous movement, but hard times inevitably demand this of them on occasion. Some may pronounce themselves unable to go on and ask to be left behind to die. If no alternatives exist and the lives of others are endangered by a band's lessened mobility, this wish may be granted.

It has been suggested that the willingness to feed and care for the elderly is a major factor in the maintenance of bands which, as larger groups, lessen the burden of providing such support (Peterson 1972). One group of Western Desert people is known to have carried a lame man for about two years until he could support himself with the aid of a crutch. Peterson suggests that the territorial anchoring of bands stems from the strong desire of old men to remain as close as possible to their natal estates and to die in or close to the area of their birth; they thus become the nodal points around which bands form. As noted in Chapter 3, the men are motivated by strong sentiments of attachment and by deeply felt responsibilities they have toward the caretaking and maintenance of sacred rituals, sites, and objects belonging to the estate.

Old people who feel that their lives may be coming to an end prefer to die close to their birthplace so that their spirit will be spared a long journey back to its original home. I have never heard old Mardu talk about their impending death or express fears or uncertainties in this regard. They seem to accept its inevitability but not its finality, since the spirit is immortal.

DEATH AND ITS AFTERMATH

As in other societies, a Mardu death is almost always a traumatic experience for the bereaved because it evokes strong passions of grief and sometimes anger and resentment. Death disrupts the network of kin ties and social interaction and, at times, its aftermath upsets the tenor of intergroup relations. Unless the death is of a very small baby, large numbers of kin will assemble to participate in the activities that follow. Whether they adopt an active or a passive role depends on their emotional distance from the deceased and their membership of either the Activist or Mourner group.

In terms of what transpires after a death, a distinction can be made between physical and spiritual concerns, in accordance with Mardu understandings. Preparation of the body, burial, bone cleaning, and reburial deal with substance but are, in effect, subsidiary activities. The major concern is to cope with the immortality of the spirit, which is thought to be so distressed at its separation from the living that it seeks to continue its close association with them—a desire not shared by the living. This is why all the efforts of the survivors are aimed ultimately at ensuring the return of the spirit to its resting place permanently.

The intensity of emotion generated by a death depends considerably on the social status and age of the deceased. Neither the very old nor the very young are mourned as long, loudly, or intensely as those adults in the prime of life and older children who are suddenly lost. The deaths of socially integral people leave large gashes in the social fabric because, by middle age, they have built up a widely ramifying network of interpersonal ties. Regardless of their social status, however, the deaths of all but the very young are treated in much the same way in terms of the procedures followed.

Activist relatives must send messengers with news of the death to as many other bands as can be located in the general vicinity, so that their members can assemble to pay their respects and assist with the proceedings. Since most members of a deceased person's band are closely related, and therefore Mourners, more distantly related Activists from other bands assume responsibility for the tasks associated with the disposal of the body. For their efforts, they will eventually be recompensed by the Mourners, in the form of foodstuffs, hair-belts, and other gifts. If a person becomes seriously ill and death appears imminent, messengers may have already gone to summon others to the camp, and those who assemble cry and wail for the afflicted relative. This response might seem like a pessimistic prejudgment of the outcome, but to the Mardu it is a gesture of concern and a reflection of the social worth of the individual.

When death actually occurs, loud and emotional wailing breaks out and people of both sexes attempt to inflict bloody scalp wounds on themselves with whatever sharp object is near at hand. Despite their own grief, Activist relatives must intervene to prevent excessive bloodshed and keep a close watch on the Mourners. When more people arrive, there are renewed outbursts of grief and self-injury. Some of the newcomers will attempt also to strike some of the close relatives of the deceased as they sink to the ground and embrace them in loudly expressed grief. Whereas older children take no active part and view the emotional and turbulent events with an air of seeming disinterest, small children and babies usually react with fright and loud crying.

When the wailing finally subsides, non-family male Activists carry the body well away from the camping area, which everyone abandons shortly after. It will not be occupied again for some years, initially because of the alleged presence of the spirit of the deceased and later because the site will arouse unhappy memories among the surviving relatives. Activist men dig a rectangular hole about three-feet deep, line the bottom with leafy bushes and small logs, then place the body inside. Hair string or bark is used to tie one arm, elbow bent, to the shoulder, and the legs are tucked against the buttocks. The arm that is left free allows the spirit to shoo away wild dingoes that may want to eat the body. To lessen the chance of this happening, the grave is left well covered with branches, logs, and heavy stones. If the deceased is male, his spears and thrower are broken and stuck upright in the ground close by; if a female, her digging stick is left. These signals enable others to avoid the grave.

Before leaving the grave, an old Activist relative who has known the deceased well will address the spirit, saying things like, "Don't look back again at your wife and don't think about your children. Keep away from the camp and don't follow us. You have to go the other way, to your own waterhole." The burial party then returns to the camp, where the rest of the Mourners lie assembled, wailing. The Activists throw leafy branches over the "dead" Mourners, perhaps in a symbolic burial, for the latter remain still for several minutes until told that the deceased has been buried properly and that they must now leave. The Activists burn most of the remaining belongings of the deceased (lest they serve as reminders of the death, and perhaps also to avert the possibility that the spirit will come in search of its gear). A dead man's personal secret-sacred and other ritual paraphernalia will later be passed on to members of distant groups as part of the gift exchanges that occur during big meetings. Since spirits of the dead (*guurdi*) are believed to be resentful—therefore malevolent or even quite dangerous—people stay well away from the place of death until the reburial occurs, some time between about six months and three years later. The name of the deceased is henceforth taboo, and in reference he or she is termed *bugurra* (the dead one). Should some other person carry the same or a similar sounding name, it will no longer be called. Instead, they become *gunmarnu* or *nyabaru,* terms with a meaning akin to "no-name." If the dead person's name was that of a waterhole or plant or animal species, that name is dropped and alternatives are adopted.[14]

The widow and other closely related females usually cut their hair and remain anointed with red ochre throughout the period of mourning. All close relatives become *daji;* that is, they refrain from eating plains kangaroo, echidna, native cat, possum, and dingo for a period of one or two years or even longer. This taboo is forcibly ended when Activist relatives seize them and force-feed them some kangaroo fat, or at least rub it across their lips; I have seen Mardu of both sexes violently resist this, saying that they are still "too sorry" to cease being *daji*. The only explanation given for this taboo is that it comes from the Dreaming. However, one man suggested that the deceased's spirit may decide to inhabit the body of one of these animals, so close relatives who are *daji* avoid the risk of eating the dead person in animal form. The informant equated this act with cannibalism, a repellent custom allegedly practiced by far-distant peoples and by malevolent spirits.

When the time for reburial approaches, the widow is expected to gather a large group of distantly related kin to assist in the proceedings. (If the deceased is a woman, her husband will be the organizer; if a child, its parents have this responsibility.) En route back to the grave, the assembly sings songs from the Laga ritual nightly. This ritual is held only in connection with death and mourning and centers on the activities of a group of Dreaming emu-people who instituted it to mourn one of their dead. Within a mile or two of the grave, the party makes camp,

---

[14]The flexibility and dynamism of Western Desert dialects is such that groups will even replace words that are basic to their language; for example, the Warburton Ranges people changed their first person pronoun from *ngayu* to *nganku* after the death of a man called Ngayunya! (Douglas 1988)

and its members sing and dance until dusk. Next morning, Mourners gather and prepare food for the burial party of Activist men and women which heads for the grave, accompanied by the widow(s). As they draw near, the widow lights a small fire, and everyone sings out to warn the spirit of their presence. The spirit, which should be somewhere in the vicinity, will answer in the form of a birdcall. The widow approaches with a diviner-curer (see Chapter 5), whose powers include the ability to see the skeleton-like *guurdi*. He catches it and puts it inside his body so that it will not harm any of the nearby humans. The men of the reburial party go to the grave and, after wailing briefly, remove and clean the bones of the deceased. They rub the bones on their bodies and carry the skull to the widow, who also rubs it against her body. If foul play was suspected in the death, the men examine the bones and gravesite for clues. They look closely for wooden slivers; if any such foreign bodies are located, they scrutinize them for a *ngamiri* (signature mark) that will identify the attacker. They may also examine a lock of the deceased's hair which the widow cut and kept for the inquest. Should any clues be found, the diviner-curer will send out the deceased's spirit to locate the killers. The spirit may use a little bird, which will perch on the shoulders of the man or men responsible. This identifies them to the watching spirit, which then informs the diviner-curer. Close male relatives of the dead man may later decide to mount a revenge expedition against the alleged killers, but if the latter are identified as malevolent spirit-beings, nothing can be done.

The bones are reburied in a small hole, their final resting place, and the main grave is filled in. The party returns to the main camp and a feast is eaten. A meeting is held to decide the widow's new marriage partner, a "B" of the dead man. The older the widow, the greater her say in the decision, although ideally she should abide by the wishes of her brothers and her late husband's patrikin.

The spirit, which has been trapped inside the diviner-curer, may remain with him for some time acting as a spirit-familiar, or it may sometimes visit its living kin to warn them of some impending dangers. Inevitably, though, it must return to its place of origin because the living have fulfilled their responsibilities toward it. It will then remain in its home, immortal but separated from the realm of the living and visible to them only during dreams. It may or may not remain vindictive toward human beings, other than close kin whom it is believed to be incapable of harming. It watches over its home area and may cause illness among strangers who venture too close; in other words, as a spirit it continues its guardianship of certain sites and objects in a carryover from its human state. The Mardu believe that most spirits of the dead soon "settle down," and it is not *guurdi* but the malevolent spirit-beings which have existed on earth since the beginning of the Dreaming that cause most illness and misfortune.

With the final return of the spirit comes an eventual balance. The *guurdi* that returns is a different entity from the *jijigarrgaly* (spirit-child) that emerged to enter its mother and begin life as a human being, but the cycle is nevertheless completed, and the spirit lives on, as all spirits must.

5 / The Religious Life

This study began with an account of Aboriginal worldview and the "spiritual imperative" which emphasized the primacy which Aborigines accord to religion. The imperatives embodied in the Dreaming are the Law, which situates the origin and ultimate control of power outside human society; that is, as emanating from the withdrawn but still watchful creative beings of the spiritual realm. From their human "descendants," these beings demand conformity to the Law and the proper performance of ritual. In return, they will ensure the reproduction of earthly society through a continuing release of life-giving power into the physical and human world.

Everywhere in Australia, Aboriginal religion is firmly grounded in the land, whose physical features are regarded by Aborigines as indelible proof of the world-creative powers of Dreaming beings as they transformed themselves into the objects of the natural world.[1] Mardu religion, like that of other Aborigines, was elaborated over time by their human forebears, yet is credited by them to the creative genius of Dreaming beings. It has become the key integratory force that shapes their lives and imbues every facet with powerful motivations and meanings. Whatever cultural and social elements we as outsiders may deem logically prior and pre-eminent in terms of guaranteeing physical survival (for example, the ability to find water or to track game), the Mardu deny them primacy. They see these elements instead as but constituent pieces of a comprehensive and eternal religious design, handed down from the Dreaming through countless generations.

All the memorable happenings of the Dreaming epoch are encoded in one or more "vehicles" through which the religion is made manifest and enables its carriers to learn, practice, and transmit its rich content. Besides the land itself, religious knowledge resides primarily in living actors, mythology, songlines, rituals, sacred sites, and a variety of movable paraphernalia. This account of Mardu religion is focused primarily on the diverse but closely interrelated nature of these elements and their significance for society.

---

[1]These sets of transformations, and the "objectification" of Aboriginal culture that results from them, are described well in Munn (1970).

GENDER AND RELIGION

At the outset, it is important to place in broad perspective the respective contributions of men and women to Mardu religious life. Initiated men are principally responsible for the maintenance of society's well-being through religious activities. Regardless of the extent of community participation, all such activities can be viewed as contributing to this general well-being. However, men say that the performance of secret-sacred, men-only rites is crucial, and women do not appear ever to dispute this assertion either publicly or in private (cf. Bern 1979, who notes the absence in Aboriginal Australia of rebelliousness on the part of women against the dominating ideology of senior men). The Mardu do not rank rituals or particular religious activities on a scale of importance or efficacy; all are equally powerful because they derive ultimately from the Dreaming. However, secret-sacred rituals and others that include secret elements are especially significant in that they entail the display and use of objects whose great power, danger, and sacredness derive from their intimate link to the Dreaming. Most of these objects and associated songs, dances, and usages are under the exclusive control of initiated males.

In Mardu mythology, some of the creative beings were women, and many sites and stretches of territory are associated with female Dreaming beings such as the Seven Sisters, or Minyiburru. Women, as members of estate groups, share with men a strong concern for the care and nurturance of country and have specific responsibilities toward certain sites associated with Dreaming beings. Many are at a disadvantage, however, in that "residence" rules favoring patrilocality take them away from their natal estates some time after marriage (most often to men of different estates), making it more difficult to carry out their duties in respect of their home estate and more likely that they will become increasingly active in the affairs of an estate or estates in their husband's territory.

Mardu women possess religious lore not shared with men and have their own secret-sacred objects and rituals, some of which are considered by all Mardu as highly dangerous to men. As with their menfolk, an important part of women's lore consists of traveling rituals shared and performed widely across the Western Desert and acquired most often during "big meetings" in the normal course of intergroup exchange. Yet the total body of Mardu women's ritual does not approach, either in size or scale, that of the men, and exclusively female rituals occupy much less time and energy than do male rituals. Significantly, during the time of most intense religious activity, at "big meetings," initiated men dictate the scheduling of events, and women must accommodate their ritual timetable to that of the men. There are a number of rituals which call for women to remain in their camps, immobilized and with heads covered, under the close surveillance of old men, for the duration of the proceedings. Some other rituals require women to be confined to the camping area, unable to leave even to obtain water or food for hours at a time. Men suffer no such restrictions at the hands of women, the only exception being in the case of certain secret-sacred women's rituals where the presence of senior men is required to sing the songs, but the men cannot, on pain of serious illness or death, turn their heads to look at the women's dancing or the associated sacred objects or witness their return to the camp.

In joint religious activity, senior men seem to revel in their "masters of ceremony" role, which includes controlling and directing women, and they allow women very little autonomy. Nevertheless, women play a vital part in ensuring the success of the Mardu religious enterprise. They are active participants in many rituals, but even when not directly involved they provide major logistical support by gathering and preparing food and attending to the domestic life of the camp while men are preoccupied with ritual. Many rituals are public or contain segments that can be performed in the camp area, where women and children can attend; in some performances everyone is free to sing and dance. Women also significantly contribute to many men's secret rituals. Their main task is the grinding and preparation of seedcakes which are then cooked by male elders and served at the special feasts that are a common and integral part of these rituals. Most women who attain the rank of "cook" are middle-aged and older, active in the leadership of women's rituals and well regarded by the community. They are selected by the male cooks, in consultation with their female counterparts, and this elevation enhances their status. However, food preparers of both sexes may include younger people who have been causing trouble of some kind. Their selection is a punishment aimed at bringing them into line by giving them much of the hardest work, while the older male and female cooks act more as supervisors. Here, the imposition of ritual tasks and related specialized knowledge is used as a sanction: people are, in a sense, being punished with knowledge which—as power—carries with it inescapable responsibilities (M. Tonkinson, personal communication).

Women are involved in many activities associated with male initiation and, although their roles seem secondary to those of men, their participation is essential. They and their children represent the life of the camp—the normal society from which a novice is removed, to be later returned as a new social person. In their public displays of grief at the "death" of the novice and their celebration of his safe return, women actively reaffirm his social worth and adult status in the community.

In a passive sense, too, women and children provide a vital baseline for the men's dichotomizing of life into dangerous-exclusive and mundane-inclusive aspects. Bern (1979) suggests that women are located in the Aboriginal social formation as antithesis, in that they are permanently excluded from the secret life of the initiated men. For youths, in contrast, this exclusion is temporary, awaiting only their physical maturation before they gain initial entry into men's secret life. The exclusion of women could be interpreted as a device of jealous males intent on reinforcing their sexual identity, solidarity, and superiority over women. However, Mardu society reveals little or no anxiety among members of either sex concerning their status vis-à-vis the other; pollution beliefs, for example, are inconsequential and so do not influence the tenor of male-female relationships. Male ideology asserts that there are spiritual forces too powerful and dangerous for anyone other than initiated men to deal with. This conviction, which gives men's religious life much of its excitement and tension, leads to a great many proscriptions and activities aimed at insulating the rest of society from these deadly powers.

Among the Mardu, then, the dominant values exhibited in those many facets of the religious life requiring male-female coactivity are harmony and interdependence—but with men calling the tune.

MYTH, RITUAL, AND SONGLINE

The media of myth, rite, and song are three of the many through which Aborigines gain an awareness and appreciation of the Dreaming and its overwhelming significance to their past, present, and future existence. These interdependent media are but different modes of expressing basically the same profound truths about how the cosmos is constituted and how harmony among its major elements— the human, natural, and spiritual realms—must be maintained.

The discussion that follows has a twofold aim: to delineate the major characteristics of each medium, using some illustrative examples, and to examine their interrelationship, highlighting the differing possibilities they present for individual and group manipulation and for the inclusion of new knowledge.

Mythology   In volume and detail, Mardu mythology embodies more information about the Dreaming than any other medium, and much of what people come to know of the creative epoch derives from this source. From an early age, children are told stories that recount Dreaming happenings. Such myths are most often brief accounts that explain the creation of some prominent feature of the landscape or tell how something came to be as it is now. Thus, they learn why, for example, Manganya the echidna has spines (he was pincushioned full of spears in a fight with Gadabuda the lizard-man), why Gaarnga the crow is black, why Garlaya the emu cannot fly, and so on.

In addition to these short "situational" myths which pay little attention to the physical setting, there are longer descriptive narrative myths that center on the wanderings of well-known creative beings. These recount the many exploits of the Dreaming heroes: their encounters with others, their hunting and gathering, and the ways in which they imprinted themselves on the landscape through their creation and naming of the many sites they visited. Many such creative acts are intentional, for instance, when a being digs for water and thus creates a major waterhole; but there is also equally important yet unintentional creativity as when Gunagalyu the snake-man leaves a winding creekbed in his wake or when the depression left by the sleeping bodies of the Wayurda possum-people becomes a huge claypan. In both their mundane and ritual activities, the Dreaming travelers were not only creating the natural environment and its inhabitants and resources, they were also preenacting much of what was to become the Law of their human descendants.

Because narrative myths tell of things secret and dangerous as well as mundane Dreaming events, some of their detail is known only to initiated men. When women tell them, no sacred objects are mentioned and, at such times, men may exchange knowing looks or whisper asides to the anthropologist, such as: "That wasn't a spear the owl-man threw at the Ngayunangalgu cannibals, it was a sacred board and that's why the whole mob died instantly"; or "Those Minyiburru women left behind grinding stones at that waterhole, but they were really sacred stones; they're still there and that's why women and children can't go into that place."

By Western dramatic standards, these myths lack excitement and tension, dwelling as they do much of the time on the naming of places and the movements of ancestral beings from one spot to the next. Yet, because many tell of journeys covering hundreds of miles of desert, through areas that some Mardu may not have seen, they broaden people's cosmological and geographical worldview and allow them, intellectually at least, to "know" those areas. In the same way, narratives bring alive and make immediate the landforms created by ancestral beings in areas that are familiar to the Mardu. The myths also evoke and sustain strong emotional ties to the land.

More important, though, is the possession of ancestral and conception totems (see Chapter 4), which link every person directly to the great Dreaming powers. Many ancestral totems are widely shared and generate feelings of spiritual kinship with others, elsewhere, who were left behind by the same Dreaming beings. Totemism operates simultaneously in time and in space, to link the past to the present, and humans to the Dreaming, to the land, and to one another. In so doing, it reinforces among Mardu a pervasive awareness of wider social unities and shared cultural identity, fostered by a huge cast of Dreaming beings and the vast expanses of country through which they traveled.

The excerpt that follows, taken from a long narrative myth, is included to convey some feeling for the content and structure. It is part of the exploits of Two Men, who were cross-cousin "brothers" and close companions; as lizard-people, they traveled widely in the desert (see Chapter 4).[2] The major events detailed below occurred in the heart of Mardu territory. One of the elders who narrated this myth also made a crayon "map" of the area (at my request), shown in Figure 5-1. The setting is south of Lake Disappointment, in and around the Durba Hills (Map 3).

> Two Men traveled on and made camp at Dibil waterhole. Next morning, they got up and went hunting. Spotting some dingoes lying in the shade, they crept close, then speared and killed them. They gutted them, threw away the guts, picked up the livers, then threw them down and they turned to stone. . . you can still see the livers at that place. They then went and cooked and ate the dogs. They named that spot Bunggula-manku then headed off in the direction of their home country. On the way they camped at Birli rockhole, then went on to Jiluguru, their main camp. There they put down all the sacred things they had been carrying with them on their travels, and went hunting in the afternoon. They climbed a high sandhill to sit down and rest; as they sat they untied their beards (which they had bound with hair string), which unrolled along the ground. The Milangga brother's beard was shorter. Their beards turned to stone; you can see those two rocks there now. They returned to camp and lay down, but a large rock was blocking the sun so they split it open, and called it Mulyayidi. They carved three clubs and left them in the sand to dry out while they hunted for meat. When they got back they saw that the clubs had turned into snakes—"quiet ones" (probably rock pythons, which are harmless). They fed some meat to the snakes, then left them and the sacred things and went on a hunting campout, to Binbi. Then they got up and went east, toward another waterhole called Yirrajiwarra, where they camped . . . I don't know . . . maybe three nights.
>
> Guriji, the mother of one of them, had followed their tracks into Jiluguru. Seeing that they had left, she tracked them to Binbi and saw that they had camped there, then followed their tracks until she spotted them in the distance, lit up by lightning being

[2]A different segment of the same myth is related in Tonkinson (1974:73).

carried on the head of Barrmalgunda, the Lightning Man, who happened to be close by at the time. She put down her seedcakes (the food she had been carrying for them), kept herself hidden as she crept closer, then in a crouching run, closed in and grabbed them. She wailed for them (because she had not seen them in such a long time), and they in turn cried for her. Then she picked them up in both hands, sat them down, went back and picked up their food, then gave it to them. They ate all of it. Then they got up and she put them on her shoulders and headed off toward home. She carried them "half way" then stood them up at a claypan, called Bulyubulyununja. She then picked them up, one under each arm, then carried them away to her own camp where she put them down—never to return. Guriji's husband, Gamurubul, who had been out hunting, had killed some meat for the Two Men, and was lying down in his bush camp when he saw the Lightning Man, whom he thought may have taken his children away. Next morning he got up before dawn, tied up the meat with some bark, then set off. Not far along, he came across some tracks and said, "They are surely Guriji's! Perhaps she's taken them and gone!" He tracked them to their home camp and saw that they had left their sacred things there. He followed their tracks. "Which way did they go?" he asked himself. He followed them to Binbi and beyond, until he finally saw that they really had been taken by their mother. He cried, saying, "Here is where their tracks end; she grabbed them and headed northward." Then he left everything he had been carrying and began following in their tracks, forever.[3]

These great Dreaming beings went up into the sky at the conclusion of their lives on earth and became heavenly bodies which can still be seen.

Since there are literally hundreds of myths known to the Mardu, it is impossible to convey here the diversity of content that coexists with their striking uniformity of structure. But whether long or short, narrative or situational, all myths aim to evoke a vivid awareness of the power and reality of the Dreaming. Since education among the Mardu is not formalized, the inculcation of mythology occurs informally, and the telling of myths has no special place in the framework of ritual life. Yet, there are times and situations when it is felt appropriate to recount them, for example, when people are taken into territory previously unknown to them or when newly found or imported objects, dances, rituals, and such, are seen for the first time. Myths thus contextualize, incorporate, and connect isolated elements into the broader scheme of things. Also, because they provide some sort of reflection of reality, myths can function as guides to action—but not invariably, since the creative beings were "law breakers as well as law-makers" (R. Berndt 1974:15).

Ritual   Questions of power, reciprocity and the maintenance of good relations between humans, spirits, and the natural world loom large in all religions. Because greater-than-human powers are believed to lie in the spiritual realm, effective communication is essential if attempts at manipulation or control of these powers through ritual are to be successful. In Aboriginal belief, the Dreaming powers have long since withdrawn from direct contact with the physical realm, yet they remain immortal presences with a strong interest in their human descendants. In Mardu understanding, if they obey the Law and perform the appropriate rituals correctly, these acts will bring about automatically a reciprocal flow of life-force from the

---

[3]Details from this myth are beautifully depicted on a wooden figure carved by the same elder; see Mountford and Tonkinson (1969).

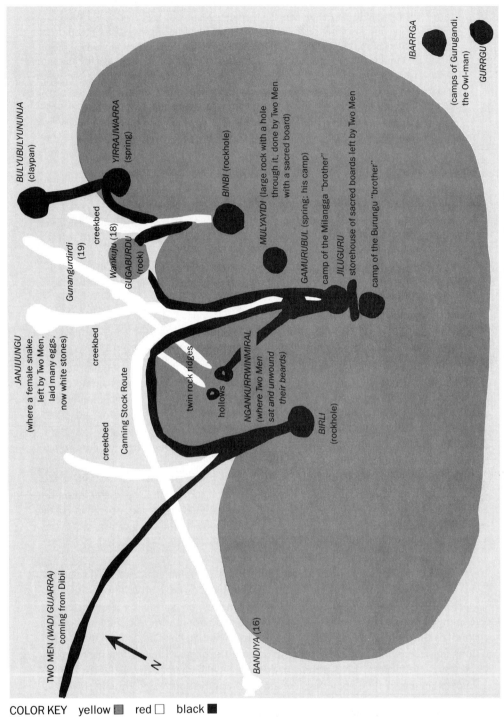

Figure 5-1. Crayon drawing of the travels of Two Men (Wadi Gujarra) in the Durba Hills area.

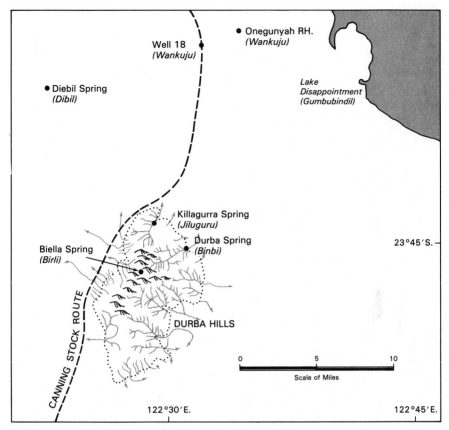

Map 3: The Durba Hills area.

spiritual realm. An element of manipulation always exists, but has more to do with individual acts than with collective rituals, which are directed much more broadly toward assuring an ongoing flow of power into the human realm. The Mardu do not believe that the Dreaming beings are involved in direct acts of reciprocity, but they presume that if they abandon their rituals and the Law, the flow of life-force from the spiritual realm would cease, and with it, life on earth. However, this view is expressed only in answer to the hypothetical question of the anthropologist; it is not a topic of speculation among the Mardu, who consider the possibility beyond comprehension.[4] When the Dreaming powers wish to communicate with the living, they use spirit-beings as intermediaries which are sometimes encountered by Aborigines during dreams or ritually induced states of altered consciousness.[5] The transfer of new knowledge, which is power, takes place via these spirit-beings, whose impingement on human affairs is taken as proof of the existence and continuing interest of the Dreaming powers in the human world.

---

[4]For the effects of contact with whites on this concern, see Chapter 7.
[5]These beings are identified as *jijigarrgarly* (spirit-children), but the stem *jiji* (child) here connotes their small size, not an ignorance of religious lore.

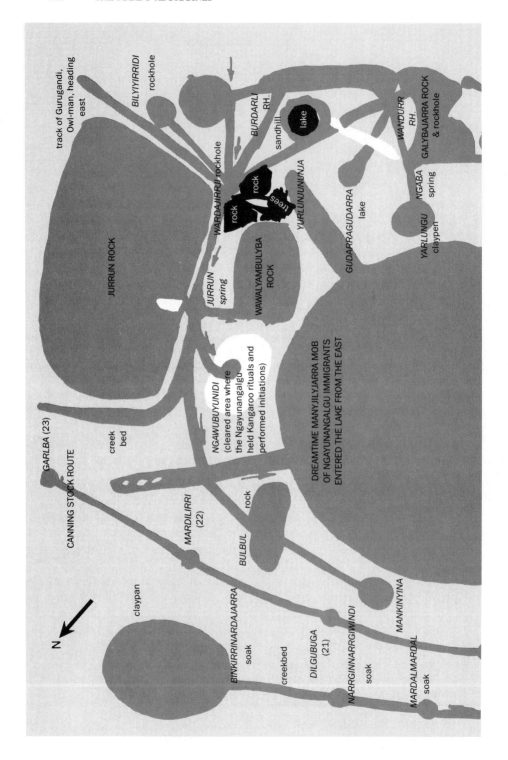

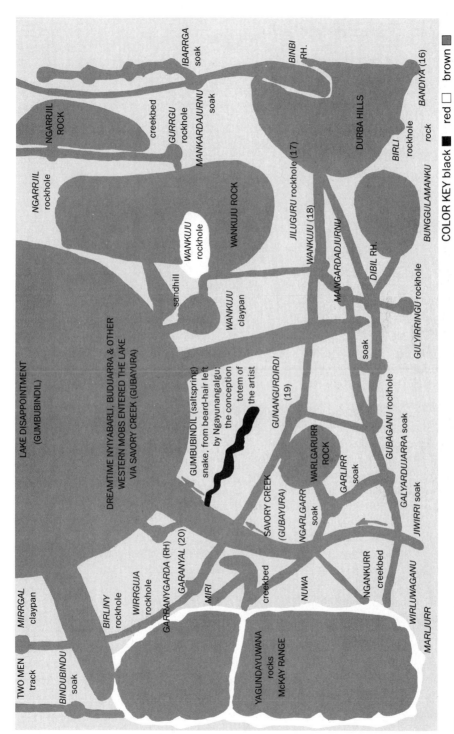

Figure 5-2. Crayon drawing depicting the Lake Disappointment (Gumbubindil) area.

Small boys decorated with white-ochre rainmaking designs in readiness for a ceremonial welcome at a big meeting.

(a) *Individual Ritual.* Individual ritual acts can take place virtually anywhere, at any time; most are socially approved and occur in public. They may be performed by anyone who knows the correct technique or invocation for attempting to secure some desired result. The motivations for such acts are many and varied: some danger is perceived; a vexatious weather condition, often connected with spirit-beings of some kind, is warded off; or some desired weather (for example, rain) is encouraged. In situations such as these, diviner-curers are favored as performers because of their allegedly greater magical powers, which include the ability to detect evil spirit-beings. They can use their magical objects to catch troublesome spirits, scare off human or spirit intruders, and so on. Their activity may include talking to or shouting at some spirit, singing songs, waving their arms, dancing, selecting certain objects or substances that will discourage or encourage continuance of some condition, and perhaps directing the behavior of others present. These ritual acts are usually spontaneous. For example, a diviner-curer leaps up and "slices" a strong wind that is disturbing a ritual, thus diverting it around the fringe of the assembled group; a large thundercloud on the horizon may prompt several men and women to sing appropriate rainmaking songs as they beckon the cloud toward them, perhaps waving small bundles of bird feathers which attract the attention of the rain spirits that are believed to compose the cloud. Such acts, most often carried out with a minimum of formality or drama, are commonplace in the lives of the Mardu.

The unseen or spiritual is just as real as the visible and physical in Aboriginal understanding, so, as with many other peoples in the world, they make no significant distinction between natural and spiritual realms. All Mardu ritual acts reflect a confidence in their ability to exert a measure of control over aspects of their world. If the strong wind persists or the thundercloud refuses to come closer, there are always reasonable explanations for such failures. Yet winds do die suddenly, and thunderclouds often approach, so there are always successes to reinforce and justify ritual acts.

(b) *Increase Rites.* One crucially important kind of ritual which involves few actors, yet indirectly affects the lives of all desert people, is the "increase" rite.[6] Scattered throughout the desert are *jabiya,* sites which the Aborigines believe are the spirit-homes of many different varieties of plants and animals, left there by the Dreaming beings. At each site, which can be as unspectacular as a small flat stone or a hole in the ground, innumerable spirits of that particular species are thought to reside—awaiting only the summons of their human guardians (male estate-group elders in whose territory the site is located) each year to emerge and be plentiful.[7] To the Mardu, fertility has nothing to do with insemination, pollination, and so forth. It results from human actions which evoke a reciprocal response by spiritual forces. Within the estate of every group, there is at least one such site; therefore, all groups have an important responsibility to perform the relevant rites properly each year. If a particular species seems to be in short supply during a given season, suspicion of inadequate performance is cast onto the group in whose estate the increase center of that species is found. Distant groups may be prompted to send messengers with a small sacred object as a gift or reminder to the guardians and the spirits.[8] Should there be no people in the area of a *jabiya* at the appropriate time, which is shortly before the expected appearance of large quantities of the species, this presents no problem. The local elders can always visit the site in dream-spirit form and "bring out" the spirits. In much the same way, men associated with rain centers can bring rain from the center to their territories or to wherever it is needed.

The rite itself is short and uncomplicated in most cases, consisting mainly of a cleaning of the site (and perhaps anointing it with blood) and singing in addition to spoken requests and exhortations by the visitors. As the following example shows, the association of site and species stems from a Dreaming incident that resulted in the metamorphosis of that species into stone, a tree, or some other physical form. A mythological validation always exists for both the association and some of the form that the ritual must take. Because increase rites are so localized, no two are identical, although in general structure and intent they are homogeneous throughout the desert.

Bajirrganya is an emu *jabiya* that consists of a clump of rounded stones with a large stone close by, said to be metamorphosed eggs and their emu mother. Wirdun, an

---

[6]This term is commonly used to describe such rituals, which were performed in much of the continent (Arnhem Land being a notable exception). While it is true that the Aboriginal guardians commonly request large quantities of the species to emerge and be plentiful everywhere, their main concern is to ensure the continued widespread availability of needed resources.

[7]For some species there is more than one spirit-center, but these tend to be widely separated.

[8]This object is called a *yumbu,* which is also the name of sorcery objects associated with "contract" killings. This suggests that an element of threat is present, though Mardu men claim that this kind of *yumbu* is "for food, not killing." (See pp. 131–133 for a discussion of sorcery.)

ancestral eaglehawk-man of the Banaga section, who was left-handed, saw the mother on her nest one day while he was out hunting. He crept up to a gap between two long rocks, behind a tree, and threw a spear at her, but he missed. The Two Men, who were also out hunting, happened along at that moment and scolded Wirdun, telling him that if he killed the emu there would be no more to lay eggs in the future. So Wirdun desisted, and the eggs and emu mother later turned to stone.

The guardians, who may or may not include men with totemic links to Wirdun or emus, gather together whichever initiated men are available in the area at the time and visit the site prior to the emu egg season every year. The men prefer to go in a large group because the spirits are thought to respond favorably to the presence of many people. One of the guardians stands exactly where Wirdun did and throws a spear in the direction of the "nest" with his left hand. The group then approaches the site and the men clean all around it. One of the elders then steps forward and addresses the emu spirits inside the *jabiya,* thus: "We want emu eggs. Make plenty. Give us lots. We want some for eating, some for emus—for meat! Keep them coming! You will do it because we all came to see you and to start you."

The implication of the essential verbal element of the increase rites is that the spirit-beings of the species concerned, as "kin," must automatically respond—generously—to such requests from their human guardians and others who came in good faith and have carried out their part of the bargain.[9]

It is not difficult to appreciate the great cultural significance of increase rites. They demonstrate the extent to which, for Aborigines, religion itself is a technology, a "mode of production," the essential prerequisite for animal and plant fertility and, thus, for human survival (cf. Hamilton 1982; Tonkinson 1988a, 1988b). This contradicts the situation among most hunter-gatherer peoples, where " . . . much of the reproduction of the means of subsistence is left to nature . . . hunters live more or less with nature as a given" (Lee 1979:117). Aborigines not only see themselves as unique and clearly set apart from the rest of nature, they view both natural and social reproduction as within their control and dependent upon a ritual mode of production. Increase rites prove that the ingredients of the "good life" must be religiously produced and reproduced, not treated as naturally given. Additionally, the geographical spread of increase centers ensures a regional sharing of responsibility, thus underscoring the fact of interdependence throughout the desert. Each group looks to many others, near and far, for the reproduction of physical resources and of Western Desert society as a whole. This is why the practice of sending a *yumbu* object can be seen as symbolizing both complaint (a tacit allegation of inadequate ritual performance) and admonition.

(c) *Collective Ritual.* The high points of Mardu life are the big meetings, notable for their intensified sociality and the great excitement and emotional and physical energy that they generate among performers and spectators alike. However, there are many other times during their travels when the Mardu stage rituals that involve smaller gatherings. Their repertoire consists of a large variety of rituals, many of

---

[9]All ancestral beings are considered to be kin of the living, but are elderly and respected kin to whom some deference and respect must be shown. In reference to them by kinship, Mardu use only terms for first and second ascending generation levels; for example, "F," "MB," "FF," "FM," and so on, implying status inequality in the relationship.

which are also performed by other desert groups. Such shared rituals usually center on the exploits of widely traveled ancestral beings. This common knowledge and performance of most of the major rituals testifies to the continuous diffusion of religious lore that occurs among Western Desert peoples. This does not mean, however, that every group performs the same set of rituals. Just as each has a body of local mythology which is not widely known or shared beyond its estate, there may also be rituals (in addition to increase rites) which are associated with a particular local area and with Dreaming beings who did not travel widely and may be little known by distant groups.

This kind of ritual may be owned collectively by the group in whose territory the associated Dreaming events occurred and whose totemic connections with these particular beings are probably therefore strongest. Performance rights to these rituals may be withheld from other groups, in which case their restriction to a home area serves as a magnet to draw distant groups to be initiated into them at periodic big meetings held there. The senior men (or women, in the case of exclusively female rituals) who are the acknowledged leaders for a ritual of this type decide as a group if and when they will allow the transfer of the necessary ritual paraphernalia and performance rights to others. The same is true of new rituals derived from dream-spirit revelations. Performance rights for these remain restricted until those in control decide to release them, usually after a newer ritual is composed.

The most common stimulus for ritual is the encountering of neighboring bands, which temporarily increases the population sufficiently to allow for adequate performance of rituals that require more personnel of various statuses than are available in a single band. The decision as to which rituals to perform would depend on many factors such as the presence of people with authority to direct a particular ritual, the locality and its totemic associations, the greater popularity of some rituals than others, the availability of paraphernalia needed for proper performance, and recent events such as the death of a close relative, which may prescribe the performance of an appropriate mourning ritual, or the arrival of novices being taken on pre- or post-initiation journeys of revelation.

Many rituals are ideally suited to general performance, regardless of the number of people available. In many, both women and men sing the songline and dance, and a minimum of paraphernalia is needed. In some, only men sing the songs, and only women dance; in others, women and children dance—or perhaps women and girls, not boys. In most dream-spirit rituals men and women sing, men do most of the dancing, and, in a concluding section, men dance with secret-sacred objects, unseen by the women and children.

At the other extreme are wholly secret-sacred rituals that exclude all opposite-sex members and the uninitiated, apart from novices who are currently being inducted. Most such rituals are men's, and are held in men's country, well away from camping areas. More common than wholly secret-sacred rituals are those comprising both secret and non-secret sets of activities, for example, some of the rituals associated with circumcision (Chapter 4). In certain of these composite rituals, men's secret rites are held in the bush while male and female "cooks" prepare a ritual feast, and the rest of the community is secluded under male supervision some distance away. In the case of the Ngaawayil rainmaking ritual, when the secret bush rites are concluded for the day and the feast is ready, the rest of the community assembles at the ceremonial ground close to the camp to greet the men in ritual fashion upon their return from the bush. After the men have eaten (women do not eat at such feasts), the ground becomes the scene of much singing, dancing, and boisterous rainmaking activities that continue well into the night, with the entire community present (see Tonkinson 1974).

To illustrate an important Mardu ritual that contains both secret and non-secret elements in its structure, a brief description is given of the Nyarnayi. This ritual, which has not traveled far, is based on the Dreaming exploits of a kangaroo-man, Manggurdu, and his pursuers who are in two groups: first, a large mob of bird-men, "featherfeet" killers (*jinagarrbil,* literally "feet-tied," referring to the footwear used to disguise their tracks), who are of many different species; and second, a mob of cannibal-men called Wajayija. These creative beings are said to have traversed a wide area to the south of Lake Disappointment during a long and eventful chase after Manggurdu, their *gunka* (law-breaker, victim). The Nyarnayi ritual has over fifty associated dances and hundreds of songs, all dealing with the theme of ritual killers and their successes and failures. Men say that when a featherfeet expedition is organized to pursue and kill someone guilty of a grave offense, preparations must include songs and other elements from the Nyarnayi.

There are two distinct locales for Nyarnayi performances, the camp area and a secret bush ground. Activities alternate between them, with nonsecret performances at the campground every evening and daily sessions at the secret ground, attended by initiated men and perhaps some novices. To begin the sequence, which may continue for a week or more, there is an evening session at the campground, which lasts about two or three hours.

The men sit in a circle around a small fire, with another larger one a short distance away on the side opposite to where the women and children form a semicircle; the latter neither sing nor dance. The men, undecorated the first night, beat time on the ground with clubs or thick sticks. After the singing is underway, men leave the circle to dance, in ones, twos, or larger groups, using movements and gestures appropriate to the ancestor(s) being portrayed. These dances are brief, lasting rarely more than a couple of minutes. They elicit much laughter in the audience, which shows its approval of good dramatic performances with a trilling sound that Mardu make to indicate strong appreciation of some act well done. To conclude the session, the women and children are sent back to the camping area, with instructions not to look back; then, in a secret-sacred dance, a man portrays owl-man's wife, who is calling out and looking fearfully around her as she travels in search of her mate. In the evening sessions that follow, most of the men wear body decorations from the day's performance. Some women will dance around the circle of men in their typical *nyanbi* style (Chapter 4) for some time prior to the men's dances. The variety of men's dances increases, and two secret dances usually conclude the session after the women and children have left. The duration of the evening performances may also lessen toward the end as the men become progressively more tired from the daily singing and dancing activities.

The secret sections of the Nyarnayi are structured very much like the Kangaroo ritual (Chapter 4). The men leave camp in a group sometime during the morning and disappear into men's country for the rest of the day. At the Nyarnayi ground, they form a circle and begin singing. The several elders who are the acknowledged leaders for this ritual will have decided the previous evening which dances are to be performed. In consultation with other middle-aged and older men, some of whom intend to dance, they choose some younger dancers from among those still learning the ritual. Early in the afternoon the dancers leave the circle to decorate and prepare the objects that they will need. They work out of sight of the men who remain to form the audience and supply the musical accompaniment when the dances eventually take place. The task of constructing the various dancing paraphernalia may take several hours, although in dances featuring the younger men, little is worn or carried besides body designs.

Late afternoon, when the dancers signal that all is ready, growing excitement manifests itself in the singing which becomes loud and spirited as the dancing is due to begin. In the hour that follows, as many as twelve different dances, each with its appropriate song, may be performed. These range from solos, to pairs, to large groups. The dances differ widely in form: in some, the performers merely walk toward the audience; in others, the actors are required to crouch or lie down, which restricts their body movements, and the emphasis in the dance is on subtle movements of the chest and shoulders; still other dances call for rapid arm and leg movements.

Almost everyone laughs loudly when an old man dances as a Dreaming woman whose anus and vagina are hot and sore from a sorcerer's attack. He appears in the distance, carrying a firestick in one hand as he laboriously advances; with the other hand, he frantically fans his rear end as he turns it toward the audience. A keen sense of humor pervades all Mardu activities, including ritual. There are very few occasions so awe-inspiring or momentous in their religious significance that laughter and joking would be thought out of place.

The "big" dances that come at the end of each day's performance may not be witnessed by the newest initiates, in keeping with the idea of initiation as a process of gradual revelation. As in most other rituals, the opening Nyarnayi dances are considered of lesser import and are danced by the younger men who are in the early stages of learning the ritual. Anyone who makes trouble or who fails to hunt diligently risks the ignominy and shame of being held back or even excluded from such rituals. Normally, however, young men are eventually selected to perform more and more important dances.

The one or two dances each day that the initiates are forbidden to see will probably involve dangerous paraphernalia, or they may involve no objects at all, but depict a happening of major mythological importance.

The Nyarnayi has a particular charcoal and ochre body decoration for each animal and bird being depicted, but it is notable for the variety and beauty of the thread-cross ornaments worn or carried by the performers. Made from grass, sharp sticks, or sacred boards into frames onto which hair twine is threaded, these facepieces, headdresses, thread-crosses, and other items are all representations of what the Nyarnayi beings themselves wore when they traveled.[10] Toward the end of the Nyarnayi sequence, the watching initiates are surrounded and harangued by the older men, who remind them of their obligation to reciprocate by hunting and to uphold the Law, and who scold them severely for their real and imagined shortcomings. Careful not to let the young men see their grins and suppressing laughter at their own witticisms, the older men mount a ferocious verbal onslaught, trying to outdo one another with salvos such as: "Leave the

---

[10]This category of objects is characterized by its impermanence, since a thread-cross can only be used once and must later be dismantled. The hair twine with which it is threaded, however, is rolled into balls and may be reused indefinitely.

Madimadi decorated and ready to perform a Nyarnayi dance.

women alone until your penises are long enough for the job!" or "Keep your minds on the Law, not what hangs between your legs!"

Typically, the initiates are not told why they have been brought into physical contact with sacred objects at the end of the dancing; old men say that this helps protect them against human and supernatural attack, no doubt through a transference of the life-force that is inherent in all such objects. During this initial exposure to the Nyarnayi, the initiates learn little of the meanings of the ritual, except for its association with featherfeet bird-men and their search for victims. But through repeated attendance in later years, the young men will learn the songs, dance the dances, and fill in for themselves the gaps in their knowledge of what it is all about.

(d) *Ritual Categorization.* The Mardu distinguish between two types of ritual: *mangunyjanu* (from the creative period) and *bardunjarrijanu* (from the dream-spirits).[11] Most rituals belong to the first category; that is, they are believed to have been instituted by ancestral beings and, therefore, are essentially Dreaming products. Every few years one or more men will be "given" a new ritual during sleep when a person's *bardunjarri* (dream-spirit) leaves the body and wanders. Sometimes it encounters spirit-beings who, as intermediaries between the withdrawn creative beings and the living, may reveal a new tune, song, dance, or sacred object. Because the Aborigines attach much significance to their dreams, a man will usually disclose his dream to others, but usually not until a half-dozen or more songs and other information have been "found," lest the spirit-beings become angry or jealous and decide against making further revelations. Excited, and perhaps rendered hypersuggestive by what they have been told, other men may soon dream about similar happenings or themes and wake up remembering songs or dances that they, too, have been given during their dream-spirit experiences. Women, too, may "find" songs and report these to their husbands for inclusion in the ritual. What happens in dreams, then, is the transfer of new knowledge in such a way that the eternal truths and powers of the Dreaming are brought into the here and now.

The ritual that is finally built up has a distinctive tune, body decorations, set of dances, and thread-cross designs; its songline may have a hundred or more verses.[12] Women and children learn the songlines by listening to the men, and these songs become popular, being sung spontaneously, regardless of whether the ritual is performed. Only a small number of the dances, and perhaps songs, are kept secret; it is with these that the sacred objects are displayed. This occurs at the end of each evening's performance when one of the dancers throws a firestick as a signal to the women and children to face away from the ground and cover their eyes.

The great appeal of these rituals is that they require minimal preparation, no special grounds, and relatively small groups can stage them effectively. They remain under the control of those to whom they were revealed until such time as their "owners" decide to hand them on to another group. With this transfer, their travels begin and, most significantly, time and space operate to transform them from the modern *bardunjarrijanu* to the eternal *mangunyjanu*. By the time they

[11]The dream-spirit is said to resemble an eaglehawk when in flight; however, when traveling in this form, a man's legs become wings, his testicles become eyes, and his anus his mouth, in a kind of back-to-front transformation that is said to protect the traveler in the event of likely encounters with malevolent spirit-beings.

[12]For a detailed description of a dream-spirit ritual, see Tonkinson (1970).

reach groups hundreds of miles away on the opposite side of the desert, they are "from the Dreaming," timeless, powerful, and stripped of all information regarding the circumstances of their relatively recent creation. This process is almost certainly how most of the huge corpus of Aboriginal rituals originally came into being.

Among the group that originates it, a dream-spirit ritual is relatively short-lived in terms of full performances because in a year or two it will be supplanted by a newly "found" or borrowed dream-spirit ritual. Yet the songs are remembered indefinitely, especially if they have a popular and catchy tune. A notable feature of Mardu life is how readily and often men and women will break into song. Although favorite choices are often dream-spirit songs, men like to sing from their repertoire of several thousand secret-sacred songs when they are out of earshot of women and children.

A further basis for Mardu ritual classification is the rather obvious one of function or purpose. As R. Berndt (1974:5) has noted:

> The most important ritual manifestations in Aboriginal Australia were those concerned with initiation, revelation (that is, post-initiatory rites at which only postulants and not novices were present), fertility (for example, increase of various natural species and of man, and seasonal-renewal-rites), and death (that is, extended or delayed mortuary rites).

With some kinds of ritual there is a clear-cut primary purpose, one that the Aboriginal actors readily identify; for example, to bring up a particular species at an increase center, physical initiation, causing rain to fall, separating a deceased's spirit from the living, and so on. They may also mention more general functions that these and other rituals fulfill, such as engendering good feelings among the participants, bringing together different groups in ideally harmonious union, transmitting the Law to younger men, acquiring strength and protection against malevolent forces, and so on. If the many functions that are discernible to an outside observer are added to this list, it is obvious that any given ritual simultaneously contributes to or fulfills a diverse range of functions, most of which are complementary and mutually reinforcing in their effects. (The political ramifications of ritual are discussed separately in the final section of this chapter).

Songlines   Singing is an integral part of almost all Mardu collective rituals. The songline traces the route taken by Dreaming travelers and dramatizes, albeit cryptically, their activities, both notable and mundane. Songlines are also a celebration, in lyrical and dramatic form, of the interplay of land and the forces of nature with Dreaming powers. Through the learning of songlines, which contain both geographical and mythical referents, Mardu are familiarized with many hundreds of sites they may never have visited, yet all become part of their mental map of the desert world. Because ancestral beings traveled from waterhole to waterhole much of the time, song sequences imprint knowledge that may have practical value should people be traveling in the area depicted. They may also provide vital clues as to what dangerous or sacred sites must be avoided in distant territories.

A song may contain anywhere from two to a dozen words and, when performed during a ritual, is repeated many times over. This combination—few words and much repetition—obviously helps people memorize songs; a much more difficult feat is that of keeping the songs in correct sequence. At the same time, the singers must remember to delete any that mention the birthplace, home base, or name of any person who has recently died. The singing of such a song would bring a sudden and painful reminder of the death, thus distressing close relatives in the audience. A characteristic common to Mardu songs is the obscurity of their meaning. In a literal translation, they reveal very little, yet are full of significance to those who have acquired the relevant knowledge over time. The following illustration is from the Ngaawayil rainmaking ritual:

(a) ii burnunya burnu ngajinya ngaji yuwanya yuwa
    lightning stones   *to me?*   *give give*

    Explanation: The two major rainmaking ancestors of the Dreaming, called Wirnba and Garbardi, met up and exchanged rainmaking stones (sacred) as a gesture of friendship.

(b) ii warlurmaliny warlurmaliny garbungga garbungga Minganbula ngarinja
    rainclouds   *daytime*   *(Place name)* *lying*

    Explanation: Rainclouds, flat and long, are sacred wooden objects, seen in the daytime at Mingan waterhole. They lay across the ancestor Wirnba's chest as he traveled around, creating waterholes and bringing rain to the land.

It should be noted that some of the major rituals performed by the Mardu (the Ngaawayil, for example) are sung in dialects or languages of people in distant areas; singers may therefore be unable to identify with certainty many of the words. What matter are the main details and themes and the intensity of performance, which can enhance the excitement of the ritual greatly.

In their singing, the Mardu employ a great variety of tempos. Although each songline has its own distinctive tune, almost all require a very wide vocal range for both men and women. The often guttural and nasalized singing of Aboriginal men, who frequently punctuate it with screams, whoops, grunts, and falsetto ululation, is very impressive and has been described as ". . . completely different from most other vocal qualities of the world" (T. Jones 1965:367). The sung word is so different from the spoken, so distorted in pitch and stress, as to be almost unrecognizable. The impact of a large group singing is dramatic, especially in loud or strongly accented songs that have bold percussive accompaniments. Purely instrumental music is absent, and virtually all dancing is accompanied by singing. It takes young men many years to build their repertoires to the level of their elders. The Mardu also have a category of songs known as *nyirrbu* which are composed by men or women from everyday happenings of many different kinds, for example, a flood, a lost lover, a hunting incident, a fight, and so on. Because many of these nonsacred songs have a locational referent, they accentuate the intersection of the natural and social environments in human terms by uniting contemporary events with places in a way that complements the mythical dimension.

The Interrelationship of Myth, Ritual, and Songline   Myths speak to the wonders and dramas of the creative epoch; major songlines trace ancestral tracks and accentuate Dreaming happenings in lyrical fashion; rituals vividly reenact founding dramas, bringing human actors and the spiritual realm into close association—these religious elements are alike in emphasizing both human and spiritual relationships to the land and to the physical realm in general (cf. R. Berndt 1974:19). All three elements also share an explicit connection to the Dreaming, but the nature of their interrelationship is far from a simple one-to-one arrangement and, in fact, there is considerable autonomy among them. Most myths have no related ritual or songline, although the reverse is not true. In any given ritual, the associated myth and songline may share clear thematic similarities, but the songline is no mere mnemonic for the myth, such that the latter could be reconstructed from the former. Shared themes, however, may bring songlines and myths into a closer relationship than either has with other ritual elements such as dances. The words of a song generally offer no clue as to how its accompanying dance is to be interpreted; in most cases, they do not even identify the ancestral being(s) concerned. Yet, in an important sense, songlines and dances are alike in being very much more circumscribed and controlled in their performance than are myths. As public spectacles, unfolding before the watchful eyes of Law carriers, these acts of communication are regulated by the Law's requirement that they be performed exactly as handed down from the Dreaming in order to ensure the success of the ritual in triggering a release of life-force from the spiritual realm. In the narration of myths, however, the context is typically informal and does not involve a large audience. Thus, there is much greater latitude for individual elaboration and character development than would ever be tolerated in publicly transmitted songs and dances. The unity and integration of these elements of the religious life are not achieved through their tightness of fit to one another, but through their relationship to the overarching cosmic order set up by the Dreaming. The implications of these three elements for questions of ideology, dynamism, and change are discussed later in this chapter.

SITES AND PARAPHERNALIA

All sorts of landforms, large and small, stand as tangible proofs of the world-creating activities of the Dreaming beings. They and the paraphernalia associated with the religious life are alike because both are physical referents—the one fixed, the other portable—of spiritual presence, power, and potential. A timeless quality is accorded the multitude of landscape features, but they are not lifeless, being imbued with spiritual significance by myths, songs, and the fact that human and animal life alike spring from the limitless quantities of life-essence that lie scattered throughout the land. These features include, in some cases, large trees, rock carvings and paintings, and other man-made constructions such as cairns and large ground arrangements of stones, all of which are attributed by Mardu to the actions of Dreaming beings. These are the fixed referents that bind particular individuals and groups to them through strong sentiments of belonging and security.

The great variety of portable objects derive sacredness and power from their intimate association—through "actual" contact or structural similarity—with some

Dreaming event or being. As R. Berndt (1974:19) notes, they are the material vehicles through which living Aborigines seek and direct power and, through them, "life is sustained and maintained." Many, such as thread-crosses, body decorations, and carved boards, are produced in emulation of those worn or possessed by ancestral heroes. The boards are kept well hidden in caches where certain Dreaming beings are said to have first left them. Red, white, brown, and yellow ochres are all attributed to Dreaming events; but red ochre, the metamorphosed blood of those beings, is the most potent and culturally important. High-quality red ochre from a few well-known quarries is diffused widely through the desert via gift exchanges at big meetings as well as through personal networks.

The most sacred and dangerous objects are stones, varying in size and shape, some naturally formed and others obviously at one time shaped and smoothed and perhaps incised with designs. These stones are revered as metamorphosed parts of the bodies of ancestral beings or as objects owned and carried by them. Such collectively owned objects are, like sacred boards, replete with power and thus kept well hidden. Although most of them play no prominent role in collective ritual performances, they are often displayed, to be gazed at, stroked, rubbed against the body, and talked about by those fully initiated men senior enough to be exposed to them. Certain of them may be passed from group to group, together with an account of their origin and totemic association, perhaps in company with a ritual that centers on the being(s) from which they derive. As gifts, they symbolize the ultimate in generosity and help ensure the continuance of close and harmonious intergroup relationships since the recipients must eventually make a reciprocal gift of objects of similar significance.

In addition to the boards and stones that are the collective property of estate-group men, every initiated male has his personal paraphernalia, kept carefully wrapped in a small bark, fur, or hair-twine bundle that usually accompanies its owner on his yearly round of movement. There will be an assortment of objects, not all of which are secret, such as hair-string bands, pearlshell pendants, bird-feather bundles, eaglehawk down, ochre, spinifex gum, and small stone knives used in ritual operations. There may also be a few objects useful for magic, such as polished stones, small bullroarers, and possibly love-magic charms. The number and variety of such items differ from individual to individual, and those having a specific ritual use may be left hidden at a particular spot and retrieved only when they are likely to be needed. As with all portable artifacts, personal bundles are kept to a minimum size and weight so as not to impede mobility and are left near camp whenever men go out hunting. Women, too, possess personal objects having similar significance, some of which may be kept hidden from men and children.

Since men frequently discover new items and receive others through exchange, one of their favorite activities whenever other bands are encountered is to display, contemplate, and talk about the objects that each possesses. Since all natural, and many man-made, objects are held to be ultimately of Dreaming origin, they invariably provoke animated discussions aimed at fitting them into the grand scheme of things through knowledge of relevant mythology and Dreaming tracks.

MAGIC AND SORCERY

Most anthropologists would agree that it is neither possible nor practicable to make a convincing distinction between "magical" and "religious" elements in any society. The above heading for this section, then, is used merely to focus attention on those individuals who claim to use human and extrahuman powers to protect, cure, or harm others.

Mabarn   Men who most often use their special powers for socially approved ends are termed "Mabarn" throughout the Western Desert; the same term refers to the magical stone or shell objects they are said to carry in their stomachs.[13] Since neither "native doctor" nor "medicine man" is a satisfactory gloss—and the somewhat more appropriate label, "diviner-curer," is clumsy—the vernacular is used in the discussion that follows. Most Mabarn inherit their special powers from their fathers, but *mabarn* objects can be obtained from others. Almost all Mabarn are men, and perhaps ten or fifteen percent of Mardu males are Mabarn. They are not required to go through the elaborate special initiations, modeled on death and rebirth, that have been reported for the eastern desert regions (Roheim 1945, R. and C. Berndt 1988, Elkin 1977). Nothing in their appearance or usual demeanor distinguishes Mabarn from their fellows and, as specialists, they practice part-time only, since all their other activities are the same as those of other men. Their distinctiveness lies in their possession of special skills, knowledge, and psychic powers that give them greater and more effective access to the spiritual realm. In their communication with the spiritual world, most are aided by spirit-familiars, usually small birds or animals, that assist them in all sorts of ways but are most useful as messengers between themselves and the spirit-beings that possess limitless magical powers from which the Mabarn draw.

The Mardu rely heavily on their Mabarn for the treatment of persistent or worrisome illness. If no Mabarn happens to be present, and the patient is too sick to walk, someone will go to neighboring bands to find one. Although individual techniques vary, all Mabarn adopt a similar approach in their treatment of illness. A Mabarn first uses his magical powers to "see inside" the patient and thus locate the source of the problem, which most often is a foreign object lodged deep in the body. The treatment consists of massage, pounding, slapping, manipulation, and applying pressure with hands (and sometimes feet) to the body, as well as biting and sucking; its purpose is to remove the lodged object. If a patient is feverish, "bad" or "hot" blood is removed by sucking and left in a shady spot to cool down, thus cooling the patient.

After the initial "x-ray" examination, the Mabarn walks a short distance away to manipulate his own stomach and withdraw his *mabarn* (or one of them, since he may have many) which he blows onto in order to charge it with extra power. Approaching with his fist firmly clenched around his *mabarn,* he then inserts it into

---

[13]For this reason, "Mabarn" is capitalized in reference to the practitioner and uncapitalized when referring to the magical objects possessed by them.

the body and directs it to its target by massage or other means so that it will drive out the foreign body, which he withdraws using similar manipulation. He again walks away to examine his catch; he may then cast it away, but more often he returns to show it to the patient.[14] The fact that, to an outside observer, the object is produced from inside the patient by the Mabarn's sleight of hand should not be grounds for impugning his sincerity. He believes in the efficacy of his powers, as does the patient, who inevitably feels much better when he or she sees, for example, a one- or two-inch sliver of stone or wood that allegedly caused the trouble.[15]

Nonphysical treatment also plays an important role in a Mabarn's curative activities. For example, Wagaji, who is considered one of the most powerful and effective of the Mardu Mabarn, sometimes cures serious illness with the help of his *bibiruwarr* (butcher bird) spirit-familiar.

> Nyalbun, an old man, has been unwell for about two weeks and sends for Wagaji to treat him for worrisome pains in his chest. Wagaji examines him and diagnoses that his heart has a hole in it and is crumbling—too big a defect for Wagaji alone to fix. After waiting until Nyalbun falls asleep, the Mabarn magically removes his heart and gives it to his bird spirit-familiar to take to Lake Disappointment and leave for the Ngayunangalgu cannibal-beings to repair (see Chapter 2). In the Dreaming, *bibiruwarr* were friends and allies of the Ngayunangalgu, so they are safe from attack. The Ngayunangalgu Mabarn takes the heart, repairs it by washing it with a magical hot water, then covers it with eaglehawk down-feathers and replaces it on the surface of the lakebed where it is soon retrieved by the spirit-familiar. On receipt of the repaired heart, Wagaji inserts it magically through Nyalbun's head while he is still asleep. The old man subsequently makes a rapid recovery, after the Mabarn gives him a full account of the cause and treatment of his ailment.

Mabarn are also called upon to recover missing objects, predict future events, explain unusual phenomena, and protect people against nonphysical attack. Their ability to detect the presence or influence of malevolent spirits or featherfeet killers makes them invaluable in a variety of ritual and mundane situations. Mabarn are said to travel inside whirlwinds or as dream-spirits on raftlike arrangements of sacred boards. Sometimes they travel at the head of a group of people in dream-spirit form, riding on the back of a magical hair string that becomes a snake in flight. The leadership of Mabarn on such trips is said to be highly desirable because on visits to distant areas the likelihood of encountering evil spirits is high. Without Mabarn to help them avoid such meetings and protect them from attack, dream-spirits may be weakened or even captured, in which case the body that they have left will sicken and eventually die. During performance of the Ngaawayil rainmaking ritual, for example, in order to "bring up" the rain which follows the travelers back to the area where the ritual is taking place, it is essential that male participants be taken in dream-spirit form to visit the many waterholes where the dangerous

---

[14]Mabarn "throw" and "retrieve" their own magical *mabarn* as well as other objects in a variety of situations; they look for signs on the returned object that will provide information. For instance, a circumcision knife is "thrown" just prior to its use; if it returns "bloodied" then it cannot be used, lest the novice bleed to death. Mabarn also throw their *mabarn* to scout ahead and to detect the presence of any evil spirits or featherfeet that may be lurking in the vicinity.

[15]It is interesting that the name given to objects "fired" by sorcerers and evil spirits is the same as the generic term for sacred boards, whose great power can be harnessed for either good or evil ends.

rainmaking ancestral snakes still live. Mabarn and people who have the rainmakers as their ancestral totem and will, therefore, be recognized by their spirit-kin, ride at the front of the hair-string "snakes." This assures the travelers of a safe journey in and out of the waterholes, because the snake ancestors are pacified by the presence of the Mabarn.

Mabarn most often work alone, but sometimes they join forces with others—on difficult cases or whenever the community at large is thought to be threatened in some way:

Five weeks after his circumcision, Mani seems weak and his wound is not healing as rapidly as it should. One of his guardian "grandfathers" claims to have seen Mani whispering to someone, yet no one could be seen anywhere near his camp at the time. Two Mabarn have treated him; still, he seems listless, and it is suspected that his spirit has been stolen. Two more Mabarn are called in (it is big meeting time and a large group is assembled), and the four experts go to work using their *mabarn* to scrutinize the novice and his camping area. They are agreed: a malevolent spirit (male but with breasts) is hiding underground and has indeed captured the youth's spirit. The Mabarn first move some distance away, in different directions (but not in one another's firing line), using leafy branches to dust a clear path from the camp to where they stand to withdraw and "fire" their *mabarn* at the spirit, which is underneath the camp (the novice has been moved to one side). Witnessing this, I am amazed to see a small whirlwind appear a yard in front of one of the Mabarn as he stands pointing his *mabarn* between clenched hands. The whirlwind then moves unerringly (uncharacteristically) down the path he has cleared and straight through the middle of the camp. (When I later comment enthusiastically on this phenomenon, my listeners simply shrug their shoulders as if to say, "Naturally! He's a Mabarn, isn't he?") When all four have fired their *mabarn,* they assemble at the camp and confer. They "see" that they have hit the evil being and it has fled, leaving behind the novice's spirit. Mani recovers quickly.

If a person is gravely ill, several Mabarn may mount a combined offensive against the forces deemed to be responsible for the problem. At such times, a Mabarn's task is to convince the patient that his power is greater than that of the people or spirits being held responsible; if he cannot do so, death may soon follow. I have witnessed the death, within a few days, of apparently healthy Mardu who have announced that they are "finished" and have succumbed despite repeated efforts by Mabarn (and trained medical staff, in the contact situation) to cure them.

When Mabarn work together, there appears to be no sign of jealousy or rivalry among them. No specific recompense is required for their service, but grateful patients may give them food or some other gift in return for their treatment. Other people may at times be somewhat in awe of them, but the Mabarn neither earn nor seek special privileges or higher status in recognition of their undoubted powers.

Dreams and dream-spirit travels play a major role in every Mabarn's diagnosis and treatment of individuals and in many of the activities carried out by them for the common good. However, dreams are important in everyone's life, and people who seek treatment from Mabarn often do so after self-diagnosis. A recurrent theme in Mardu dreams involves an attack by one or more evil spirits throwing missiles, some of which the dreamer is unable to dodge. Any adult who has a disturbing dream may take it as a bad omen, just as good dreams about great successes in hunting or gathering activities will soon come true. Dreams and a variety of other signs act as motivators or inhibitors of action. For example, seeing or hearing certain birds at certain times indicates some impending danger, such as featherfeet lurking somewhere nearby. The occurrence of nerve twinges or throbbing in different parts of the body is taken as a sign that someone in a particular kin category is ill, or dead, or will arrive soon. For instance, *milyga,* a twinge in the groin, indicates that an "elder brother" or "spouse" is thinking of you; *wimalwimal,* a heart twinge, means that a "mother's brother" not seen for a long time will be encountered soon; *dagarldagarl,* an itching in the nose, is a premonition of a serious fight or a death. Taken together, these many signs constitute a kind of "sixth sense," commented on by many observers of the Aborigines, who have noted a seemingly uncanny ability to know when deaths have occurred among distant kin and to foretell other happenings.

Love Magic   The practice of individual love magic is not common among the Mardu, who claim that the techniques, objects, and rituals they possess were all obtained from other areas. Members of either sex may use it to attract a lover or rekindle strong desire between marriage partners. In secret activities carried out by one or two people, special songs are sung and the name of a desired one is spoken, usually over something belonging to that person. If the practitioners are men, they may swing small bullroarers at a secluded spot, for the sound will penetrate the head of the victim and fill her with passionate desire for the performer of the magic. All such techniques are thought to cause the person who is the object of them to become so crazed with longing for the practitioner that they will capitulate.

The Mardu sometimes perform one of a number of large-scale rituals, widely known across the Western Desert, that have strong love-magic connotations. These may or may not involve both sexes in the same place at the same time. Their aim is a more generalized enhancement of sexuality among the participants, brought about by the sexually explicit and erotic dances and songs that are performed. Although the pairs of dancers are of the same sex—and in many performances they simulate intercourse, much to the delight of the audience—the ritual is explicitly aimed to arousing heterosexual desires.[16]

Sorcery   Mabarn are said not to practice sorcery against close kin and associates, but they are sometimes allegedly involved in its practice against people in distant groups. Because the community image of its Mabarn is decidedly positive, their periodic resort to sorcery is presumed to be warranted and to be directed against some wrong-doing outsider. Any man (but never a woman) who possesses the necessary objects and techniques is capable of working sorcery; however, as the practice is usually condemned, Mardu men always deny that they have ever engaged in it. Since sorcerers usually work alone and in secret, the practice is detected most often by its effects (sickness or death) rather than its performance.

---

[16]Male and female homosexuality appears to be absent from Mardu society, apart from occasional mutual masturbation among adolescent males. There is, however, much homosociality in that those members of the same sex whose kin relationships allow a lack of restraint often engage in physical displays of affection.

Except for the very young and very old, whose deaths may not be suspect, other deaths are considered unnatural, the work of either human or spiritual malevolent forces. The Mardu believe that malevolent spirits, called by the generic term *malbu,* were probably already on earth when the Dreaming beings arrived; although most *malbu* were later killed off by the creative beings, some remained to cause humans grief. Variously described as hairy, long-toothed, and cannibalistic, the most dangerous *malbu* live in areas far distant from Mardu country. The more local spirit-beings, who inhabit several known and avoided sites within the area, are thought to be much less inclined to harm grievously their living "countrymen," unless of course someone inadvertently comes too close to their home. As noted earlier, some Mardu claim such beings as their ancestral totem, having been left behind by them. Groups of evil spirits that are associated with certain kinds of illness are mostly located in distant places, so when, for example, an influenza epidemic hits a band, the local Mabarn will soon know which group of beings is responsible.[17]

Proof of the activities of either *malbu* or human sorcerers is the removal of a foreign body from a sick person. If countermagic fails and the victim dies, the inquest that eventually takes place can have minimal social consequences, as for example when spirit-beings are identified as the killers. Alternatively, it can lead to accusations and counteraccusations, physical violence, dire threats, and sometimes the organization of a revenge expedition—a group composed of the victim's close male relatives who attempt to track down and execute the alleged killer. Significantly, the Mardu claim that resort to countersorcery is rare among them. Instead, they prefer an open confrontation with the alleged killers at the public dispute-settlement session that is a feature of the early stages of every big meeting, where a large assembly can judge the merits of their accusations. However, Mardu also tell of featherfeet expeditions sometimes being mounted. These involve elaborate ritual preparation of the members, including the upward dislocation of the little toe of each foot so that they will act as "eyes" to prevent the expedition member from stepping on dry sticks that would break and alert the victim. Also, the travelers wear small sacred boards strapped to the back of each leg to "lighten" it and thus enable them to move fast and far without fatigue.

According to Mardu Law, disputes within the band or local group should be settled openly, face to face, not by sorcery. However, as Mardu point out, it is not inconceivable that a few people of bad disposition could harbor such great resentment after a conflict that they resort to *yumbu* sorcery. This is a "hired killer" variety, named for the small length of hair string that the hirer spins from his own beard and hair, then attaches to a small bullroarer or wooden "killing stick" with a piece of spinifex resin. Wrapped securely in a feather bundle, the *yumbu* is delivered to a distant Mabarn ally by a trusted messenger of the hirer, together with the intended victim's name. If the Mabarn keeps the *yumbu,* he is accepting the contract.

---

[17]People whose senility involves sometimes erratic and disturbing behavior may be thought to have become *malbu.* It is sometimes privately suggested that the reason for certain people's behavioral eccentricities is that they are true *malbu* who had been substituted for a human child in infancy.

Much alleged individual sorcery is of the "firing at a distance" variety. The sorcerer creeps to within sight of his victim, but remains hidden. He points a specially "primed" wooden object, most commonly a cigar-shaped pointed stick with snakelike markings burned onto it, from which *miyu,* a force akin to a ray of light in appearance, travels underground and up into the body of the victim. Sacred boards are also effective as sorcery weapons because of their great power. The preparation of such objects includes anointing them with certain substances, singing, and chanting the victim's name over them. Because the risk of backfire is great, users must be careful not to hold them with one end pointing to any part of their own body, lest they themselves sicken and die. Various forms of exuvial sorcery are also alleged to be practiced.

I have seen objects identified as *yumbu* and many killing sticks in the possession of Mardu men, who invariably say that they have obtained them from some distant area and have never used them themselves. The very existence of such objects (in addition to unexpected deaths) strongly motivates Aborigines to accept the reality of sorcery. The Mardu do not live in great or constant fear of sorcery; yet, if serious conflict disrupts normal social relationships, the possibility of someone resorting to sorcery must enter people's minds and, after a sudden death, it is prominent in *ex post facto* rationalizations. As a theory of causation, it fills a large and disquieting gap left open because the mythology supplies only a general explanation for human mortality.

DYNAMIC ELEMENTS IN THE RELIGIOUS LIFE

Stanner (1965:214–15) has noted the existence of two complementary emphases in the concept of the Dreaming: "the fixation or instituting of things in an enduring form, and the simultaneous endowment of all things [including humans and their condition of life] with their good and/or bad properties." The Dreaming is thus of fundamental importance because it set for all time the parameters of a way of life which, in its essence, Aborigines perceive as unchanging. In their view, none of these essential elements alters, because the Law is continually upheld and the founding patterns are thus perpetuated. Nowhere does their ideology admit structural change as a possibility. On the contrary, the emphasis throughout Australia is on continuity of present and future with past, and the notion of progress does not exist.

A few observers of Aboriginal culture (for example, Strehlow 1947) appear to have accepted as fact its static nature and to have attributed the changes that do occur to contact with whites. They depict the Aborigines as incapable of independent thought and innovation. They have taken ideology at face value and confused its heavy emphasis on fixed and immutable patterns with the realities of a life many of whose elements make change inevitable: highly mobile and flexible groups and total reliance on oral cultural transmission for its perpetuation. In precontact Aboriginal society, such changes were rarely radical and always occurred within an existing religious framework for action, so the Aborigines very rarely had their adaptive abilities severely tested. In one of his most insightful statements, Stanner (1966:168) has written, ". . . they welcomed change insofar as it would fit the forms of permanence"—that is, as long as it was congruent with the spiritual givens of their way of life.

The question remains as to how such congruence can be guaranteed. The secret lies in the existence, in Aboriginal societies, of a kind of cultural redundancy, since a close examination of the religious life leads inescapably to the conclusion that there is almost nothing essentially new under the sun. Among the Mardu, a newly revealed or imported ritual, when dismantled into its many constituent elements, will reveal a uniqueness of tune, body pattern, song wording, and design of some of the associated thread-crosses. Yet virtually all other components—seating arrangements, dance steps, spatial configurations, raw materials in use, and so on—are already familiar from their use in various other rituals performed by the Mardu. In other words, there are a number of basic ritual components common throughout and beyond the Western Desert, forming a large store of possibilities to be selected from and rearranged in the creation of each "new" ritual, which is a unique recombination of these preexisting elements. Since the possible permutations are virtually limitless, the Aborigines can continue to develop new variants. Stanner's "forms of permanence" are these basic elements. So, while a tune will be new, it is never *radically* different in its pitch and rhythms from all the others. The body patterns are distinctive, but only slightly so. The song words are unique, yet the way they are sung, in what contexts, and with what accompaniments, are all shared with some other rituals. Stanner (1966), in his classic study of the Murinbata Aborigines, posits a fundamental characteristic of change within stability in both myth and ritual and presents strong evidence to refute the notion of a static traditional religion. Maddock (1969), in a study of northern Australian rituals, has reached a similar conclusion: new ritual constitutes a unique sequence, achieved by a novel recombination of extant ritual "bits."

Four related aspects of the dynamism that is internal to Mardu religious life are the diffusion of new rituals, songlines, and objects among groups within the desert; ritual innovation at the local level; discoveries of sacred objects; and the exploitation of myth's inherent flexibility.

Diffusion   The clearest evidence that the religion of the Mardu is lively and dynamic is provided by the central role of diffusion and the continuous exchange of lore with their desert neighbors. The focus for diffusion is the big meeting, held in emulation of the Dreaming beings who instituted and exchanged rituals and objects on many occasions when their paths crossed. People look forward to them for many reasons in addition to the excitement of ritual participation and reunions with distant friends and kin. There are novices to be inducted, marriages to be arranged, new objects to be seen, stories to hear or tell about long journeys that a few people have taken to a distant area, and so on.

At big meetings, it is not only through the acquisition of new rituals and sacred objects that religious understandings are deepened and broadened. The benefits of mobility and of a curiosity that impels men of adventurous spirit to embark on journeys of enlightenment far afield are passed on to their fellows at such gatherings. There, in an atmosphere of heightened emotion, they are assured of a rapt audience which shares vicariously in the drama. The new knowledge thus obtained will in time be relayed to others in a never-ending process of diffusion. Not only physical journeys, but the equally valid travels of the dream-spirit form part of the information exchange. People dream about places known through myths and from the descriptions of others, as well as those sites that are known physically. The many songs that dream-spirit rituals comprise are examples of innovation resulting from an expanded individual consciousness.

Innovation   Local innovation refers to the composing of new rituals as a result of dream-spirit journeys. These rituals, revealed to humans by spirit-being intermediaries of the spiritual powers, invigorate the life of the band and occasion great enjoyment among its members of all ages. Although individual dream-spirit rituals wax and wane in popularity, their existence suggests a profound truth to the Mardu: the great creative powers endure and remain concerned and interested in human life. More important still, they reward human conformity to their Law by regularly revealing these rituals to responsible humans.

It is true that individuals are not credited with ritual creativity, but they nevertheless have the vital task of translating piecemeal information into highly structured and integrated ritual wholes. The bones of "divinely" inspired elements are fleshed out into the ritual body only through the cooperative endeavors of human actors. Denying an innovatory function to the individual effectively removes a potential source of status differentiation among men who so strongly express an egalitarian ethos in their claims to be the equal of other men. Instead, enabling powers are kept concentrated in the spiritual realm, and the grand life design embodied in the Dreaming is thus protected from egotistical and potentially subversive impulses of individual humans. As the Mardu aptly put it, "Everyone is under the Dreaming," or as an Arnhem Land man remarked, "We are always running to catch up with what has been done before" (Morphy 1988:249).

Discoveries   The discovery of sacred objects is likewise not hailed as an individual accomplishment, since it too is revealed or hinted at through signs that prompt an individual to respond. Men tell of encountering spirit-beings during dreams, who tell them to go and look in some spot where they will find something important left by Dreaming beings. Again, the resulting revelation of the find to other initiated men, with a description of where and under what circumstances it was found, transfers the matter from an individual to a collective context. There, consensus is sought, and the "true" religious meaning of the find is assessed on the basis of available mythological knowledge of the discovery's location and the characteristics of the object—shape, size, color, and so forth. For example, any natural or incised concentric circle motif strongly suggests its connection with Dingari beings (see Chapter 3).

One very significant aspect of such discoveries is that they remind the Mardu of an incompleteness in their knowledge of all that transpired during the Dreaming. For example, it is believed that ancestral beings did not always leave clear evidence of their passage through certain areas, so some of their movements are unknown. In the case of most newly found sacred objects, their shape may be sufficiently general to allow identification with ancestral beings already known to have traveled or lived in the same area where the objects were found. For instance, an egg-shaped stone is easily linked with any of the vast numbers of different egg-laying beings. Yet some objects have characteristics so distinctive that they could have been left only by one particular being or group. Thus, their association is now established with the spot where objects identified with them were discovered. In this way, important new knowledge is acquired which must lead men to anticipate some later revelation of further corroborative proofs.

The practical and political implications of this kind of incorporation are considerable. To take one example, the Ngaawayil ritual is "owned" and controlled by groups living in the Percival Lakes area (Map 2), many of whom claim descent from the major rainmaking beings of the Dreaming. People wanting to participate in the ritual had to make the journey to one of the sites in that area because the Ngaawayil had not been passed on to groups in other areas. Eventually, when enough Mardu men had attained the highest Ngaawayil status, they were given permission by its leaders to construct the special grounds and perform the Ngaawayil in their home area. They were given some rainmaking stones and other sacred paraphernalia needed for its proper performance, since the rainmaking ancestors were not known to have traveled in Mardu country and thus to have left objects behind there.

Not long after the new ritual was established among the Mardu, very large cylindrical stones were discovered in several different places. These were positively identified by senior men as varieties of secret-sacred rainmaking stones, proving that the rainmaking beings had not only been in this area, but had left for the Mardu valuable repositories of their power. Because of these discoveries, the Mardu men are convinced of their fitness to hold the Ngaawayil successfully, since its associated beings can now be counted confidently among their own. Also, they have reinterpreted some of the more obscure Ngaawayil songs, which identify neither the location of what is being sung about nor the characters concerned. These songs are now cited in support of contentions that the event depicted took place in Mardu country. When character interaction occurs, it is interpreted to refer to an encounter between a rainmaking ancestor and one closely associated with the Mardu area.

Mythology and Incorporation   How does this kind of new knowledge find its way from individuals and the periphery into the core collective structures of the religious life? In view of the highly proscribed nature of ritual and songline and the pervasiveness of a strong ideology of nonchange embodied in a static cosmic order, this question must be posed. The answer lies principally in the nature of mythology, which serves as an ideal vehicle of incorporation because of its inherent flexibility. This characteristic openness has long been recognized by writers on religion. As R. Berndt (1952:52) has observed:

> Mythology presented verbally . . . no matter how conventional the structure of the society, shows a certain amount of flexibility, since the only means of presenting, and thus of preserving it, must be the individual members of that society.

Stanner (1966:84–85) suggests that myths have inspirations and a logic of their own and, more importantly, considerable dramatic potential: "Every myth deals with persons, events and situations that, being less than fully described, are variably open to development by men of force, intellect or insight." This could explain why protagonists in myths are often vague and ambiguous characters. Because of this variability in myths, there is no such thing as a single correct version, although a concern for consensus certainly exists with respect to the most important details of plot in major narratives. Those present at a telling would take into account the narrator's sex, approximate age, totemic associations with, and knowledge of, the stretch of country that forms the setting for the action being described (R. and C. Berndt 1970).

The flexibility of myth allows for more than the embellishment of details of character and plot. Myths are capable of extension and expansion to permit the inclusion of new information that comes to light as the result of revelations by spirit intermediaries and also from the finding of new objects and the subsequent deduction of new links between sites and creative beings. In an apt summation of the major role of mythology in human society, Burridge (1969b:417) notes, in reference to the myths of the Tangu, Melanesians of Papua New Guinea: "Not only do the Tangu use their narratives to think with, and think from, but in their narratives new thoughts are deposited." The Mardu know best and in greatest detail the myths and sections of longer narrative myths that deal with happenings in their home territory among ancestral beings to whom they have the closest connections of "descent." They know less of those of distant areas, however, and their grasp of the mythology associated with imported rituals is more sketchy. In learning the ritual's songline, they usually gain a good idea of the sequence of major mythological events, but individual knowledge is more variable as to detail.

To return to the Ngaawayil example, the brevity and imprecise nature of the mythology of the rainmaking beings, added to its lack of close correlation with either songs or dances in the ritual, allowed Mardu men to develop it. They have amplified the myth to incorporate the appearance of the rainmakers in Mardu country and to add details as to some of their activities there, including meetings with local beings. Through the discovered rainmaking stones and the reinterpretation of certain songs, those Mardu groups in whose territory the finds were made have enlarged the myth of the rainmakers and have made some of it their own. This appropriation of knowledge is both religiously and politically important, since it strengthens the claims of these Mardu to proprietorial rights. Since such rights include their use of the ritual to attract other groups, desirous of eventual acquisition, to big meetings held in their estate, these Mardu reap the status benefits that accrue to the host group. Thus, there is an interesting contrast between the denial of individual creativity and the appropriation and manipulation of myth by groups for political and prestige ends.

Knowledge is not finite, since there is always something more to be revealed to the Aborigines, and there are gaps in totemic geography that allow new proofs of ancestral activities to be accommodated. It is perhaps therefore incorrect to describe the cosmic order of the Mardu as unified, if that word connotes finality and completeness.[18] There must always be gaps, and the dynamism that enlivens their

[18]Stanner (1965:165) says of the Murinbata that "there were only workings towards system and transient captures of unity" in a society that "while being caught up in change and development, was segmented into like (but not identical) and unlike (but not independent) parts that had to compete for many of the scarce goods of life, and to do so under . . . a set of principles no one of which covered all real-life situations."

religious life is a result of continuous effort toward closure—an impossible goal, since its attainment would really mean stagnation. Yet, the Aboriginal worldview admits of no concern about gaps or incompleteness; instead, one gains an abiding impression of harmony and rightness and an unshakable conviction that no contradictions of any consequence exist. The human, plant, animal, and spiritual inhabitants of the cosmos are perceived as interdependent parts of a single domain, beneath the all-embracing canopy of the Dreaming.

RELIGION, POLITICS, AND HIERARCHY

Considering the pervasiveness of religion in Mardu society, its possible relationship to inequality and to competition for power requires examination as part of a religious dynamic.

In addition to the gender dichotomy discussed earlier in this chapter, most rituals feature different male and female status hierarchies, and the division of labor that takes place is based largely upon these. People of both sexes "rise through the ranks" by repeated ritual participation over a period of years and by the satisfactory performance of their allotted roles. Among initiated men, there is a hierarchy of statuses which form the basis for a generalized division of labor that operates in the context of ritual. First are the "cooks," the older men who prepare the many different ceremonial feasts, act as advisors and directors of most rituals (and perform the most important "big" dances), and are guardians of the caches of sacred objects. Next are the active middle-aged men who are responsible for the mechanics of ritual activity. They transmit directives from the "cooks" to the statuses beneath theirs and perform specific tasks such as butchering game and dividing seedcakes for ritual feasts, caring for sacred paraphernalia in the storehouses, performing many important dances, and leading the hunts that are integral to all rituals.[19] The third status level is that of the "leg-men," not yet in their forties, who assist the second-level men in a variety of tasks and have major roles as hunters and supervisors of novices, whom they discipline when necessary. The lowest level is that of the partly initiated young men who are novices. They must remain silent and do exactly as they are told during rituals. Men of the senior "cook" status together choose worthy candidates to join their ranks and, in collaboration with those of the second status, select new members for that level.

It should now be clear how the religious system sets up hierarchies within and between the sexes and how effectively initiated men can use it to promote male exclusiveness and assert their superiority over women. Yet, does it allow senior ritual leaders to transfer power or authority derived from the religious domain into the mundane world? Also, does it create "horizontal" inequalities among different estate groups or language-named units? Is religious lore a scarce resource that is used by different groups in competition for regional preeminence? Do the various

---

[19]The sacred boards are heavily greased with fat and red ochre to protect them against termites. They are always kept carefully hidden, not only because they are extremely dangerous to women and children, but also because it is believed that strangers may wish to steal them and concentrate their great power in order to kill an enemy, using sorcery.

Mardu groups use religion as a political mechanism for boundary maintenance, the reinforcement of ethnocentrism, and the promotion of in-group solidarity? These questions touch on an important topic that has been, in recent decades, the subject of vigorous debate among scholars of Aboriginal Australia: whether or not Aboriginal societies are more accurately characterized as egalitarian or hierarchical in nature.[20]

The terms of the debate were brought into sharp focus by Bern (1979), who noted a neglect by scholars of two vital aspects of Aboriginal society: the political structure of religion and the existence of accumulable wealth in the form of ritual property (including powerful secrets) as well as the productive and reproductive powers of women.[21] Bern's central argument is that inequalities defined within religion set up the conditions for dominance in the rest of the society and that there is a "spill-over" of the power and authority of ritual leaders into everyday social and political life. There is strong evidence in support of Bern's argument for the presence of hierarchy in some parts of the continent. There are significant regional variations (and some important differences within regions, such as Cape York), suggesting that both ecological and cultural factors are germane to boundary maintenance, competition, and hierarchy (cf. Chase 1984). In Arnhem Land and western Cape York, for example, competition may become prominent at two levels: individually, among senior males, and among corporate groups, such as clans, operating above the level of family and band. Such political struggle is mainly centered on rights in women and ritual property (cf. Keen 1978, Sutton 1978, von Sturmer 1978, Sutton and Rigsby 1982, and Williams 1987). Marked inequalities of this kind seem to be characteristic of societies which, unlike the Western Desert, have corporate kin groups interposed between the family-band level and the society at large, together with other features conducive to the generation and maintenance of hierarchy, for example, small patriclans (around thirty people) with strong mutual interests in a cluster of neighboring sites, localized cult rituals, and a high degree of local endogamy (Sutton, personal communication). None of these features is found in the Western Desert, where, although the estate group has a core of patrikin, its members are widely scattered, membership criteria are broad, the major cults are shared regionally, and local area endogamy is the exception, not the rule.[22]

In some resource-rich regions, where population densities are higher, ranges smaller, and boundaries less permeable, localized corporate descent groups such as patrilineal clans or subclans may assume great cultural importance. Ritual property that constitutes title to land, and other ritual prerogatives, is jealously guarded, and punishment for offenses involving them is extremely severe (Williams 1986:94). Under such conditions, the illegal appropriation by one group of another's totemic

---

[20]For summaries of the issues, see R. Berndt (1965), Bern (1979), Hiatt (1986), Williams (1988).

[21]Woodburn (1980, 1982), writing about egalitarianism among hunter-gatherer peoples, categorized Australian Aboriginal societies as atypical precisely because of what he saw as significant inequalities generated via the maintenance and transmission by senior males of long-term rights over females. Tonkinson (1988b) tests Woodburn's model against Western Desert evidence, but finds it inapplicable there because of a variety of factors which inhibit the generation of such inequalities.

[22]On regional contrasts, Sutton and Rigsby (1982:158) offer the comment that ". . . Western Desert people display a more flexible, individualistic and religion-cast approach to invoking attachment to land than do their more sedentary, clannish and secular counterparts on the coasts and in the uplands."

clan design or songs is cause for a major feud, with injury and sometimes deaths resulting (cf. Warner 1937). Ritual politics are thus fraught with competition or outright conflict, and intergroup boundaries may be tightly circumscribed and defended. Exclusiveness of this kind is something the Mardu and their desert neighbors cannot sustain, and it may help explain why "cult lodges" are absent and social totemism (the linking of a social group to a particular animal, plant, and so on) is unimportant. The overriding significance of Mardu totemic associations lies in their linking of *individuals*, rather than social categories and groups, to the life-sustaining spiritual realm. Even members of the same estate group may have different ancestral totems, as noted earlier. Totemism, like ritual, cuts across other memberships and therefore dilutes rather than reinforces parochial tendencies among Mardu groups.[23]

Although the *potential* for domination exists in all Aboriginal societies, among the Mardu this is not realizable as a permanent condition. Dominance and the monopolization of the means of production by individuals or groups are inhibited by a combination of ecological, social, and religious factors, which instead generate strong interdependence at all levels of Mardu society (cf. Tonkinson 1988a, 1988b). We have seen how, in everyday life, the rules of kinship are not normally over-ridden, and the only status inequalities (apart from those based on age) derive from the operation of kinship and have a strongly egalitarian flavor. When male-female hierarchy is invoked, as in domestic strife, it is a temporary manifestation rather than an intrinsic property of behavior between spouses. It should also be clear, from the description earlier in this chapter, that regionalism provides the very foundation for Mardu ritual life. With every group, the same totemic geography that binds it to its estate and fosters pride and solidarity among its members also links them to all their neighbors and to other individuals and groups in distant areas through the many ancestral tracks that criss-cross the desert and thus unite distant groups in shared ownership of, and responsibility for, the associated lore. Similarly, in both their structure and operation, collective rituals demand close cooperation and shared labor inputs among the various groups.

In the case of ritual hierarchies, the control exerted by senior men and women over younger members of the same sex is a generalized one, not concentrated in the hands of a powerful few; it therefore cannot form the basis for sustainable individual claims to the leadership of groups. Not only is ritual leadership context-specific and therefore highly variable, but there are many "bosses," so their authority is also diffuse. Even in ritual contexts where control by mature men over younger adults is total, the major message they seek to impart is the dominance of spiritual powers, outside the human realm, to which all must submit if the legacy of the Dreaming is to be perpetuated. Even the oldest and wisest men and women are only go-betweens

[23]Maddock (1982) discusses the tension in Aboriginal societies between forces promoting parochial-ism and those that reinforce an outward-looking "universalism." He shows how the widespread "owner-manager" distinction operates to deny "owner" descent groups autonomy in the performance of their own rituals, since the active involvement of "managers" (drawn from different groups, but related to the "owner" group through females) is essential. In recent times, this division has been a prominent and contentious aspect of Aboriginal land claims in the Northern Territory (cf. papers by Hiatt, Keen, and Morphy and Morphy, in Hiatt, ed. 1984; Maddock 1980, 1983a, 1983b; Bern and Larbalestier 1985; Neate 1989).

or "vehicles" for the maintenance of the Law. It follows, then, that being of senior ritual status does not give men or women the right to assert their authority over others outside the religious domain. In line with their strong sense of equality and autonomy, people say that the Law is everyone's boss, not other people.

In the context of intergroup relationships, these status hierarchies, like so many other institutions and practices, cut across local groups and kinship networks as if anticipating the dangers of parochialism and local group exclusiveness in a drought-prone and marginal habitat. The relatively even distribution of basic food and water resources inhibits the potential for significant differentiation in power among the various groups, and they enjoy an equality of opportunity to create valued social capital. All groups are free to compose new rituals, and the exclusive performance of each group's own dream-spirit rituals when visitors are hosted must enhance its status among its neighbors and reinforce local solidarity. Yet the hoarding of such capital would be tantamount to a refusal to share, which is (ideologically, at least) unthinkable to the Mardu, so the urge to retain, in many cases, yields to pressure from other groups. Prestige, then, accrues from the generous release of the ritual into the regional network of exchange.

Throughout the Western Desert, there is an elaborate code of host-visitor etiquette which accords superior status to the role of host. In some other parts of Australia, this combines with control of resource-rich territory to generate hierarchical ordering akin to the famous Melanesian "big man" system (cf. von Sturmer 1978). In the Western Desert, however, uncertainties of rainfall and the practice of rotating big meeting venues among many estates counteract such tendencies. Also, restrictions on the rights and the movement of visitors are lifted prior to the commencement of ritual activity, and major decision-making is undertaken by senior men from all groups present, who consult from time to time with a similarly mixed group of women about the complex logistics of co-ordinating public activities. Thus, as the larger "community" asserts itself, the host-visitor status distinction loses its force.

During these periodic but vitally important gatherings, the dominant division of the assembly is into two merged alternate generation levels (see Chapter 3, Figures 3-4 and 3-5). To the extent that these two groups compete, they do so as equals, whereas the status inequality separating initiated men from the rest of society is unmistakable. Yet, in both cases, ritual competitiveness and the control of the religious life by initiated men are subsumed within broader and compelling imperatives demanding cooperation and correct performance if society is to endure. Men's and women's interests are thus conjoined, as are those of the older men and the younger initiates, leaving little room for the unequal segments (women and younger men) to develop a rebellious counter-ideology, even if they so desired.

Underlying these strong cultural values is an undeniable ecological imperative. Highly irregular and unreliable rainfall makes it essential that social structures minimize, rather than create, physical or social boundaries. Where such boundaries do exist, they must be permeable; survival may depend on unrestricted access to the territories and resources of others (cf. Gould 1982). The maintenance of a very broad cultural horizon, such a notable feature of Western Desert peoples, is both cause and result of a flexible society characterized by a relatively unrestricted flow of people and ideas. The openness of Western Desert society is not a function only of the religious system, of course; the ramifying and cross-cutting bonds of kinship, social category, language, and marriage all operate to transcend local parochial interests and inhibit tendencies toward rigid boundary maintenance. In the desert, hegemonic tendencies must do battle with the social realities of small groups scattered in low density across vast spaces.[24]

[24]This expansiveness of worldview is noted by Strehlow (1965:131), when he contrasts the comparative lack of cultural conservatism among the Western Desert peoples with the intense conservatism of the Aranda of central Australia: ". . . the Western Desert nomads, whose wanderings frequently took them into the lands of distant tribal groups, remained open to the suggestions of their neighbours, and even of other 'tribes,' in religious, social, and artistic matters. Unhindered by the rigidity of outlook that results from centuries of residence within safe hunting grounds, the Western Desert people borrowed religious concepts, social norms, and artistic practices freely."

6 / Living the Dream

In Aboriginal understanding, the legacy of the heroic world-creating labors of the Dreaming beings is encoded in the Law. This blueprint envisions an ideal world wherein human beings remain under spiritual authority, yet accept responsibility for perpetuating the founding design; in other words, they must not only live out the master plan, but they must also live up to it if the cosmic order is to remain intact. The Dreaming is, in effect, a key cultural symbol which provides both a "model of" reality and a "model for" Aboriginal conformity to its dictates (cf. Geertz 1973). The challenge faced by Aborigines is, of course, not unique, since human social life everywhere is a product of the tensions between two major domains: a normative system—the shared body of values and rules of expected behavior that reflect an ideal—and the lived realities of everyday existence. Added to this is the perennial human struggle between assertions of individuality and social pressures demanding conformity to a wider interest group. Addressing these tensions in the context of an Arnhem Land society, Hamilton (1981:152–153) reaches a conclusion that has general applicability in Aboriginal Australia:

> The centripetal forces of sociability and the centrifugal ones of self-assertion, individuality and aggression are mediated by customary behaviours—the giving and receiving of food and women, the control of aggression through ridicule and interference, and the control of excessive individuality by pressures to conform to traditional role expectations formed early in life.

Real life, which is always less orderly, more complicated, and less predictable than the normative system would have it, is made imperfect by many factors, not the least of which are the foibles of idiosyncratic human beings. Small-scale societies like those of the Aborigines, which were relatively isolated and homogeneous, would seem to have had the greatest chance of maintaining close congruence between the ideal and actual. In the Aboriginal case, especially, the host of rules surrounding such basic institutions as kinship, social categories, marriage, and ritual suggest an emphasis on order and formality that strongly favors the collectivity over individual self-interest. Yet, nowhere can the fit be perfect, and Aboriginal societies are certainly no exception. To answer the question of how well the domains of the ideal and real approximate or diverge in Mardu life, attention in this chapter focuses mainly on norms and values, and conformity and conflict, at both individual and group levels.

At the end of the last chapter, a large number of factors favoring a cooperative ethos among the Western Desert groups were discussed. The consequences of a marginal environment have considerable bearing on the ability of the Mardu to live out the Law as bequeathed them by the Dreaming, particularly with respect to maintaining harmony within and between groups. We must thus keep in mind a society traditionally made up of small, separated, highly mobile bands, characterized by a very low population density and behaviors that maintain this kind of spacing as the status quo. The lack of crowding and the relatively low level of sustained interaction among different groups contributes greatly to the reduction of tensions beyond the level of the family unit. Another major factor which lowers pressures to conform is the ease of withdrawal by individuals and families from a band or larger temporary aggregation in anticipation of, or in response to, conflict. Hamilton (1981:153) has rightly identified this aspect of mobility as "the deepest and most significant freedom in Aboriginal society." Conflict, particularly of an interpersonal kind, is nonetheless unavoidable, and there is no doubt that for the Mardu its effective management and containment is a major social concern; this is indicated by the presence of a large number and variety of cultural conventions to deal with it.

THE IDEAL AND THE COLLECTIVITY

All ideal Mardu social attributes are embodied in the dictates of their Law. The Law defines the good life, and religion not only acknowledges the human realm as being under spiritual authority but also affirms the need for humans to accede to terms laid down and fixed for all time in the Dreaming. Fortunately, nothing in nonliterate societies gets captured and frozen forever by the written word, and social norms tend to retain sufficient flexibility to allow people to conform without feeling stifled or overly constrained by rules.

At all levels of society, the value system places great emphasis on reciprocal obligation and interdependence, reinforced through the sharing and exchange of religious and mundane elements. Such exchange is promoted by conventions of hospitality, to be freely given as long as visitors are peaceful in their intentions and observe the correct etiquette. Travelers who come upon a distant band as *ngajarri* (strangers) should never enter the camping area; instead, they sit within sight of it and wait until local men go to greet them. Once the nature of their visit is known, they are taken into the camp for a *milyanggul* (formal introduction). Only after the various kinship links are known can interaction occur between members of the two groups. The visitors will be given food, and perhaps a ritual will be organized in their honor. If they include men traveling without wives, and there are local women of the appropriate kinship category available, such women may be lent to them. The visitors may reciprocate with gifts of food or other objects immediately, but this is not necessary or expected. According to the ideal of generalized reciprocity, the same hospitality would be expected of them at some future time when they are called on to assume the role of host.

The many conventions surrounding the statuses of host and visitor reflect the importance both of proper behavior when in some other group's territory and of generous hospitality as hosts. The ideal big meeting features an early, equitable, rapid, and relatively bloodless settling of outstanding disputes between individuals or groups wanting to air grievances or to seek redress for alleged wrongs. Thereafter, the emphasis should be on harmony, enjoyment, and a flow of valued goods, ideas, and rituals among participating individuals and groups. Through initiatory activities and exchanges, new alliances will be forged and existing ones reinforced, with the promising and giving of females in marriage as an important feature. When the meeting ends, everyone should disperse fully satisfied with what has transpired.

In the complex orchestration of these major assemblies, authority and control rest ultimately with the collectivity of fully initiated men present. The men know that the women and the uninitiated will cooperate and that women will play a major role in the provision of food and water and the supervision of children during ritual proceedings. Leadership roles will change as one ritual ends and a different one is organized. Within such circumscribed contexts, orders can be given and will be carried out but, unless novices are involved, there will be a complete absence of authoritarianism, for the essence of relationships among adults of the same sex is an unstated equality. As Maddock (1982:166) notes, "egalitarian mutuality" is the governing principle, but among the Mardu it never fully submerges the asymmetries that are basic to many kin relationships. The norms of kinship are virtually never ignored, whatever the context, so it remains the key determining factor behind social interaction. Thus, a leader for a particular ritual could not tell someone to whom he defers, such as a "father" or "mother's brother," to do something. Instead, he would indicate that something needed to be done, and the relative concerned should take it upon himself to do it or, alternatively, an intermediary whose kinship link permits it would convey the request. In general, the demeanor of men playing the role of director should be somewhat diffident and open to suggestion, rather than authoritarian; in fact, they will be as nondirective as it is possible to be and still get the activity organized.

In contrast, when dealing with young men whose initiation is not yet complete, their elders take advantage of ritual contexts to be stern and demanding in their demeanor.[1] They play the role of taskmaster and tutor, expecting absolute obedience as they forcefully remind the young men of how much remains to be known and how all of this precious knowledge must be paid for with gifts of meat. Ideally, the only possible response on the part of the young men is dutiful compliance and willingness to reciprocate for these acts of empowerment. The young men will accept their subordinate status in religious affairs for several obvious reasons: they are virtually certain of their eventual succession to power; this is the only possible route to the attainment of full adult status; and they already enjoy compensations in the form of contributory roles in ritual and the opportunity to act as guardians of younger novices entrusted to their care. Thus, although dominated from above, they

---

[1]This harsh attitude toward young novices contrasts markedly with that shown toward mature, fully initiated men who do not yet know the ritual in question. There is enthusiasm and excitement when objects are shown, but much less theater and no scolding or assertion of dominance; also, the initiators convey much more information and detail concerning the ritual to their fellows.

have the opportunity to exert authority over those below them in the male hierarchy. Wives will have already been promised to them, and their bachelor status is not one of celibacy. They therefore know that it is just a matter of time, patience, and conformity until marriage, the eventual attainment of *nindibuga* (wise one) status, and an influential place in the society are theirs.

REALITY AND THE COLLECTIVITY

Mardu society consists of somewhat isolated, small groups of closely related people—highly mobile yet solidly grounded by multiple ties to certain localities in one or more estates. This condition fosters a measure of solidarity that finds expression in some ethnocentric attitudes and a rather inward-looking, parochial ethos. People are distrustful of the motives of strangers and are prone to attribute negative, even nonhuman, behaviors to those distant groups about whom very little is definitely known but of whom much is certainly suspected. This suspicion of strangers and fear of revenge expeditions, added to strong beliefs in various malevolent spirits, engenders in Mardu society extreme caution about surprise attack. This is reflected in such matters as the choice of campsites (always on clear, open ground to lessen the possibility of a successful sneak attack by featherfeet revenge expeditions), the trust in their dogs as detectors of strangers in the vicinity, and the frequency with which ritual activity suddenly grinds to a suspenseful halt when something is allegedly seen or heard nearby, and all available Mabarn go out to investigate. Many signs, for example their totemism beliefs (where things in nature can turn out to be spirit-children in disguise), tell the Mardu that all is not what it appears to the eye to be and that their cosmic order contains both beneficent and evil forces. One only has to embark on a dream-spirit journey, or attend an inquest, or consult a Mabarn, to confront either or both kinds of force. The security of being in one's own country and among familiar kin appears to counteract any tendency to be obsessively concerned about imminent assault by persons or forces unknown—unless a person has broken the Law or is traveling in country far from his or her habitual range.

If there are dangers "out there," but they are minimized the closer one sticks to familiar territory and to life among those most like oneself, then ethnocentric attitudes are bound to exist. At a superficial level, local ethnocentrism surfaces in humorous comments and asides about differences in dialect and custom. The relative homogeneity of desert culture nonetheless encompasses these variations, which, after all, are religiously validated, having been deliberately established by the creative beings of the Dreaming. More seriously, when disruptions occur at the intergroup level, the dichotomy between "we of one country" and "they who are different" may activate boundaries and exaggerate differences. The breach could result from an actual event, as for example, when a member of one group elopes with the wife of a member of another or when a serious quarrel results in bloodshed. Alternatively, it could be the result of an alleged offense, such as a sorcery attack, the theft of a sacred object, an attempted featherfeet attack or ambush, neglect of an increase center, failure to reciprocate adequately or Lawfully for something, and so on. The attribution of most deaths to sorcery, plus the belief that close relatives cannot resort to this practice, means that scapegoats are sought among outsider groups, probably those with whom there has been some prior trouble.

If the guilt of individuals is beyond doubt, as in the case of most elopements, resolution of the problem can be attempted with the consent of members of both groups concerned. The threat to social order that is posed by such offenses is conceded by all, and few would stand in the way if the wronged man and his close relatives invoked self-help to punish the pair. Like all small-scale acephalous societies, those of Aboriginal Australia lack centralized institutions for political control, such as chiefs, judiciary, or other formal bodies that could deal with litigation and render judgments binding on all parties. For this reason, intergroup conflicts, in particular, may be difficult to resolve. If the men of both groups cannot arrive at a course of action acceptable to both parties, the only solution is to delay adjudication until the next big meeting. There, the dispute can be aired with both sides free to put their cases to the large assembly, which is the closest physical approximation to "community" that the Western Desert people achieve. Should illness or death strike a member of either group during the interim period, though, sorcery accusations are almost certain to be directed at people with whom there is already a difference awaiting resolution.

There is no ethnographic evidence of any longstanding intergroup animosity akin to feud among the Mardu, and no word exists for either feud or warfare in their language. The absence of localized, solidary corporate groups contesting resources and maintaining boundaries, in addition to the ecological realities of an arid and demanding physical environment, would make such organized, sustained hostility virtually impossible. Predictably, then, most Mardu accounts of conflicts are phrased in kinship terms and are situated on an interpersonal or interfamily rather than intergroup level. Instead of feud-inducing behaviors, the arena of intergroup conflicts is dominated by measures aimed at achieving as rapid, peaceful, and binding a settlement as possible.

One of the most important of these expiatory measures is for people to defuse tensions by physically punishing a guilty member of their own group or, if the offender is a man, to induce him to face the wronged person or group. Once actually confronted by his accusers, the culprit will step forward without having to be pushed, in line with a strong Mardu value that personal responsibility for question-able behavior must be assumed. Unarmed except for a shield, he will be showered with spears and boomerangs, or his punishers may close in and wound him with clubs and jabbing spears, until he is injured to their satisfaction.

> Jadu, a bachelor in his late twenties, was repeatedly warned by his own kin to stop pursuing and copulating with two young "wrong" ("ZD") women from a neighboring band. After several meetings between the groups concerned, where he tried un-successfully to justify his actions, his three older brothers ordered him to *gandulajanam-ba*, to stand in the open and face his punishers. He immediately did so and used his shield effectively to parry almost a dozen spears, thrown mostly one at a time by five of his "EB." As they closed in, only his older sister Wunda and two other "EZ" attempted to intervene to protect him. Even they could not prevent him receiving two spear wounds in the thigh and several very severe blows from clubs.

If members of two groups stand off and begin trading missiles as well as verbal insults, women of the two groups, aided sometimes by men who act as peacemakers, will soon intervene. Those whose role does not call for incitement converge quietly but very determinedly on the combatants, dislodging spears from throwers and doggedly clinging to weapons until the conflict de-escalates into verbal abuse or successful attempts are made to shift the venue to men's country, where the Law forbids fighting. Much such conflict is highly ritualized, with gradations of escalation and the certainty of intervention by others should a spear fight eventuate. Uncontrolled exchanges are usually short-lived, but quite fierce and frightening—to spectators as well as combatants. When missiles begin to fly, the outward composure displayed by men in deflecting or sidestepping them defies description.

Short of physical combat—or following it, if cool heads have not prevailed—there are other measures useful in effecting binding settlements. The most serious and powerful, usually resorted to only after a serious intergroup rift, is an exchange of sacred boards.

> The normally rather orderly dispute-settlement session at one big meeting erupted into chaos when a heated verbal exchange of accusations and counteraccusations of sorcery, leveled between a Gardujarra and a Manyjilyjarra group, suddenly became physical and escalated into a wild spearfight involving almost all the men present. Many boomerangs were thrown and several men on both sides were badly cut, as were several women who had intervened. When calm returned, a meeting of all the men decided to settle the dispute for good by means of the cutting and exchange of sacred boards. The following morning, men of the two groups went out together and spent two days cutting and shaping two huge wooden boards from a rivergum tree; each measured about sixteen-feet long by eighteen-inches wide. Once properly shaped and smoothed, they were ceremonially exchanged, then carved, a task that was to take the two teams of men weeks to bring to a conclusion. They worked in separate locations in men's country. Once both sides had completed this mammoth task, they reassembled for a communal feast, wherein each group ate seedcakes and meat provided by the other. Having feasted, they then exchanged the two carved boards in a gesture designed to end for all time the conflict that had divided them. Any attempt to revive animosities between the two groups would henceforth be considered unthinkable, because the Dreaming beings who settled their disputes in like manner never again fought each other.

The penis-holding rite is another important method that men adopt to prevent or atone for conflict. It is also used by travelers to "pay for" their entry into the territories of distant host groups and into ritual activities there. At the same time, it is an affirmation of peaceful intentions and the right of the visitors, by virtue of having been subincised, to be present at secret-sacred business.[2] In this simple rite, men of one group sit with heads bowed while men of the other walk among them and grasp each by the arm, pressing their penis into the palm of his hand so that the urethral incision can be felt. If a man stands in the Mourner relationship (see Chapter 3) to the one who is offering his penis, he cannot comply and so will not allow his arm to be raised; instead, he will be tapped on the shoulder or head. Should all men in the seated group refuse to allow their hands to be raised, this

---

[2]When this ritual takes place in the camp area, men will first signal women and children to lie down and cover their faces, since they are forbidden to witness the proceedings.

signifies rejection of the conciliatory gesture and physical violence would ensue. According to senior Mardu men, however, such an outcome would be extremely rare. Acceptance of the gesture, signified by a reciprocal act on the part of the receiving group, is virtually always assured.

Nyubamarda is described by the Mardu as a female equivalent of the penis-holding rite and sometimes occurs in association with it. The rite entails the women of one group being sent by their men to lie face down for several seconds on top of every man (face up) related to them as *nyuba* or "spouse." Later, the men concerned must reciprocate with gifts to the women. The *nyubamarda* of this kind that I witnessed all took place just prior to the start of rituals at big meetings. In this context, both *nyubamarda* and the penis-holding rite are assurances of trust and goodwill that "open up" the proceedings and make for a successful meeting. Should they occur as atonement for some conceded wrong, however, the women may be sent to have sexual intercourse with men of the offended group.

The existence of intergroup disputes suggests that strains toward the kind of ethnocentrism or suspicion that exacerbates differences do indeed exist in desert societies. Yet, the fact that there are so many measures directed toward the effective settlement of such disputes also indicates that people are at pains to prevent the resulting conflicts from escalating or enduring. In this endeavor, the Mardu are aided by the many elements that militate against extreme boundary maintenance by providing strong linkages above the level of the local group or band. Among the most potent of these are the norms of classificatory kinship, friendship, and affinal alliance, and the unifying authority of a shared Law. There are also the survival functions inherent in mutual hospitality and unfettered access to natural resources in both lean and bountiful times.

THE IDEAL AND THE INDIVIDUAL

When the Dreaming beings laid down the life design to be followed by their human descendants, they specifically excluded their own frequent excesses and included only those exemplary behaviors that are now highly valued in Mardu life. The ideal person is someone who shares unselfishly and without hesitation, who is generous (*mijigurlu,* meaning "having blood") without making an issue of it or asking for return, and fulfills ritual and kinship obligations without question. He or she is an active provider as parent, child of aged parents, and in-law, shows compassion for others and respect for their individuality and integrity, and demonstrates a close attachment to family and to homeland. In behavior, the worthy person is unassuming and not overly aggressive, egotistical, or boastful. Status in Mardu society is very much a matter of the fulfillment of kinship obligations in the style suggested by these ideal behaviors.

With the exception of the diviner-curer or Mabarn, all adults of the same sex possess a very similar range of skills and technological knowledge. Individuals who excel at certain tasks may be admired and respected for their greater ability, but this is not made the basis for status differentiation. Likewise, individual status is quite unrelated to the acquisition or accumulation of material possessions. The older vigorous man who successfully lives with four wives or possesses immense religious knowledge is admired but not envied, since these are achieved statuses and have little effect on his everyday dealings with others.

In subduing egotism to the cause of society and imbuing its members with valued attributes of personality and behavior, the Mardu would seem to have an uphill battle, given the extreme permissiveness that typifies their child-rearing practices.[3] They rely on the development of individual self-regulation, which is achieved through socialization, enculturation, and the internalization of conformity and of the emotions that facilitate it. Before he or she can walk or talk, a small child is pressured to share food with others. Throughout its childhood it should be constantly told of its kinship relationships to others and of behavior that is appropriate for each kin category. Through entreaty, ridicule, threat, withdrawal of support, peer-group pressure, and so on, the child will learn to conform. From the models that surround it in the immediate family and band, it will learn about sex roles and the division of labor. Yet the keys to self-regulation lie in a child's development of certain powerful emotions central to Aboriginal culture everywhere: a strong sense of compassion (*nyarru*) which will impel it to be generous and to look after others; shame/embarrassment (*gurnda*) which will inhibit it from many antisocial or immoral behaviors; and a deep-seated yearning (*gujil*) for family and home estate, which will draw the wanderer back there throughout his or her lifetime. After childhood, the protracted period of initiation will serve to induce in the male total acceptance of, and commitment to, the religious life. This should occur in such a way that a young man, having the enormity of the secret life revealed to him, will experience neither skepticism nor an urge to rebel.

A rapidly developing sense of shame-embarrassment will induce boys and girls to begin conforming in early adolescence to appropriate kinship behaviors without over-coercion from adults. The telltale signs among big boys and girls are an awkwardness and self-consciousness in certain social situations where interaction with adults is involved. The more rapidly maturing girl will have made this transition at a younger age. Ideally, she will enter marriage well equipped with the necessary work skills and ready to obey the wishes of her husband and any older co-wives. She should be hardworking, dutiful, and willing to accept the primacy of his sexual rights over her. She should have internalized these marital values so well that their periodic reinforcement by means of verbal or physical abuse at the hands of co-wives or husband is rarely needed.

In sum, the properly socialized Mardu man and woman should need little in the way of external sanctions or compulsion to maintain their conformity to the Law. The kinship system provides them with the parameters for most anticipated social interaction, and religious precepts supply additional guides for participation in ritual activity.

---

[3]Hamilton (1981:150) notes that this permissiveness is less extreme than it appears. In reality, it is tempered by subtle, non-punitive but effective pressures on children that produce in them certain attitudes (for example, to regard sharing as natural) that will lessen conflict and by a basic attitude which assumes that "humans are 'naturally' sociable and generally agreeable to maximising others' benefits as well as their own."

THE REALITIES OF INDIVIDUAL BEHAVIOR

No close observer of Mardu society could fail to affirm that under normal circumstances the great majority of adults of both sexes are agreeable people of pleasant disposition. This positive assessment does not preclude another equally valid one: both men and women have a capacity for rapid and passionate arousal of emotions to a violent pitch, seen most often in either anger or sorrow. At such times they may attempt to harm themselves, as when grieving over the sickness or death of a relative, or they may vent their anger on others in conflicts. Great anger can suddenly well up over seemingly minor matters, resulting in quite intense confrontations between individuals. Yet such outbursts are not a defining characteristic of everyday life. What is most notable about them is how rapidly they subside and how very quickly the precipitating incidents seem to be forgotten. In some cases, the person who provokes a confrontation may be held responsible by those present. In others, some nonhuman force is deemed to be at work, as when a pregnant woman is "pushed" by the spirit-child within. In still others, the person is commonly acknowledged to be *ngagumba* (mad) and therefore unable to help his or her behavior. In most cases, however, individuals are held fully responsible for such acts, especially if they break the Law. Certain emotions are considered likely to lead people into trouble if not kept under control: strong dislike (hatred seems too severe to describe it), *migu* (jealousy, covetousness, envy), promiscuity and unbridled sexuality, malicious gossip (and its mate, tale-carrying), and *yurndiri,* which I translate as "aggressive sulking."

These emotions can be very upsetting to people, who refer to this state of disturbed well-being as *wirla ngarnda* (sick stomach), a reflection of the importance of the stomach as the locus of Mardu emotions. Being upset connotes a dissatisfaction that demands some kind of action, from either the distressed person or those held to be the cause of it. Becoming *yurndiri* is one of the most interesting of the many ways possible to make other people aware of one's distress. A few people who tend to be disagreeable much of the time are said to be permanently *yurndiri* and, in their case, this affliction is generally ignored. It is a natural condition among children and seems more common among men than women, especially in contexts of informal meetings and matters arising from ritual activities.

> It is midsummer, and a big meeting is ending. A full series of Ngaawayil rainmaking rituals has just finished, and about thirty men are gathered for the distribution of various items of rainmaking paraphernalia to members of different ritual status levels. Among these objects are some fifteen large pearlshells, presented to the Mardu Ngaawayil leaders by some northern visitors in return for hair belts and spears that had been given to their group at an earlier big meeting. The distribution is being carried out by men of the highest level of the Ngaawayil status hierarchy, and these eight elders discuss each shell and the likely recipients before making a final decision, whereupon the shell is formally presented.
>
> Didi was given a smallish shell; he sits slightly apart from the rest of the assembly, fingering the shell and seemingly muttering under his breath. Only two shells, large ones, remain to be presented, and it is clear that neither is meant for him. He suddenly stands

up, noisily grabs his several spears and boomerangs, and stalks off as rapidly as the soft sand of the large creekbed will allow him. A few men nudge one another, and a couple call out, "Didi! Come back! What's the matter?" But he pretends not to hear.

About eighty yards away, he turns, drops everything but his thrower and a single spear, which he loads and makes as if to throw in the direction of the men. He grabs a boomerang and makes as if to throw it, amid a chorus of shouts, "Leave it, leave it! Come back here and sit down!" Didi addresses them: "What about me? I've been a good man for this rainmaking; I worked hard; every time; you don't see me lying around in camp; I hunt, I sing, I keep the ritual going! No one thinks about me. I'm nothing, that's all. You're on your own next time around, you lot!" Having said his piece, Didi gathers up his gear and turns to walk away. The men shout back, "Old man! [*a term of respect, since Didi is in fact middle-aged*]. Don't be that way! Come back here. You're a good man for this business . . . everyone knows that. Don't be worried; come and sit down." Didi pauses, then slowly returns, to sit silently some twenty yards away, nervously pushing sand away from where he is sitting. There is a rapid, whispered consultation among the Ngaawayil leaders; one of them, Labayan, gets up and goes off to where his bundle of personal belongings is stored, in a tree fork on the creekbank. He takes one of his large shells, walks back and presents it to Didi, who appears quite satisfied and says nothing more.

The resort to *yurndiri* behavior signals that someone has a grievance which is upsetting them, and it focuses attention on them so that they can react by making their problem public. This action saves a person the great embarrassment of broaching the matter first. The Mardu, men and women, are extremely reluctant to address gatherings face to face, and most find it a painful ordeal. I once watched a man speak to a gathering of men with his head down, voice lowered, and his back to the circle for the entire duration of his lengthy speech. Some of the more outgoing and influential middle-aged and older men have less difficulty at such times, but public oratory is not highly valued. Most such gatherings typically begin with short speeches by two or three men proclaiming their complete ignorance of the matter about to be discussed! Appropriate verbal style in such situations is a quiet, self-effacing, and rather apologetic delivery, such that others will utter reassurances and words of encouragement, such as "No! Don't hold back; you're alright; that's a straight word you're giving us; we know you; you're a good man; go on; we need that good talk; keep on talking!" People are always heard out, and every effort is made to obtain consensus when decisions are being made at these *ad hoc* gatherings. However, what "consensus" really means is that those who have been arguing against the majority refrain from raising their objections publicly, so the matter may not be finally resolved at this point.

The marked reluctance of Mardu to deliver speeches to assemblies probably explains why so much airing of disputes among band members takes place at night. Each participant shouts from his or her camp, under the secure cover of darkness, and these exchanges can go on for hours. In the dark, people's confidence seems to increase, and the chances that weapons will be thrown if tempers fray are minimal. It is a memorable experience to sit in a camp in the middle of one of these sessions, surrounded by disembodied voices and wailing, yelping dogs, trying to identify the speakers and anticipate the drift of the conversations on a pitch black night relieved only by stars and the glow of small campfires. In a society whose members are scattered in small groups most of the time, much public "oratory" is confined to such occasions.

Violent conflict would be extremely disruptive in these normally closely knit bands, so there are strong pressures for upset people to keep the airing of grievances at a verbal level. Yet, particularly within domestic groups, a quick-tempered outburst may lead to blows being struck and, sometimes, women are severely beaten by their husbands. Verbal exchanges may prompt physical abuse when a woman swears at her husband and thus embarrasses him in front of other nearby families, who are certain to be watching and listening with intense interest. There is no such thing as a private altercation, but when a husband beats his wife, others are most reluctant to intervene regardless of their assessment of whether such action is justified. Close kin intercede to restrain a man only if he appears to be seriously injuring his wife. The superior rights of men in marriage are undisputed, but women can and do arm themselves and fight back.

> Bumana wanted to take Galidu, a young widow, as a second wife. Balu, Bumana's first and hitherto only wife, widely reputed to be a jealous woman, was incensed and threatened to leave him if he did so. She claimed that he had no right to the widow, since her elder brothers had not yet authorized her remarriage. One night during a big meeting, Bumana went and seized Galidu (who concurred) from her camp and took her back to his own. Balu delivered a withering verbal blast at them both, then stalked out of the camp. Bumana, angered by her jealous outburst, followed her and began beating her with a club. Although badly bruised on her neck and back, Balu managed to grab a club, with which she slammed Bumana across the shins, felling him like a stone. By the time he had hobbled back to his camp, Balu had sent Galidu on her way with several uncontested blows of the club, and there the matter ended.

For women to initiate physical attacks on their husbands is considered bad form. Such action earns them little in the way of community sympathy, regardless of their motives. A bad-tempered man who habitually mistreats his wife without good reason may prompt her "B" and "F" to intervene on her behalf. If he continues in spite of such warnings, she may leave him and go back to her own people, who are not then likely to force her to return to him. They may strongly suggest that she rejoin him, but can offer no guarantee that she will not run away again.

The Mardu say that fights between co-wives are uncommon because the older wife is "in charge of" the younger and should be obeyed. Yet when co-wives are close in age and when, as is often the case, a man favors one over the other as a sexual partner, jealousy may inflame passions and a fight erupts. Women fight each other with great violence at times, wielding clubs or digging sticks to inflict bloody scalp wounds, or else using hands and teeth as weapons. Although women's fights within or between families are usually regarded by the local community as less serious than men's, and are viewed in many cases as light entertainment by men, their ferocity may cause other women to intervene. If the altercation persists, men will shout at the combatants and order them to desist, only to be ignored by the women until physical intervention occurs. Perhaps even more than their menfolk, Mardu women show a remarkable capacity to drop the matter once the air is cleared. On several occasions, I have seen women relaxed and chatting amiably together who still bore bloodstains from wounds inflicted on each other a day or two before.

There are many fewer conventions covering female than male conflicts. The most notable is the requirement that a woman who is clearly at fault must bow her head and accept the first blow uncontested. She thus admits guilt and offers "satisfaction" to her opponent, regardless of who actually fares better in the club fight that ensues. The only men's weapons that women are permitted to use in fights are clubs. A young woman who commits the serious offense of having sexual intercourse deemed incestuous in terms of the kinship system must bear almost the entire burden of blame. She stands alone and faces the savage attack of the young man's "M" and "Z."

> Binya, a young woman in her late teens, took the opportunity of a big meeting assembly to renew an affair of a few years earlier with Jimin, a bachelor in his early twenties, and her distant "S," an incestuous relationship in Mardu terms. Caught once, the couple was loudly berated by both sets of close kin, but they persisted and were discovered a second time within a week. They ran away into the bush but finally returned to the camping area just before dusk of the same day. Jimin's "MZ," seeing Binya's approach, picked up a large stone and ran at her, hitting her on the head with such force that she sank to her knees. She got up, blood streaming down her face, but made no effort to resist as five or six of Jimin's "M" and "EZ" beat her with clubs and fists, while screaming abuse: "You rotten little bitch; you're an animal, you copulate with your own son; you're hungry for penis, any penis, even your own family's; you have no shame; we'll kill you for this; you're mad!" Only after she had been severely beaten and deeply shamed did her mother and "Z" go and drag her away from the frenzied, screaming attackers.

The sheer ferocity of such attacks is understandable when the seriousness of such affronts to social stability and the Law is considered. Regardless of genealogical distance, for a "mother" and her "son" to behave like this threatens the entire structure of kinship and social categories, and such excesses cannot be tolerated.

When men fight each other, the unstated aim of the many conventions surrounding their conflicts is to allow maximum opportunity for the dispute to be aired verbally. This takes place in an atmosphere of great public drama and menace, so that honor is seen to be satisfied, but with a minimum of physical violence. The pronounced ritualization of such conflicts is evidenced by the ability of both observer and actors to predict the sequence of events in many cases. However, the unexpected often occurs.

> Old Bimulyara had for some time barely tolerated the obvious interest that Magun, a distant bachelor "B" was showing in Bimulyara's favorite wife, Damuji. One day when Magun refused to move away from Bimulyara's camp, the old man flew into a rage and called him all the insulting names he could think of. Humiliated, Magun immediately called Bimulyara out for a fight, and both men armed themselves. Magun chose only to rattle his spears and shout, since he knew his case, as an outsider who had joined the band to spend time hunting for his future in-laws (his betrothed was still a child), was a weak one. The old man threw two spears at him, and he easily dodged them both. Jadajada, the father of Magun's betrothed, threw one spear in his direction, but only as a token gesture calling for an end to the conflict. Meanwhile, Damuji, the wife who had been having an affair with Magun, was attacked by Majal, her "FZ," for allegedly causing the trouble. The two women exchanged several hard blows. Then Gidu, Majal's brother, threw two

boomerangs in the direction of old Bimulyara, because Bimulyara's wife had just injured his sister.

Virtually all the events to this stage were predictable in some measure. However. . . .

> Gidu's second boomerang, thrown short so as to bounce high and clear Bimulyara by a wide margin, did so and was caught by the wind. It whizzed back into a fleeing group of spectators and sliced into the scalp of Babagada, a tough old woman with an iron constitution and an incredibly sharp tongue.
>
> Outraged, Babagada snatched up a club and ran headlong at her "YB," Gidu, cursing him en route then belaboring him about the shoulders and back with the club while he stood, very shame-faced, and accepted the blows. The original conflict was by now forgotten, as Babagada's daughter's husband Wilyan suddenly entered the arena in support of his "WM," who, by this time, had been pushed to the ground by Gidu, who had decided that she had punished him enough. Wilyan sank his jabbing spear deep into Gidu's thigh. No further heavy blows were struck after this because of the many men and women who milled around and separated all the combatants.

Another event that frequently changes the course of a hitherto controlled encounter is when some man who has been quietly watching suddenly becomes enraged by something that is said, or by what he considers to be an unwarranted intrusion of someone who is supporting one combatant against the other. He snatches up his weapons, dashes into the open area (where most fights take place, away from campsites a little), and launches a couple of boomerangs and a spear before the surprised onlookers can run and hold him back. His supportive stance, called *burndurrini* (standing up for/taking the place of), can lead to a rapid escalation of a fight—especially if other men consider his intervention unwarranted, perhaps a mere excuse to air some personal grievance against one of the original combatants or their active supporters.

Whatever has prompted the violence, many spectators intervene to separate the fighters and prevent them from launching weapons, so as to bring the conflict back to a verbal level. As noted earlier, women play a crucial role in physically restraining men. They dislodge spears from throwers with sticks or hands, snatch boomerangs and clubs and throw them away, and cling firmly onto the men. It is a common sight during fights to see a man vainly trying to shake off two or three women, dragging them along the ground, kicking and hitting at them but quite unable to free himself. Perhaps one important reason why men are forbidden to fight during secret-sacred activities is the absence of women (in addition to the fear of upsetting spiritual powers). Without the most often restraining and calming influence of women, men might have to put their weapons where their mouths are, so to speak, with doubtless bloodier and more dangerous consequences. Women are equally capable of inciting men to violence in certain disputes. Older women, especially, sometimes break into a side-skipping dance and accompanying shouting that are highly inflammatory—an emotional and fervent encouragement to violent conflict. Women's primary roles, though, are to restore calm so that more reasoned resolution of disputes can be achieved.

Given the closeness of the kinship links involved, there are usually interested third parties among the men, and they too endeavor to bring conflict quickly to an end. They help ensure that both parties obtain a measure of "satisfaction" from it, signaled by a mutual willingness to say so, or at least to engage in a ritualized exchange as final settlement. This exchange can take the form of a penis-holding rite, gifts, temporary bestowal of sexual rights to their women or, after a serious dispute (for example, a spear fight between two full brothers), the cutting, carving, and exchange of sacred boards. If one man is clearly in the wrong, he must carve the board or boards cut and shaped by the offended party.

When a dispute arises from an obvious or admitted offense, the wronged person obtains satisfaction from the exposure of the offense to public notice and the punishment and group censure of the offender. In fact, very few transgressions can remain private in this society, where the ground can be read like a book, and gossip is a common and acceptable practice. A Lawbreaker has the option of removing himself from the band for a time, but this act may not resolve the problem; instead, it may only prolong dissatisfaction until an inevitable confrontation some time later. A prudent withdrawal may, however, increase the chances that the ultimate clash will be less physical than it would otherwise have been. Perhaps the fear of sorcery or of revenge expeditions prompts most Mardu to stay and confront the problem. The worst an offender can expect under normal circumstances will be a clubbing and some spear thrusts at his thighs. The multiple spear wound scars that every mature Mardu man and woman carry (and dismiss as of no account) attest to the popularity of this form of punishment. The jabbing spear is favored because it can be guided precisely to its target, whereas thrown missiles are far less accurately delivered. Throwing spears are rarely aimed at the upper body, since their use against people is intended to wound, not kill.

When there is no clear offense or admission of guilt by either party to a dispute, both are likely to derive satisfaction from a conviction that they got the better of the other or that community sentiment favored them rather than the other. A rapid and relatively bloodless clearing of the air defuses tensions while providing an exciting and diverting interlude in people's lives. The seeming disinclination of the Mardu to bear grudges or harbor smoldering resentment rests in large part on their many conflict-management conventions. These operate to bring about a "good feeling in the stomachs" of the principals, a sense of satisfaction, vindication, or finality that endures long past the immediate aftermath and survives the test of later calm reflection.

In all conflicts, regardless of scale, circumstance, or particular idiosyncrasy, the various roles played by those present—and the extent of their involvement or avoidance—have much to do with kinship, as was noted in Chapter 3. Depending upon their kinship relationship to the combatants, there are those who should chastise, who restrain, who substitute for and defend, who inflame, who appeal to reason and calm, and so on. For example, if a person is so enraged that he persists in attempting violence and refuses to calm down, drastic action may be called for. A man who is *manggalyi* (initiator) or a *wumari* (wife's mother)—if either is present at the time—may enter the fray to confront and even touch him. This action, unthinkable in normal life because the relationships concerned are of strong avoidance, should so shame the man that he comes to his senses and calms down immediately.

For the outsider, a knowledge of the kin relationships of those involved in a fight generally proves to be a reliable guide. But in the heat of the moment people may forget or ignore kinship norms. In this case, prediction of their likely behavior is based less on kinship than on a knowledge of their personalities and of how they react under aggravation and stress. Information of this kind is stored in each person's biographical "file" of all others with whom he or she interacts at some stage in the normal course of life.

In other words, the kinship system is indeed a fairly reliable guide to expected behavior, but it is no straitjacket. Nevertheless, if the gulf between Aboriginal kinship norms and actual behavior were compared crossculturally, it would appear to be narrower than in most other human societies. The notable closeness of fit is attributable to the small scale of Aboriginal society, its marked stability, and the undisputed primacy of kinship statuses.

In terms of the ideal values outlined above, it is evident that in everyday life most Mardu display them in abundance—unselfishness, an unquestioning willingness to provide and care for relatives, affection for children, behaviors favoring cooperation over conflict, and a quiet unassuming manner devoid of public boastfulness or egotism that intrudes upon others. Also characteristic are a gregariousness, a love of animated discussion and repartee, and a keen interest in what transpires in all dimensions—social, natural, and spiritual—of their cosmic order. Above all, most Mardu face the world with a sense of humor which is rarely suppressed and a readiness to laugh uproariously at themselves and others alike.

Circumspection and restraint are of course present in dealings with certain categories of kin, but there are plenty of other kin with whom humor can be generated and enjoyed. The superb skills of mimicry that facilitate their hunting activities are put to humorous theatrical use in parodying the mannerisms and characteristics of their fellows. The more extroverted comics sometimes reduce their audience to helplessness with devastatingly accurate, but cunningly exaggerated, renditions of someone's peculiar gait or voice. Or they may suddenly jump up and act out the parts in a story they are telling which involves people known to their listeners. Should a target of this humor happen to be present, he or she is expected to take it in good fun and share in the enjoyment of the occasion. Personal afflictions—a limp, deafness, blindness, erratic behavior—are also parodied, in what might be branded sick humor in some other cultures. Among the desert people, however, such afflictions are facts of life that are often used as labels, both as terms of address and reference; a crippled person may be addressed as *mugundu* (lame, cripple), a blind person as *bamburu*, and so on, with no insult intended or taken. Certainly no attempt is made to pretend that such conditions do not exist or to shun people because of them.

The fact that people can maintain such a spirited and positive outlook in an environment as tough and uncertain as the desert speaks volumes for their strength of character and their great confidence in the Dreaming and the Law, which answers life's biggest questions and attests that the human spirit is invincible. It is conceivable that jollity, warmth, and ready laughter are really only masks hiding some inner pain or insecurity, but if so, such distress has remained remarkably impervious to the scrutiny of outside observers of the desert people. In this respect Aborigines are like most other hunters and gatherers, whose traditional worldview has struck many anthropologists as basically optimistic and life-affirming.

There is no concept of suicide among the Mardu, nor any evidence of warfare, sexual perversions (bestiality, child molestation, and such), vandalism, or cannibalism. Theft and murder are both rare occurrences. As noted above, there is anger, spite, jealousy, violence, and cruelty at times, to name some of the negative aspects of life. Yet the magnitude of the absent evils seems to be far greater than that of the problems that are sometimes present. Above all, the Mardu respect the individual, and their society allows ample recognition of the uniqueness of each person.

As Burridge (1973) notes, the self-same elements in kinship, totemism, social groupings, and social categories that unify and incorporate the individual with others operate simultaneously to differentiate, separate out, individualize, and make unique that person. The individual thus represents an amalgam of statuses that is like no others in its entirety, yet shares every constituent element with certain other people.

For young men, there is also the profound reinforcement of their individuality during circumcision, when they become the focus of attention and the *raison-d' etre* of the entire big meeting. True, their sudden and drastic entry into the life of men entails uncertainty, fear and even trauma, so they must sometimes feel humbled. Yet they surely cannot help realizing that all this is for them, and that for a time they are the center of the Mardu social universe.

It is true that individuals are denied authorship of their own creativity in favor of spirit-beings as the fount of all power and knowledge. This restriction would seem to be an affront to individualism and a major blow to the ego, but such is the nature of Mardu worldview that great advantages can be gained by having human beings submit to a larger spiritual purpose. As individuals or members of groups, people are not passive receptors of the Dreaming legacy, but must actively fulfill their part of the bargain if the design for life is to be forever replicated. Passive obedience there must be, but it is never enough. Through ritual activity, those who hold the key to communication with the spiritual realm share a great responsibility for maintaining the fertility of the human and natural worlds.

Mardu men accord themselves greater ritual responsibility, higher status, more power, and more rights than women. It is a society in which male interests generally prevail when rights are contested and in the centrally important arena of religious life. As in most societies, however, there is a discrepancy between ideology and reality, between *de jure* power and *de facto* influence. Thus, no unbiased observer could fail to see the important roles that Mardu women play in the affairs of the family and band, despite their exclusion from the secret rituals of the men. They, as a group, accept their situation, assured in the knowledge that their contributions as child-bearers, providers, partners, and religious actors are vital and that the Dreaming validates their place in society.

CONTESTING THE DREAM

"Living the dream," as described in this chapter and throughout those preceding it, refers to an age-old acting out of the spiritual imperatives of the Law, when Australia was the exclusive and huge domain of a single people, the Aborigines, who followed basically the same mode of adaptation for many millennia. The

Papuan and Macassan adventurers who "discovered" the north coast prior to the European invasion left their mark, but no immigrant communities, for their homes were elsewhere, and the wish to return was obviously compelling. Their transitory presence caused no ripples in the surface of Western Desert societies far to the south and, for a long time after the European invasion began in earnest in southeastern Australia, no hint of that invasion was given to the desert people. Inexorably, though, the whites spread across the continent, even into the forbidding interior, challenging "the dream" and forcing Aboriginal societies into totally unprecedented dealings with them. The invaders dislodged the indigenous people from a position of certainty and control at the center of their desert universe, relocating them structurally, then physically, on the wretched margins of a powerful and unyielding Western society.

The next, and final, chapter outlines the main features of this momentous one-way journey that has taken the Mardu into a world which contests their Dreaming-derived certainties every day and demands from them an unceasing accommodation to forces more powerful than themselves. All that has been described in this study now switches to the past tense, because the Mardu dream has, decades since, been caught in the web of a larger social and cultural order—the nation-state of Australia.

The fact remains, however, that no full understanding of contemporary Mardu life is possible without an appreciation of how "traditional" elements have continued to shape Mardu reactions. The Law has provided them with the strength of purpose to manage the huge transformation that has taken place as a result of their adoption of a sedentary lifestyle under white domination. For this reason, the final chapter is concerned as much with continuities as with change in describing how two cultural systems remain locked in a struggle whose outcome will decide the fate of the Mardu as a distinct cultural minority in Australian society.

7 / Europeans and the Mardu Response: 1900–1990

Until only a century ago, the Mardu were the undisturbed owner-occupiers of a vast desert domain, unaware that there was anyone else on earth except for shadowy "strangers," potentially hostile but incorporable via the limitless web of kinship. Yet even strangers were nonetheless *mardu,* a label that, in its most inclusive sense, meant "human being." Significantly, the European invaders whose coming shattered Aboriginal autonomy and the certainty of life under the Dreaming were never called *mardu,* being so different in appearance and behavior that they had to be placed in a separate category—eventually conceded as human, yes, but Aboriginal, never. The reaction of the Mardu to this unfathomable phenomenon, for which their Dreaming master plan had allowed no place whatsoever, was to situate the newcomers outside their moral universe and thus separate the two groups into distinct domains of power, whose boundary was so much clearer and less permeable than any they had hitherto known. The Mardu understood well the origin, nature, and workings of power emanating from the spiritual realm of the Dreaming, but had no explanation for that which accompanied the whites and emanated from various possible sources, such as "the government" or "God." Their Law offered no strategies for the understanding or control of the behavior of the aliens, so, to them, it stood "outside the Dreaming." In relating what has happened to the Mardu since first contacts occurred with whites, I use their attempts to sustain the Mardu-"Whitefella" dichotomy as a conceptual focus in analyzing accommodation and change.

This account of post-contact change and contemporary Mardu life is focused mainly on the community of Jigalong, where most of the Mardu eventually settled after leaving the desert.[1] Today Jigalong is a community of between 250–300 Mardu and a dozen or so whites. Once quite remote and isolated, it is now only a hundred miles by dirt road from the massive iron-ore mining operation and town of Newman, where in 1990 about eight thousand whites live (see Maps 1 and 2). This chapter follows a roughly chronological sequence in discussing notable phases in the transformation of Mardu society: migration and the end of nomadism; the pastoral frontier; the mission era; community incorporation and "self-management;" the mining challenge and the outstation response; and the present situation. Interwoven with these phases is an assessment of the successes and failures of Mardu adaptive strategies in a period of accelerating change.

---

[1]The history, evolution, and structure of this community are detailed in Tonkinson (1974), a study of post-contact changes centering on the mission era and tracing developments into the early 1970s.

ABORIGINAL MIGRATION AND THE FRONTIER

As noted in Chapter 2, early European exploration of the desert produced such negativity among those who survived the ordeal that no attempts were made to settle there. Safely ensconced in their forbidding land, the Western Desert people were never overrun by whites and were thus spared the terrible fate that overtook many other Aborigines, especially in the more fertile and accessible southern regions where the European invasion quickly took its toll through disease, mistreatment, and a shattering of spirit. A century or more after many Aboriginal groups had all but vanished, Western Desert societies were still thriving. The Mardu thus had time to become aware that their isolation had been breached and to adjust to the realization that theirs was not the only culture in the world. The desert remained uncolonized, but the spread of the pastoral frontier from the west eventually took it to within fifty miles of Mardu territories, and the building of a stock route through the center of their land brought them to a greater awareness of the intrusion of a powerful new "other" into their social universe.

First contacts between Mardu groups and the early explorers were mostly brief and non-lethal, but some Aborigines suffered violence at the hands of the parties of whites who between 1906 and 1909 surveyed and built the Canning Stock Route (Map 2). This thousand-mile chain of wells connected northern pastoral areas to the railhead at Wiluna. Its subsequent use by drovers was rare, but the wells—many of them dug in established Mardu water sources—were used by the Aborigines. The route itself later became a kind of funnel for their north-south movement and eventually for an exodus to settled fringe areas. There was no forced removal of the Aborigines, but the erosion of their freedom to choose whether or not they wished to initiate or maintain contact with the whites was beginning, and the invasion of the desert by introduced animals must have begun affecting their food resources. Their ensuing exodus stemmed from a combination of these disturbances and led eventually to the physical abandonment of their homelands, but without severing their emotional and spiritual ties. Although it appears that, initially, curiosity was an important motive for contact, in hard times the attraction of the whites' food and water must have been strong. Among some of the last immigrants, fear of Aboriginal revenge expeditions was cited as a motivating factor, in addition to the more commonly expressed desire to be reunited with close kin in the settlements. The last of the Mardu left in the mid-1960s and, for the first time in millennia the desert proper was empty—but not for long.[2]

The majority of Mardu headed westward, and many of them eventually came to identify Jigalong as their new home. It had come into being as a maintenance depot and camel-breeding center on the No. 1 Rabbit Proof Fence (completed in 1907 in a futile attempt to stem the spread of these introduced animals, which quickly

---

[2]The last two Mardu still living a "traditional" nomadic life were rescued from a soak in drought-stricken Manyjilyjarra country east of Lake Disappointment at the end of September 1977. Wari and his "wife" Yadungga had remained in the homeland long after their relatives left, because they were wrongly married and feared punishment, according to the Mardu from Wiluna who successfully located them. Their discovery was accorded widespread coverage in the Australian media, under headlines such as "Last of the Desert Men" and "The End of a Way of Life" (*The West Australian,* October 4, 1977).

multiplied to plague proportions). Jigalong was not the first point of contact for most Mardu, however, since a few outlying pastoral leases were situated along the most traveled route in from the desert. At these places, the initial contact pattern was of periodic brief sojourns, followed by a return to the old nomadic life; but it was eventually reversed to a more settled existence punctuated by brief returns to the desert heartlands. This major transition was caused by a subtle process whose implications could never have been sensed by the Mardu: the link between increasing involvement with, and a growing dependence on, an alien economy. They had rapidly acquired a strong desire for tea, flour, twist tobacco, and sugar—as several Mardu have described it, "We were captured by flour and sugar" (Ken Lance, personal communication). Also eagerly sought were iron and steel tools, flints, and other useful and portable material items. In exchange for such objects and food-stuffs, the Mardu had their labor potential and sexual access to their women to offer the frontiersmen, who, as bachelors living in lonely isolation, had strong desires for both.[3]

The frontier in the pastoral areas west of Mardu country was predominantly peaceful. Although the few whites had superior weaponry, their ability to retain their Aboriginal labor, especially in the early years, depended on the maintenance of amicable relationships; ill-treatment was reacted to with violence, or more commonly, the overnight disappearance of the entire Aboriginal workforce. As more and more Aborigines were displaced by pastoral activities, or were forced in off the desert in bad times, their care and sustenance became a problem for the state government. It instituted a system of "rations," regular issues to "indigents" of what by this time had become staples—tea, sugar, flour, and tobacco. There were also periodic allotments of blankets and clothing. Wherever it was still possible, Aborigines supplemented European foods by hunting game and collecting bush foods. Men mastered the skills of stock work and did menial tasks such as wood-chopping. Many young women became domestics, whose privileged access to the homestead and intimate relationships with white pastoralists advantaged them in unprecedented ways.[4] Many became better English speakers than their menfolk and came to occupy a mediating role between the two groups of men. Sexual use of Mardu women was common, but abuse provoked risks of retaliation by their male kin and the loss of the Aboriginal labor force at that station (the Australian term for ranch).

The Jigalong maintenance depot, which was staffed by two bachelors, attracted local Aborigines and so became a ration point with food and other items being issued in return for casual work by able-bodied men and women. Most of the Nyiyabarli, who were the traditional inhabitants of the Jigalong area, had already drifted to sheep and cattle stations further west when Mardu began to arrive at Jigalong in the 1930s. As elsewhere, there was still high mobility between Jigalong, surrounding stations, and the desert, but as further groups of desert immigrants arrived, a more settled community of Mardu was taking shape. Virtually the only

---

[3]Some pastoralists (ranchers) traded food, tools, and so on for dingo scalps, on which the state government paid bounties. Dingoes were declared vermin because they were suspected of attacking sheep and cattle.

[4]For an account of the changing status of Mardu women from traditional to contemporary times, see Tonkinson (1990).

whites they were encountering were rough-and-ready frontiersmen, who drank, smoked, swore, and sought Aboriginal women as sexual partners; such men provided Mardu with their initial images of the aliens.

THE MISSION ERA: 1946–1969

Jigalong became a mission station when, following the closure of the maintenance depot in 1945, the state government offered the site to a Protestant group which had been searching for somewhere to minister to the spiritual and material needs of desert Aborigines. In its quarter century of life, the mission failed to become a viable concern evangelically or economically and, much of the time, the situation was one of unstable accommodation marked by considerable tension between the two sides. At Jigalong, the gulf between typical European frontier values and behaviors and those of the fundamentalist missionaries who came upon the scene much later was so great that the Aborigines put them into a category all their own—"Christians," as distinct from "Whitefellas." As with the pastoralists, the situation entailed inequalities of power generally favoring the whites, but also mutual exploitation. Many of the Mardu worked for the missionaries and, in return, they received food and other rations and were left with much free time. Unlike the "Whitefellas," however, the "Christians" placed the children and teenage girls in dormitories under close supervision and attempted to make converts of them. They encouraged them to reject their own culture, which to the fundamentalists was entirely the work of Satan and so had to be destroyed if the desired Baptism of the Holy Spirit were to occur. Thus were the battle lines drawn, but at least two factors favored the whites: their superior political power, sanctioned by government laws and manifest in the seemingly almighty police, and the fact that the Aborigines had become heavily dependent on the rations and other services provided by whites, weakening their resolve to return to a more arduous existence in the desert. Also, a younger generation was emerging for whom Jigalong, not the desert proper, was "home," their primary locus of attachment.

On the positive side, rarely was there any direct intervention in the domain of the camp by missionaries or other agents of the dominating society to suppress or ban aspects of Mardu culture that they opposed.[5] The missionaries were greatly outnumbered and were faced with a people they knew to be capable of violence, so despite their great desire to destroy the Law, they were reluctant to intervene physically to break up ritual activities, and they lacked the language skills for effective communication with the Mardu. The missionaries thus failed to foment rebellion by the young against their elders or to abolish polygyny or replace Aboriginal religion and the Law with Christian doctrine. In twenty-five years, they gained only one committed convert, but they did manage to plant at least the seeds of Christian belief in some of the dormitory children. Ironically, through mandatory

---

[5]The dormitories and school were a different matter, and there the interference was overt and sometimes violent; for example, children were regularly beaten for "speaking language" instead of English and were subject to all sorts of controls alien to Aboriginal society (Tonkinson 1974).

issues of rations (and, from 1960, payment of Social Security benefits) and provision of food and clothing, the Jigalong missionaries inadvertently promoted the Law. The Mission made it possible for a large, stable community to exist and provided its Mardu residents with sufficient leisure time to maintain an active religious life. The co-residence of members of once scattered groups led to a pooling of religious knowledge and an intensification of traditional ritual activity. What hitherto had been possible to achieve only periodically, namely optimum conditions for the "big meeting," was now almost perennially available. The only inhibiting factor was that most of the young and middle-aged men, who had developed a range of "cowboy" skills, including excellent horsemanship, spent several months a year working on pastoral leases in surrounding areas. However, their return was guaranteed because, in most cases, their wives, children, and older relatives lived at Jigalong. There, the elders acted as caretakers and organizers of ritual activity, which was carried on intermittently throughout the year. Every summer, the slack time on stations when the Aboriginal labor force was laid off, the workers returned to Jigalong to help the community plan and stage a big meeting and organize trips by large numbers of men, women, and children to attend similar functions in neighboring centers.

During this era, whether they were living at the Mission or on pastoral properties, the Mardu maintained a strict conceptual separation of the two domains of power. This dichotomy was symbolized by the settlement (*maya* meaning "house"), the locus of white power, control, and dominance, and the *ngurra* (camp, home), which the Mardu maintained as bounded Aboriginal space and not a legitimate domain for the exercise of white control (Tonkinson 1982, 1988b). Whites, of course, played their part in this separation by maintaining social distance and staying away from Aboriginal camps, while, as a rule, allowing only Aboriginal women to enter their own dwellings. The missionaries were masters in the domain of the *maya*, and Mardu rarely disputed their rights there, which included all bureaucratic dealings with the outside world on behalf of the Aborigines. At the Mission, extreme paternalism was routine, and the Mardu were never consulted in such matters; nor did they challenge this dominance which they perceived as legitimately "Whitefella business," squarely located in the other domain. These concessions were, after all, a recognition of the superior power of the whites in the new situation but, more significantly, they were considered trivial in comparison to the central concern of the Mardu: maintenance of an internal autonomy, the treasured right to conduct their own political, social and religious affairs free from overt outside interference. The primary Mardu aim was to protect the basic integrity of their Law by keeping the whites at bay, while continuing to socialize their young into the values and behaviors of the Law. During the mission era, the Mardu were largely successful in this vital aim, while at the same time coping with a host of unprecedented changes.

In the first place, sedentarization meant a total transformation of their local organization and economy. The band disappeared, and the constituent families and their descendants were now living in communities of a size formerly attained only temporarily, if at all. Their greatest freedom, the mobility that enabled people to defuse conflict by withdrawal, was now reduced (the missionaries, some of whose government funding was tied to Aboriginal numbers, were opposed to the movement of women and children out of Jigalong). With sedentarization and a changed diet, plus Western medical care, a population explosion began and created a new demographic situation and new problems. The society was rapidly becoming younger, but lacked mechanisms for controling the activities of large groups of children. Fortunately, the Aborigines who congregated at settlements like Jigalong shared a great deal as members of the same cultural bloc—notably, language, kinship and marriage systems, much of their religion, and virtually the same Law. Yet the many small differences among the various Mardu groups did not simply melt away once they had all come together at Jigalong; different groups situated their camps in a re-creation of their traditional directional orientation. After deaths, suspicions of sorcery were often aroused—and sometimes aired—between the earlier arrived Gardujarra (and closely related southern groups) and the later arriving northerners, the Manyjilyjarra (see Map 2). Even today this "northerner-southerner" division is sometimes invoked in the community. However, the experience of living together and the close cooperation entailed in the organization of the religious life, plus increasing intermarriage and friendships, prevented any hardening of boundaries among the various language-named units represented at Jigalong. By the 1960s, a new kind of solidarity had been forged, expressed in the use of the term "Jigalong mob" by its Mardu inhabitants to distinguish themselves as a community from Aborigines elsewhere. This form of self-reference contrasted them favorably against other community-based "mobs." They claimed greater conformity to the Law and a more steadfast commitment to tradition, especially in the realm of ritual responsibility and performance.

Intra-community relations were aided by the fact that none of the immigrant groups owned the territory within which Jigalong was located, its Nyiyabarli owners having vacated it after an amicable ritual transfer of responsibility for the land to the collectivity of the immigrants. Thus, there was no one estate group that could command the role of permanent host and attempt to sustain the kind of asymmetries in rights and powers that would inevitably lead to resentment and strife. The mingling of Nyiyabarli sacra with those of the immigrants created a new, hybrid *yinda* (main place) that gave all of them shared proprietary rights and guardianship responsibilities for the Jigalong region.

Despite the emergence of this new form of parochialism, the powerful bonds of a shared culture continued to overshadow it as each community linked with the many others scattered around the desert periphery. The traditional tendency to conceive of an almost limitless desert society persisted, and social horizons were considerably widened by improved communicative networks that arose after contact. Everyone had close kin, many allies, and friends in neighboring communities. Inter-community mobility has remained at a high level, with informal visits, formal visits for big meetings, and the Law still taking precedence over "Whitefella business" of whatever kind. Considerable mobility was thus maintained, but by vehicles enabling large groups to cover long distances in relatively short times, despite frequent breakdowns en route. Big meetings now sometimes include visitors from many hundreds of miles away—from groups which may never have met in precontact times. Youths are sometimes flown across the desert in chartered planes to be circumcised at these gatherings.

Once they had settled, the Mardu were constantly forced to adjust their behaviors and expectations in all manner of ways. They adopted clothing, entered a rations economy which later became increasingly cash oriented, subsisted largely on bought foods, put their children in schools, gambled with cards as a major leisure activity, used clinic and hospital facilities, hunted with rifles, made increasing use of motor vehicles, and so on. Yet, these changes were, for the most part, viewed by the Mardu as largely peripheral to the important things in life and therefore easily coped with. They retained a basic tradition orientation and saw their situation more in terms of continuities with the past than disruptive or irrevocable change. The Mardu were able to maintain their most highly valued norms and behaviors: the kinship system and associated behaviors; the religious life, exemplified in ritual and initiatory activities; and intercommunity cultural diffusion. The missionaries took care of certain basic needs and, together with the government teachers, kept Mardu children well under control, thus enabling the elders to devote more time to the important task of maintaining the Law.

By the end of the 1960s, the population of Jigalong had risen to 350. This trend accelerated after 1968 when, following the extension of award wages provisions to Aboriginal workers in the pastoral industry, most were laid off. At the mission, both sides continued to maintain their standoff, each feeding on negative stereotypes of the other but for different reasons. The missionaries used the "irredeemably sinful character" of the Aborigines as an excuse for their continuing failure to gain converts, while still soliciting support from their church; while the Aborigines exploited the Christians' ignorance of Mardu culture and of much that went on in the Aboriginal domain to maintain a strong boundary between themselves and the whites. Decreasing outside support and chronic staff problems plagued the mission and, even before it finally ceased operations at the end of 1969, it was forced to abandon the dormitory system and surrender its tight control over Social Security payments (pensions, child allowances, and so on) to the Mardu recipients. This lessening of paternalism came at a time when important changes occurred on the national scene that were to have considerable consequences for all of Aboriginal Australia.

THE RISE OF ABORIGINAL SELF-MANAGEMENT

By the beginning of the 1970s, the tempo of change in Aboriginal affairs was quickening at an unprecedented rate. A booming national economy that had left Aborigines marginalized and neglected as it raised the living standards of the white majority aroused the consciousness of many Australians. Unspoken assumptions about the rights of the British colonists to dispossess and trample on the indigenous minority, without treaty or compensation of any kind, were being called into question more effectively. Among Aborigines, particularly in the major cities and towns of Australia, black political consciousness and action were galvanized;

loud protests and reminders of a long and continuing history of injustice were receiving considerable media coverage. Implicitly racist policies of assimilation or cultural absorption came under increasing attack, and most state governments moved to dismantle restrictive legislation affecting Aborigines. A 1967 national referendum gave the federal government the right to legislate nationally in all matters affecting Aboriginal people and allowed for the establishment of a Federal Department of Aboriginal Affairs which was to play an increasingly major role in the implementation of new policies in such fields as community development, health, and housing.

The Mardu were far removed from the mainstream of this altered consciousness, but their isolation was decreasing. Following four years of stagnation and uncertainty after the mission ceased operations, a new era suddenly began. The catalyst had been the election of a Federal Labor Government in 1972, the implementation of its policy of Aboriginal self-determination, and a large infusion of funds into the Department of Aboriginal Affairs. These changes began to affect Jigalong when, at the urging of government officials, it became a legally incorporated Aboriginal community in October, 1973. The Mardu populace elected an eight-member Aboriginal council, initially all-male but later augmented in number, with women also gaining representation. The new policies dictated that the council would assume control and responsibility for much of its everyday functioning and would set its own developmental priorities. It received government grants for its capital and operating expenses, but the Department of Aboriginal Affairs hoped that a substantial income could be derived in later years from the expansion of cattle-raising activities. Such income has, in most years, constituted only a fraction of Jigalong's expenditure on maintenance and development, and the community has continued to rely very heavily on governmental financial assistance in order to continue functioning.

The Mardu were suddenly catapulted from a situation of total paternalism with respect to bureaucratic dealings with the outside world to one which demanded that they assume responsibility for both these outside concerns and the management of the community. They were totally unprepared for such a challenge yet had no alternative but to accept it. Having jealously guarded their relative autonomy in major matters relating to the Law, the Mardu were now faced with a measure of *de jure* responsibility for what they had hitherto safely consigned to the missionaries as "Whitefella" business. Most of the councilors were men of little if any formal education, and their understanding of the complexities of white society was, at best, limited. For these reasons, they relied heavily on the integrity and judgment of their white advisors who thus had considerable *de facto* power. Moreover, bureaucratic decisions concerning fund allocations and spending priorities, taken at government level, militated against the realization of local autonomy and Aboriginal self-regulation.[6]

Although, for the first time, the Mardu were being consulted as to their priorities

---

[6]For a discussion of the disparity between government policy and practice at Jigalong, see Tonkinson (1977, 1978a, 1979); at the national level, see Tonkinson and Howard (1990). Contributors to the 1990 volume also address issues relating to Aboriginal self-management, but primarily at the community level.

and wishes, and had new powers such as the right to dismiss white staff in their employ, what they most wanted was for these whites to take responsibility for a variety of problems whose existence hitherto had been masked by the presence of the missionaries, but were now emerging full-blown. Still clinging to what they saw as a protective dichotomy between the domains of the Aboriginal camp and the white settlement, the Mardu were reluctant to accept the notion that the white settlement was now *Mardu* property and *Mardu* space and that, under the new policies, *they* were responsible for the care and upkeep of much of that domain (except for government-run services such as health and education) and its transactions with the wider society. They tried with little success to persuade white staff to assume the old-style paternalistic mantle and deal with intractable, nontraditional problems of vandalism, unruly children, drunkenness, and its associated violence. Little wonder that a certain nostalgia arose for the mission era, when children were tightly disciplined, no alcohol was allowed at Jigalong, and the Mardu were not constantly being asked to deal with problems that had never existed in the desert.

The Mardu response to attempts to get them to fuse the two domains was to burden their councilors with responsibility for handling "Whitefella business," with whatever assistance they could muster from white staff, and to confine it as much as possible to the *maya* (mission/settlement) domain. For a time, this strategy for protecting the internal concerns of the Law from "Whitefella business" worked well enough, but the pressures operating to dissolve the dichotomy have been relentless as the encapsulating society has intensified its invasion of all aspects of Mardu life. Elections for the council were held annually, with a large turnover of membership. Short membership tenure was guaranteed by the tendency of the Mardu to blame their councilors for failure to solve increasingly serious community problems; besides, councilors have little chance to gain access to significant resources in terms of money or influence. Councilors, and particularly council chairpersons, are in a no-win situation as "bosses." Being designated as authority figures, they are expected to be nurturing and attentive to community needs, but are criticized and rejected if they try to contravene the egalitarian ethos by "bossing" people around in the course of addressing the problems that their electorate urges them to solve (cf. Myers 1982). Their typical reaction is to be embarrassed, then angry, and then to resign from the council.

The 1970s and 1980s saw large capital expenditure on basic community infrastructure, particularly in the areas of housing, power, and water supplies. Conditions for white residents improved enormously, and Jigalong became much less of a hardship post for them. Yet only a small fraction of developmental funding was of direct material benefit to the Mardu inhabitants, some of whom in 1990 continue to live in makeshift shelters of iron, canvas, and bushes, in generally unhygienic conditions. People have remained heavily dependent on Social Security income. For a long time, the community rejected the receipt of unemployment benefits—which the Mardu refer to as "sit down money"—but, in 1984, Jigalong joined a scheme that paid a lump sum to the community, which could then assign jobs to those registered for unemployment benefits and pay them a weekly wage from the fund.

Jigalong today. A softball game between teachers and pupils outside the school yard.

Capital expenditure on Jigalong was symptomatic of state and federal governments focusing on the less intractable challenge of alleviating material deprivation, at the expense of concern with social upheavals that, in the long term, may be far more threatening to the survival of Aboriginal culture. The issues of greatest concern to the Mardu of Jigalong were not the result of imposed change; rather, they arose from more subtle and indirect influences on social control and conformity, both within their community and in their dealings with other communities.

Conflicts and disruptions were bound to increase in the new milieu of the settlement, with large numbers of previously scattered groups now living in close quarters on a permanent basis. The transition to a cash economy in the late 1960s led to alterations in spending patterns and the rise of vehicle ownership by the Jigalong Mardu, with important consequences for mobility and for access to liquor. The arrival at Jigalong of drunken Mardu, sometimes carrying liquor, began a new and traumatic phase in the community's short history. Alcohol or similar drugs were unknown traditionally and so no strategies existed for dealing effectively with inebriated individuals. The use of alcohol among Aborigines is one of the consequences of their colonized status, as an alienated and socioeconomically deprived minority, for whom boredom and despair are commonplace. Social problems stemming directly from alcohol use remain the single greatest challenge confronting

Aboriginal Australia as a whole. At Jigalong, proven and Lawful conflict-management techniques were not transferred in this instance, out of a conviction that inebriated people are not fully responsible for their actions. The Council has never allowed the sale of alcohol there, and rules against taking it into the settlement were promulgated—but enforced only intermittently and with mixed results. Because the liquor has to be bought at outlets 100–150 miles away, drinking is a periodic activity at Jigalong, but its effects have been severe. A large number of deaths, of women as well as men, have occurred as a result of alcohol-related violence, motor vehicle accidents, and illness. The community has tried many different strategies, none successful, to deal with this most serious of their problems.

Threats of intervention by outside authorities, especially the police, have been another very worrying problem for the Mardu. The establishment of nationwide Aboriginal Legal Services in the 1970s significantly mitigated most adults' terror of the police, once they discovered that they were not godlike enforcers with limitless power (Eggleston 1977). The Mardu had always resented the missionaries calling in the police after offenders against the Law had been speared and clubbed in the traditional manner, since they regarded such action as unwarranted encroachment into the Mardu domain. Furthermore, the police have been inconsistent, sometimes arresting the Lawful punishers and sometimes the true offenders in Aboriginal terms. Some ambivalence about such outside intervention has arisen. At times when problems have been severe, the council has called in the police but the Mardu have always sensed the risk of surrendering some of their precious autonomy. Dislike of police intervention undoubtedly led to a lessening of traditional physical punishment, with a consequent relaxing of social control. Recalcitrant offenders became much less willing to accept the judgments of the community as to their guilt.[7] The clash between two different systems of law was manifested in the mission era when attempts by initiated men to claim their promised teenage wives under the Law were foiled by the missionaries, who strongly encouraged the girls to resist and threatened the suitors with police arrest if they attempted to abduct girls who were under the legal age of consent from the dormitory.

For Mardu men, this resistance was part of a growing autonomy from attempted male domination among women of all ages and has since led to younger women calling themselves by the English term, "free agents." The betrothal system was seriously eroded by the refusal of many young women to marry older men to whom they had been promised. This gave rise to a new phenomenon, the unmarried mother (cf. Burbank 1988:118–20). Such women receive a child-support allowance from the government, which enables them to be economically self-sufficient and independent, a condition that they value highly. Some young mothers have remained defiantly single and successfully resist strong community pressures to end this status, which in the traditional society existed only during brief periods of widowhood. The uncontrolled sexual activities of these young women (and young

---

[7]See Williams (1987), whose study of conflict and its management in an Arnhem Land society reveals many strong parallels with the Jigalong situation.

men) have been blamed for what people say is a greater number of conflicts in the community. Furthermore, some young women use the "free choice" of marriage partners in white society as an argument against betrothal. An earlier (and for men, less troubling) trend was for many old women to remain widows. They, too, receive a Social Security benefit and are happy to live with other widows and unmarried women in "single camps," free of the demands that marriage would impose upon them. Nonetheless, they remain firmly embedded in the kinship system, retain close ties of interdependence with their married and unmarried children, and remain staunch upholders of the Law in opposing the unbridled sexuality of teenagers. A third facet of female resistance has been the marked decline in polygynous unions in the drastically altered economy of the settlement, where the new young, strong co-wife who would contribute much labor to the household was now more singularly a competitor for the husband's attention and favors. Older first wives have frequently asserted themselves by driving out the new arrival after subjecting both her and the husband to verbal and physical abuse and refusing to be placated. This has made many men reluctant to claim their betrothed ones if they are already married, but the practice persists and sometimes the older wife is the one who leaves. Ever since the frontier station milieu began to alter Mardu male-female relationships, men have been gradually losing their traditional control over women (as well as young members of both sexes). This has generated anxiety among older Mardu men about what they see as a decline in the strength of the Law.

The young have been exposed at an accelerating rate to a whole panoply of erosive influences, including a white-oriented education system, television (Jigalong got its own satellite dish, along with telephone service, in 1988), drinking, gambling, comics, Western music, and so on. Their awareness of the role of "free choice" based on romantic love among whites has led some to question the relevance of traditional marriage rules, and to enter affairs and relationships that are wrong in traditional terms; that is, those which are either "irregular" (a "MB"-"ZD" *nyagaji* union) or "incestuous" (between categories of kin forbidden to marry under the Law). Despite fierce community resentment, abuse, and physical sanctions, some young couples have remained together. Older Mardu have always insisted that such arrangements would be brief and transitory preambles to a "settling down" with Lawful spouses, and that has often been the case; however, the incidence of long-term wrong marriages has increased, thus threatening the integrity of the kinship and section systems and social harmony.

The age of marriage for males has decreased as the period of initiation following subincision becomes increasingly truncated. This change was initially a response to competing demands from pastoralists for the labor of young men, but since the 1970s its cause is the competition for time and energy posed by community affairs and other diversions, such as gambling with cards, sometimes for large sums of money. Despite this, the young men have continued to demonstrate commitment to the religious life and the Law, and no wholesale rebellion has occurred among Mardu youth. These commitments have long been shared with strong interests in Western trappings such as motor cars, "country" and "disco" music and clothing styles, and heavy drinking and associated "macho" behavior.

Jigalong today. A group of youths.

For some of the young adult Mardu, and a number of middle-aged couples as well, another element that has competed for their allegiance is Christianity.[8] Ideas implanted while they lived in dormitories during the mission era persisted and, in the 1970s, some of these men and women, encouraged by Christian staff members and linguists, as well as by periodic visits by members of the Pilbara Aboriginal Church (headquartered on the coast), began to profess beliefs in Christianity. In a more tolerant atmosphere, consonant with Aboriginal self-management, Mardu were no longer required to renounce the Law in order to accept Christianity and so coexistence of the two bodies of dogma and behavior became possible. Mardu interest in Christianity was also bolstered in the early 1980s by the rapid, nation-wide spread of an Aboriginal Christian evangelical movement, which appealed to young people through its strongly country-and-western musical elements and to many Mardu because of the "Aboriginality" of its leadership and behaviors. The strong opposition of the evangelical Christians to alcohol seems to have great appeal to many Mardu, beset with seemingly intractable problems centering on liquor, who see in Christianity the power to save them from themselves. Here, their submission to a power that is external, higher, and greater than secular power parallels their submission to the spiritual imperative embodied in the Law—a Law

---

[8]For a commentary on an earlier ethnography centered on relations between the Mardu and fundamentalist Christian missionaries at Jigalong, plus an account of Christian influences in the community since the mission era, see Tonkinson (1988a).

which, however, offers no strategies for coping with non-traditional social problems. There is power in Christian fellowship, in demonstrating a united front against drinking, and in the enjoyment of the singing and Christian prayer meetings, but to date, theology seems notably absent as a basis for embracing the alien faith.

Apart from considerations of motivation and commitment, the time available for the concerted pursuit of traditional religious activities has been steadily eroded by wage labor and an enormously increased impingement of outsiders and externally derived priorities on the community. Large numbers of official visitors keep arriving, frequently necessitating time-consuming council or public meetings. Since the Mardu regard most such assemblies as irrelevant, many people resent having to attend them, a resistance summed up in the comment of one young man, "I don't believe in meetings." Community employment projects, which officially require twenty hours of labor per week from the otherwise unemployed, have had little success. These attempts at job creation are characterized by long periods of inactivity interspersed with short bursts of vigor and determination on the part largely of white staff concerned by the failure of even basic activities such as rubbish collection to occur. These projects, like Council meetings or station activities related to cattle raising, may also clash with major cultural concerns, such as attendance at funerals or "big meetings." The latter require long absences from Jigalong if staged elsewhere and involve the mobilization of most of the community's human resources no matter where they are held.

These many and competing demands on people's attentions have made it well nigh impossible for the Mardu to keep the two worlds apart and thus insulate the essence of the Law from alien influences. The barrier between the two domains has been steadily crumbling and, with it, the treasured illusion of an internal autonomy, which had kept intact a sense of the integrity of the Law, no matter what was going on in the other domain. It would, however, be wrong to think that the Mardu have been exclusively concerned with the threat posed by "Whitefella business." For decades, a major preoccupation has been with difficulties in political relations with some of their northern neighbors. A rift occurred in the late 1940s after Aboriginal station workers, a mixed group of desert and coastal people, took successful strike action for better wages.[9] Some abandoned pastoral work and later embarked on cooperative mining ventures, under the leadership of a white man whose vision was to unite all the Aborigines of the region into a single political group. To this end, the northerners repeatedly but for a long time unsuccessfully attempted to recruit people from Jigalong. The Mardu elders were strongly opposed to moves by certain more acculturated mixed-descent Aborigines among the northerners to modernize the Law in such ways as hospitalizing novices for the circumcision operation and allowing freer choice of marriage partners.

A large group of northerners and their white patron set up headquarters on Strelley Station, a property near Port Hedland (Map 1). Their strongly anti-government, anti-mission stance made them very critical of the Mardu at Jigalong for allowing themselves to be first, "under the missionaries," then "under the

---

[9]For an account of the genesis and growth of the Pilbara Aboriginal social movement, see Wilson (1980). The northerners are also here referred to as "the Strelley mob," named after their station headquarters; this label is still commonly used by the Mardu.

government." In the late 1960s, they managed to persuade most of the Manyjily-jarra at Jigalong to join them, thus achieving what twenty-five years of missionary endeavor had failed to do: the division of a once solidary community at its weakest point. Repeated attempts to get the remaining Manyjilyjarra and the rest of the community to abandon Jigalong failed; after 1973, much was happening at Jigalong and councilors and others began to feel more confident that they were taking control of community affairs and were not pawns of any government. In 1982, following an unsuccessful attempt to wrest control of the Jigalong community from its council, the Strelley mob's pressure on Jigalong lessened. The northerners began to experi-ence their own internal difficulties, which resulted in the same kind of dispersal into small, separate communities that has occurred with the Jigalong Mardu. One of the first such breakaway groups consisted of most of the ex-Jigalong Manyjilyjarra, who took over a desert outstation (later renamed Punmu) that had been established some years earlier by the Strelley mob as a "punishment camp" for lawbreakers and heavy drinkers. In 1983, after conflicts over resource allocation, they severed their political and economic ties with the Strelley mob. The breakaways soon realigned themselves with Jigalong through the Western Desert Land Council, an umbrella organization of desert communities that was established in 1984. The motives for this development bring us into the very recent past, a momentous phase in Jiga-long's history.[10]

MINING AND OUTSTATIONS: REGIONALISM AND FRAGMENTATION

When it came to power in 1972, the Federal Labor Government promised to address the question of Aboriginal land rights in belated recognition of the fact that the entire continent had been taken from the original owners without treaty or compensation. Vast tracts of land had long been leased cheaply by white pastoral-ists, and multinational mining companies were taking massive profits, with little or no financial benefit accruing to the Aboriginal traditional owners of the land concerned. The federal government set the tone by passing legislation for the only area in which it has jurisdiction over land. The *Aboriginal Land Rights (Northern Territory) Act 1976* was the first and strongest legislation to be enacted. Since then, several states have passed acts relating to Aboriginal land and compensation claims.[11]

In Western Australia, the establishment of an Aboriginal Lands Trust in 1972 resulted in the transfer of many millions of acres of reserve lands to nominal Aboriginal control. In the case of Jigalong, this provision covered the settlement and surrounding reserve area (a total of about a million acres), but not the traditional homelands which the Mardu had always thought of as inalienably theirs. Mardu

[10]Lawrence (1989) gives an account of political developments among the Mardu in the 1980s, and some of the detail and chronology of events in the following section draw on his material.

[11]For detailed information relating to Aboriginal land rights, see for example Maddock (1980, 1983a); Peterson and Langton (1983); and Neate (1989). By the mid-1980s, the impetus toward land rights had faltered in the face of concerted opposition from the mining industry, and the federal government abandoned its proposal to introduce national land rights legislation aimed at forcing recalcitrant states such as Western Australia and Queensland into line (Neate 1989:6).

who had been born there continued periodically to revisit their treasured haunts in dream-spirit form. During some of these visits, men would enter increase sites to bring forth the species from within (Tonkinson 1970). Emotional attachments to the desert remained strong. People would be moved to tears at the mention of a familiar waterhole or site in story or song and would regale the younger settlement-born generation with stories of food in abundance in the old days. Until the 1970s, apart from an occasional party of white adventurers following the Canning Stock Route, their homelands remained virtually undisturbed.

In 1976, hearing that the state government was considering gazetting the Durba Hills area (Map 3) for a nature reserve, the Jigalong Mardu managed to have the decision deferred by proposing the designation of a huge area of their homelands as an Aboriginal reserve to be vested in the community. A survey was done and recommendations in favor of this proposal were made, but nothing eventuated. In 1977, however, the Rudall River National Park (Map 4) was gazetted over a huge area of the Mardu homelands, without consultation with the Aboriginal traditional owners. The existence of the park was not discovered by the Mardu until 1984, during the course of a major state-government inquiry into land rights.[12]

For the Mardu, one positive aspect of this inquiry was the decision taken by desert Aboriginal groups to present a united front in pressing their claims to land by forming a regional land council in 1984. (Only the Strelley mob refused to participate.) Another impetus toward the creation of the Western Desert Land Council was the threat now posed to Mardu homelands by mineral exploration and associated desecration of sites of religious significance. The discovery that drilling was taking place in the Rudall River area, only 150 miles from Jigalong, prompted the establishment of Jigalong's first major outstation, at Parnngurr rockhole.[13] By this time, the breakaway group of Manyjilyjarra had two outstations to the north, at Punmu and Gunawarriji (Well 33 on the Canning Stock Route; see Map 2). Through the Land Council, Jigalong and the outstations began their battle to keep the miners at bay and have remained totally opposed to exploration and mining in their homelands, especially after the discovery of huge uranium deposits in a locality they had traditionally treated as dangerous and illness-inducing. Although much of the Rudall River region was the homeland of a single language-named unit, the Warnman (Map 2), its reliable water sources included

[12]The inquiry resulted in strong recommendations favoring Aboriginal land rights, which angered powerful mining interests whose exploration leases blanketed much of the state. They mounted an expensive media campaign, notable for its scare-mongering, racism, and bias, which contributed to a reduction in support for Aboriginal land rights in Western Australia (cf. Libby 1989). Even after being greatly watered down, legislation stemming from the inquiry was rejected by the State Parliament in 1985. Having had their expectations of receiving land rights raised in the course of the inquiry, Aboriginal communities throughout the state were depressed and angered by the negative outcome.

[13]In northern Australia, what became known as the "outstation movement" had begun in the 1960s. One motivation was an intensification of prospecting activities and associated desecration and alienation of Aboriginal homelands. Other motivations included improved access to funds and transport and an earnest desire to escape from the pressures of life in large white-controlled settlements. These led to a return to ancestral lands by small groups which resumed hunting, gathering, and custodial activities aided by vehicles, guns, and other Western paraphernalia. The movement has been a distancing from, but not a rejection of, the wider society. Integral to its success has been the continuing provision of needed services and material goods from the established centers (cf. Coombs, Dexter, and Hiatt 1980).

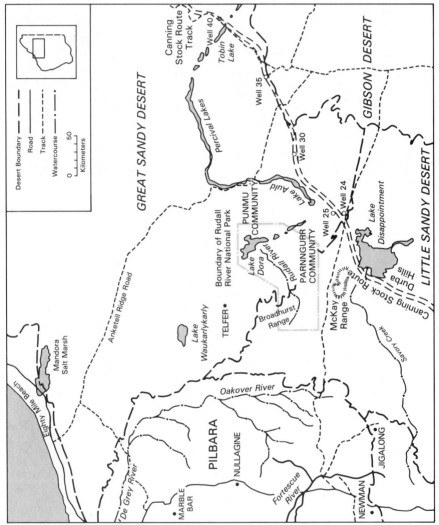

Map 4: Mardu outstations and the Rudall River National Park.

Parnngurr outstation. Mardu outside their camp.

several big meeting venues and it had served as a conduit for many Mardu who used the area during their drift toward the frontier to the west. In the view of the Warnman people, many other groups therefore have strong rights to speak for this area, and so they opted for collective representation via the Land Council. The strong support of the Mardu for a regional body, wider than a single community, is clearly in line with traditional cultural values favoring the widest possible definition of "society."

The fact that both Punmu and Parnngurr outstations lie within the boundaries of the National Park adds a state government bureaucracy, the Western Australian Department of Conservation and Land Management (CALM), to the already volatile mix of mining and Aboriginal interests. Each of these groups has its own agenda and priorities, and great differences in outlook separate them. It was hoped that a major social impact study carried out in 1989 would resolve many of these difficulties. At the time of writing, the state government has not acted on the recommendations of the report, but the Premier has vetoed uranium mining in the Rudall River area.

In the late 1980s, these outstations have received much more funding and have grown in size and permanency, though they still lack the range of services available at Jigalong, and poor roads hamper ground movement (but also discourage unwanted tourists). Several more outstations have been established by Jigalong Mardu, for the same mix of reasons—to protect valued homeland areas against miners; to achieve a measure of financial and other independence from the parent settlement, whose large size (over 500 people prior to the beginning of the outstation movement) and growing social problems had eroded its earlier solidarity; to remove young people further from pernicious influences, in particular, alcohol; and to teach a settlement-born generation the totemic geography of their ancestral homelands in an attempt to revive traditional skills and strengthen the Law. With examples of the growing independence of the large outstations in mind, more groups have been talking of a return to the desert to set up their own communities. Only time will tell if current outstation initiatives will result in seemingly permanent and successful settlements on the scale of Punmu and Parnngurr.

Jigalong in 1990 is at a momentous stage in its history, and its future as the major Mardu center is now in doubt as two contrary movements deplete its population. On the one hand, the outstation movement is producing increasingly independent communities (Parnngurr is now a legally incorporated community, with its own council, funded separately from Jigalong) which could in the future look to the Land Council, based in the town of Port Hedland, to act as their administrative and servicing base. On the other hand, a movement westward into white towns has accelerated in recent years, much to the alarm of the rest of Mardu society. In the 1970s, a few Jigalong people moved to the small town of Nullagine (Map 1) and took up permanent residence there, in a "drinkers' camp" with ready access to alcohol, and a couple of families later secured housing. More recently, a fringe camp close to the town of Newman has been attracting increasing numbers of Jigalong Mardu, whose demands for basic facilities and housing have created considerable controversy. For somewhat different reasons, neither the Shire Council nor the Jigalong Council wants them there, and both bodies have opposed the provision of facilities that will make the fringe camp into a legal, more permanent entity. Newspaper articles have suggested that the Shire's desire to exclude Aborigines from settling in Newman stems from concerns such as public Aboriginal drunkenness and violence in the town. The Shire has taken stringent measures against Aboriginal use of public facilities, including the fencing of open spaces and the removal of faucets from public water taps, thus discouraging Aborigines from congregrating in the town center and inconveniencing the many Jigalong Mardu who go there to shop. The Mardu at Jigalong and the desert outstations regard the notion of a permanent Newman community as anathema, an abandonment of the Law in the pursuit of alcohol, with its inevitable consequences of violence, surrender of autonomy to police and welfare authorities (the removal of children from their mothers has already occurred at Newman), and personal degradation under the eyes of an increasingly resentful, discomfited, and hostile white population. Some of the Newman squatters are Aborigines from other areas, and there is much coming and going, but the majority of the nearly one hundred Mardu now at Newman are from Jigalong. Many are young men and women, bored with life at Jigalong and less likely in the town camp to be punished for un-Lawful behavior, especially in regard to choice of sexual partners. On a national radio program in May 1990, several articulate Mardu women from Newman forcefully supported their bid for government housing in the town and their right to exercise free choice of place of residence. Following an inquiry, agencies of the state government have recommended the establishment of an Aboriginal "village" at a site some miles from the town itself.

CONCLUSION

The Mardu have lost their battle to keep the white world at bay, though for many older people "Whitefella business" remains less important than the need to keep the Law strong. The outstation movement can be seen as a continuing affirmation of the values encoded in tradition, whereas migration to towns represents, for the majority of Mardu who are bitterly opposed to it, a final, fatal renunciation of the Law.

Situated in the middle is Jigalong itself, and its problems exemplify the reasons behind both movements. High turnover rates among both white and local Aboriginal staff have robbed the community of the opportunity to create and carry through various projects aimed at improving the community's financial viability and physical conditions. Huge discrepancies between government policy and practice have helped keep "self-management" an illusory goal; today, over twenty different governmental agencies, each generally not knowing what the others are planning or doing at Jigalong, or even what their predecessors in the same agency have done, impinge on the community, often repeating the same mistakes. No community employment schemes have succeeded, and the place has a neglected and run-down appearance. Many of the public buildings have been poorly designed and constructed and inadequately maintained. The council has lacked the community support and the will to address continuing problems of many kinds. It has been frightened to push too hard, for example, in disciplining young people or punishing those who carry liquor, because it does not want to risk the young rebeling against the Law or drinkers deciding to move to towns, away from the Law and with constant access to alcohol. Following the inception of television in 1988, an already poor school attendance has plummeted, since children, who remain a law unto themselves, watch it until very late at night. Television has undoubtedly increased Mardu knowledge of the rest of the world and its problems, and the community is able to show locally produced videos and many other Aboriginal programs.[14] Yet their exposure to commercial advertisements highlights Jigalong's material deprivations in a wider society seemingly full of material riches and excitement. Such is the attraction of television to Mardu of all ages that sometimes the council has to shut off power to the community in order that public meetings and Law business can take place at night.

The fact that ritual activities still occur is an indication that some of the integrity and strength of traditions remains, but they are held much less frequently than during the mission era. They must compete with the greatly expanding domain of "Whitefella business," a range of social problems, trips to town, plus gambling and television and many other things, for the attention of the Mardu. The high level of communication and cooperation that the religious life demanded of the Mardu who migrated to Jigalong provided the essential backbone for the rise of community solidarity and a new sense of community-based identity. The power of a shared Law

---

[14]Likewise, the advent of videos and solar-powered radio transceivers has brought the outstations into greatly improved and enlarged contact with similar communities elsewhere in the desert as well as to larger settlements and towns. Since public telephones were installed at Jigalong, they have been very heavily used, especially by younger people, to communicate with relatives and friends in many places.

Jigalong today. Television watchers in their camp.

was strong enough to paper over the cracks caused by unease and suspicion (especially between the dominant Gardujarra and Manyjilyjarra groups) that were the inevitable residues of disparate geographic origins and local identities. The weakening of the all-important collective religious life at the settlement has led to the opening and widening of the cracks that had always existed and, as a result, the "Jigalong mob" is fragmenting into smaller groupings. Some of these reflect "traditional" alignments, as in the case of small groups seeking to establish their own outstations, but others derive from exogenous influences, as in the case of the Newman town camp community, united by drinking and a reluctance to live "under the council" or "under the Law" at Jigalong or the outstations.

The segment of Mardu society most affected by the large void created by unemployment and a lessening of the traditional religious life is the young (particularly the males), whose boredom has led to a variety of problems, from vandalism, break-ins, and theft, to illegal use of motor vehicles, drinking, Law-breaking in sexual matters, and migration to Newman where there is more action and excitement and less community censure. Having the young retain their loyalty to kin and to key Law activities and values remains paramount to older Mardu men and women, who are willing to put up with a lot from the young as long as there is a chance that they will eventually assume the heavy responsibility for upholding Mardu traditions. Other increasingly differentiated segments of Mardu society already discussed include young unmarried mothers and old widows, the major language-named groups, those on outstations versus those at Jigalong, and perhaps the small number of Christians.

Certainly, Christianity is a force that is poised ready to fill some of the void at Jigalong and provide answers for the many uncertainties now confronting the Mardu there. The notion now held by some Mardu that adherence to both the Law and to Christianity is tenable provides evidence of a merging of the two major domains— and two contrasting sources of power—around which this concluding discussion has been framed. The rapidly accelerating pace of social transformation since the 1970s has made it impossible to keep the two domains apart, and the fusion of formerly separated Mardu and "Whitefella" business demands new solutions. Elsewhere, I have suggested that:

> The challenge now is to fuse the two domains in such a way that . . . [traditional] strategies and organizations for the marshalling of resources and channelling of power can be applied to the realm of "Whitefella-become-Aboriginal" business. Certain major rituals require considerable planning, resource-management, personnel-scheduling, and coordination of various activities. If the same Law which produces these considerable skills can be extended to embrace also the requirements and activities of non-Aboriginal origin, a very productive fusion could result. Perhaps here also a large conceptual leap is required: one in which the ultimate origins of power become less important than the modes of employing it, be they derived from the Law or whites or newly invented in response to pressing needs. (Tonkinson 1988b:408–409).

However, basic economic problems remain. The desert and its periphery offer very little in the way of a resource base from which the Mardu and other Western Desert groups can develop their productive potential. Northwestern Australia is extremely rich in minerals and much development has occurred in the Pilbara region. Yet, as Rowley (1972:10) notes, such large-scale developments ". . . will pass by the Aborigines on the spot, using their services more sparsely, and with even more limited sharing of the product than has been the case with the pastoral enterprise." The huge iron ore operation at Newman created many jobs, but little effort has been made to employ or train Aboriginal labor.

Even for the Mardu now living on outstations, their retreat from alien pressures (at one level) and their advance to confront an avaricious and intrusive mining industry, at another, are in the long term no more than holding actions. For them, survival in the nation-state becomes a matter of strengthening their regional organizations, resisting the inroads of mining interests, and keeping themselves distanced from certain social problems that impede their proper maintenance of an ordered and orderly social life. It is also a matter of asserting greater local control over important institutions, such as the school. Both Parnngurr and Punmu have their own community schools (controlled by Mardu committees) which function as information and learning centers for the entire community. The curriculum is tailored to Mardu cultural concerns, such as language learning, as well as "the three Rs" of the conventional white school. The desire of most Mardu to retain core aspects of the Law certainly remains strong, but the totality of their encapsulation within Australian society and the sheer relentlessness of Westernizing pressures continue to operate as insidious and potent erosive forces from which effective escape is now impossible. Also important to their long-term survival as Mardu is the willingness of the dominant white society not only to accept, but actively to promote, pride in ethnic diversity and true cultural pluralism. In the less liberal atmosphere of the 1980s, support for Aboriginal causes declined as deteriorating economic conditions led the Australian majority to perceive a threat to its prosperity. Whatever the reason, there has been a hardening of attitudes against the continuance of special measures aimed at ameliorating the socioeconomic situation of Aborigines. The Mardu remain largely unaware of these changes in the wider society, which take place far away from them. What many of the Mardu do know is that money is scarce and that obtaining funding for community development is a slow and often unsuccessful battle. Nevertheless, they continue to evolve new adaptive strategies as they attempt to cope with the many problems now besetting them. In this struggle their basic creativity and resilience will be strong assets. It is certainly too early to pronounce their battle for cultural survival lost, but time and an enormous imbalance of power between desert people and the dominant society may well tip the scale against them.

References Cited

Allen, J., J. Golson and R. Jones (eds.),
   1977, *Sunda and Sahul: Prehistoric Studies in Southeast Asia, Melanesia and Australia.*
   New York: Academic Press.

Allen, J. J.,
   1989, "When Did Humans First Colonise Australia?" *Search* 20: 149–154.

Altman, J. C.,
   1987, *Hunter-Gatherers Today: An Aboriginal Economy in North Australia.* Canberra:
   Australian Institute of Aboriginal Studies.

Anderson, Christopher,
   1988, "Anthropology and Australian Aboriginal Economy, 1961–1986." In *Social Anthropology and Australian Aboriginal Studies* (ed. R. M. Berndt and R. Tonkinson)
   Canberra: Aboriginal Studies Press, pp. 125–188.

Barker, Graham,
   1976, "The Ritual Estate and Aboriginal Polity." *Mankind* 10(4): 225–239.

Bern, J.,
   1979, "Ideology and Domination: Toward a Reconstruction of Australian Aboriginal
   Social Formation." *Oceania* 50: 118–132.
   1988, "Structures of Inequality and the Meaning of Surplus: A Conundrum in the Anthropology of Australian Aborigines." *Anthropological Forum* 4(4): 559–573.

Bern, J., and J. Larbalestier
   1985, "Rival Constructions of Traditional Aboriginal Ownership in the Limmen Bight
   Land Claim." *Oceania* 56(1): 56–76.

Berndt, R. M.,
   1952, *Djanggawul.* London: Routledge.
   1959, "The Concept of 'The Tribe' in the Western Desert of Australia." *Oceania* 30(2):
   81–107.
   1965, "Law and Order in Aboriginal Australia. In *Aboriginal Man in Australia* (R. M. and
   C. H. Berndt, eds.) Sydney: Angus and Robertson, pp. 167–206.
   1970, "Traditional Morality as Expressed Through the Medium of an Australian Aboriginal Religion." In *Australian Aboriginal Anthropology* (ed. R. Berndt). Perth: University of Western Australia Press, pp. 216–247.
   1974, "Australian Aboriginal Religion," Four fascicles, in one volume. Institute of
   Religious Iconography, State University of Groningen. Leiden: Brill.

Berndt, R. M. and C. H. Berndt,
   1945, "A Preliminary Account of Field Work in the Ooldea Region, Western South
   Australia." *Oceania Bound Offprint.* Sydney.

1970, *Man, Land and Myth in North Australia: The Gunwinggu People*. Sydney: Ure Smith.

1988, *The World of the First Australians*. Rev. ed. Canberra: Aboriginal Studies Press.

Berndt, R. M. and R. Tonkinson, eds.,

1988, *Social Anthropology and Australian Aboriginal Studies: A Contemporary Overview*. Canberra: Aboriginal Studies Press.

Birdsell, J. H.,

1967, "Preliminary Data on the Trihybrid Origin of the Australian Aborigines." *Archaeology and Physical Anthropology in Oceania* 2: 100–155.

1970, "Local Group Composition Among the Australian Aborigines: A Critique of the Evidence from Fieldwork Conducted Since 1930." *Current Anthropology* 11(2): 115–131.

1977, "The Recalibration of a Paradigm for the First Peopling of Greater Australia." In *Sunda and Sahul* (ed. J. Allen, J. Golson, and R. Jones). New York: Academic Press, pp. 113–167.

Bowdler, Sandra,

1977, "The Coastal Colonisation of Australia." In *Sunda and Sahul* (ed. J. Allen, J. Golson, and R. Jones). New York: Academic Press, pp. 205–246.

1981, "Hunters in the Highlands: Aboriginal Adaptations in the Eastern Australian Uplands." *Archaeology in Oceania* 16: 99–111.

Bowdler, Sandra, and Sue O'Connor, in press

"The Dating of the Australian Small Stone Tool Tradition, with New Evidence from the Kimberley, W.A." *Archaeology in Oceania*.

Bowler, J. M.,

1987, "Water and Sand: Climate in Ancient Australia." In *Australians to 1788* (ed. D. J. Mulvaney and J. P. White). Sydney: Fairfax, Syme and Weldon Associates, pp. 25–45.

Burbank, Victoria,

1988, *Aboriginal Adolescence: Maidenhood in an Australian Community*. New Brunswick: Rutgers University Press.

Burridge, K. 0. L.,

1969a, *New Heaven, New Earth*. Oxford: Blackwell.

1969b, *Tangu Traditions*. Oxford: Clarendon.

1973, *Encountering Aborigines; A Case Study: Anthropology and the Australian Aboriginal*. New York: Pergamon.

Cane, Scott,

1984, "Desert Camps: A Case Study of Stone Artefacts and Aboriginal Behaviour in the Western Desert." Unpublished Ph.D dissertation, Australian National University.

Cane, Scott,

1989, "Australian Aboriginal Seed Grinding and Its Archaeological Record: A Case Study from the Western Desert." In *Foraging and Farming: The Evolution of Plant Exploitation* (ed. D. R. Harris and G. C. Hillman). London: Unwin and Hyman, pp. 99–119.

Carnegie, David,

1973, *Spinifex and Sand*. London: Penguin. (Colonial Facsimile of the 1898 ed.)

Charlesworth, Max,
1984, "Introduction." In *Religion in Aboriginal Australia: An Anthology* (ed. Max Charlesworth, Howard Morphy, Diane Bell and Kenneth Maddock). St. Lucia: Queensland University Press, pp. 1–20.

Chase, A. K.,
1984, "Belonging to Country: Territory, Identity and Environment in Cape York Peninsula, Northern Australia." In *Aboriginal Landowners* (ed. L. R. Hiatt) Oceania Monograph 27, pp. 104-122.

Coombs, H. C., B. G. Dexter, and L. R. Hiatt,
1980, "The Outstation Movement in Aboriginal Australia." *Australian Institute of Aboriginal Studies Newsletter* 14: 16–23.

Cowlishaw, Gillian,
1978, "Infanticide in Aboriginal Australia." *Oceania* 48(4): 262–283.

Dixon, R. M. W.,
1972, *The Dyirbal Language of North Queensland*. London: Cambridge University Press.
1976, "Tribes, Languages and Other Boundaries in Northeast Queensland." In *Tribes and Boundaries in Australia* (ed. N. Peterson) Canberra: Australian Institute of Aboriginal Studies, pp. 207–238.
1980, *The Languages of Australia*. Cambridge: Cambridge University Press.

Douglas, W. H.,
1988, *An Introductory Dictionary of the Western Desert Language*. Perth: Institute of Applied Language Studies, Western Australian College of Advanced Education.

Durkheim, E.,
1915, *The Elementary Forms of the Religious Life*. London: G. Allen.

Eggleston, E.,
1975, *Fear, Favour or Affection. Aborigines and the Criminal Law in Victoria, South Australia and Western Australia*. Canberra: Australian National University Press.

Elkin, A. P.,
1954, *The Australian Aborigines: How to Understand Them*. Sydney: Angus and Robertson.
1963, Personal Communication, in "Discussion: Religious and Artistic Life." In *Australian Aboriginal Studies* (ed. H. Sheils). Oxford: Oxford University Press, pp. 252–253.
1977, *Aboriginal Men of High Degree*. Brisbane: University of Queensland Press.

Elphinstone, J. J.,
1971, "The Health of Australian Aborigines with no Previous Association with Europeans." *Medical Journal of Australia* 2: 293–301.

Endicott, K. L.,
1981, "The Conditions of Egalitarian Male-Female Relationships in Foraging Societies." *Canberra Anthropology* 4: 1–10.

Flood, Josephine,
1989, *Archaeology of the Dreamtime*. 2nd ed. Sydney: Collins.

Forrest, John,
1875, *Explorations in Australia*. London: Low, Marston, Low and Searle.

Geertz, C.,
   1966, "Religion as a Cultural System." In *Anthropological Approaches to the Study of Religion* (ed. M. Banton). London: Tavistock, pp. 1–46.

Giles, Ernest,
   1889, *Australia Twice Traversed.* 2 vols. London: Low, Marston, Searle and Rivington.

Glass, A., and D. Hackett,
   1970, "Pitjantjatjara Grammar: A Tagmemic View of the Ngaayatjara (Warburton Ranges) Dialect." *Australian Aboriginal Studies,* 34. Canberra: Australian Institute of Aboriginal Studies.

Goodale, Jane C.,
   1971, *Tiwi Wives. A Study of the Women of Melville Island, North Australia.* Seattle: University of Washington Press.
   1982, "Production and Reproduction of Key Resources Among the Tiwi of North Australia." In *Resource Managers: North American and Australian Hunter-Gatherers* (ed. N. M. Williams and E. S. Hunn). Boulder: Westview Press, pp. 197–210.

Gould, R. A.,
   1968, "Living Archaeology: The Ngatatjara of Western Australia." *Southwestern Journal of Anthropology* 24(2): 101–122.
   1969a, *Yiwara: Foragers of the Australian Desert.* New York: Scribner's.
   1969b, "Subsistence Behavior Among the Western Desert Aborigines of Australia." *Oceania* 39(4): 253–274.
   1971, "The Archaeologist as Ethnographer: A Case from the Western Desert of Australia." *World Archaeology* 3(2): 143–177.
   1977, "Puntutjarpa Rockshelter and the Australian Desert Culture." *Anthropological Papers of the American Museum of Natural History* 54(1): 1–189.
   1978, "The Anthropology of Human Residues." *American Anthropologist* 80: 815–835.
   1980, *Living Archaeology.* Cambridge: Cambridge University Press.
   1982, "To Have and Have Not: The Ecology of Sharing Among Hunter-Gatherers." In *Resource Managers: North American and Australian Hunter-Gatherers* (ed. N. M. Williams and E. S. Hunn). Boulder: Westview Press, pp. 69–91.

Hallam, S. J.,
   1987, "Changing Landscapes and Societies: 15000 to 6000 Years Ago." In *Australians to 1788* (ed. D. J. Mulvaney and J. P. White). Sydney: Fairfax, Syme and Weldon Associates, pp. 47–73.

Hamilton, Annette,
   1980, "Dual Social Systems: Technology, Labour and Women's Secret Rites in the Eastern Western Desert of Australia." *Oceania* 51(1): 4–19.
   1981, *Nature and Nurture: Aboriginal Child-Rearing in North-Central Arnhem Land.* Canberra: Australian Institute of Aboriginal Studies Press.
   1982, "The Unity of Hunting-Gathering Societies: Reflections on Economic Forms and Resource Management." In *Resource Managers: North American and Australian Hunter-Gatherers,* (ed. N. M. Williams and E. S. Hunn). Boulder: Westview Press, pp. 229–247.

Hansen, K. C., and L. E. Hansen,
   1969, "Pintupi Phonology." *Oceanic Linguistics* 8(2): 153–170.

Hercus, L., and P. Clarke,
   1986, "Nine Simpson Desert Wells." *Archaeology in Oceania* 21: 51–62.

Hiatt, L. R.,

1962, "Local Organization Among the Australian Aborigines." *Oceania* 32(4): 267–286.

1966, "The Lost Horde." *Oceania* 37(2): 81–92.

1975, "Swallowing and Regurgitation in Australian Myth and Rite." In *Australian Aboriginal Mythology* (ed. L. R. Hiatt). Canberra: Australian Institute of Aboriginal Studies, pp. 143–162.

1984, "Traditional Land Tenure and Contemporary Land Claims." In *Aboriginal Landowners* (ed. L. R. Hiatt). Oceania Monograph 27, pp. 11–23.

1986, *Aboriginal Political Life*. Canberra: Australian Institute of Aboriginal Studies.

Hiscock, P., and P. M. Veth, in press.

"A Re-analysis of the Adzes from Puntutjarpa Rockshelter and the Australian Stone Tool Tradition." *World Archaeology*.

Horton, D. R.,

1981, "Water and Woodland: The Peopling of Australia." *Australian Institute of Aboriginal Studies Newsletter* 16: 21–27.

Hunn, Eugene S., and Nancy M. Williams,

1982, "Introduction." In *Resource Managers: North American and Australian Hunter-Gatherers* (ed. N. M. Williams and E. S. Hunn). Boulder: Westview Press, pp. 1–16.

Jones, Rhys,

1969, "Fire-Stick Farming." *Australian Natural History* 16: 224–228.

1973, "The Emerging Picture of Pleistocene Australians." *Nature* 246: 278–281.

1977, "Man as an Element of a Continental Fauna: The Case of the Sundering of the Bassian Bridge." In *Sunda and Sahul* (ed. J. Allen, J. Golson, and R. Jones). New York: Academic Press, pp. 317–386.

Jones, Trevor A.,

1965, "Australian Aboriginal Music: The Elkin Collection's Contribution Toward an Overall Picture." In *Aboriginal Man in Australia* (ed. R. M. and C. H. Berndt). Sydney: Angus and Robertson, pp. 285–374.

Keen, Ian,

1978, "One Ceremony, One Song: An Economy of Religious Knowledge Among the Yolngu of Northeast Arnhem Land." Unpublished dissertation, Australian National University.

1988, "Twenty-Five Years of Aboriginal Kinship Studies." In *Social Anthropology and Australian Aboriginal Studies* (ed. R. M. Berndt and R. Tonkinson). Canberra: Aboriginal Studies Press, pp. 79–123.

Keats, Bronya,

1977, "Genetic Structure of the Indigenous Populations in Australia and New Guinea." *Journal of Human Evolution* 6:319–339.

Kendon, Adam,

1988, *Sign Languages of Aboriginal Australia: Cultural, Semiotic and Communicative Perspectives*. Cambridge: Cambridge University Press.

Kimber, R. G.,

1983, "Black Lightning: Aborigines and Fire in Central Australia and the Western Desert." *Archaeology in Oceania* 18: 38–45.

Kirk, R. L.,
   1983, *Aboriginal Man Adapting*. Oxford: Oxford University Press.

Kolig, Erich,
   1978, "Aboriginal Dogmatics: Canines in Theory, Myth and Dogma." *Bijdragen tot de Taal–, Land– en Volkenkunde* 134: 84–115.

Latz, P. K.,
   1982, "Bushfires and Bushtucker: Aborigines and Plants in Central Australia." Unpublished M.A. thesis, University of New England.

Lawrence, Peter,
   1964, *Road Belong Cargo*. Manchester: Manchester University Press.

Lawrence, Robert,
   1989, "The Political Context of the Struggle for Land-Based Security in the Karlamilyi (Rudall River) Region." In *The Significance of the Karlamilyi Region to the Martujarra of the Western Desert*, (ed. Guy Wright). Perth: Department of Conservation and Land Management, pp. 1–40.

Lee, R. B.,
   1979, *The !Kung San: Men, Women and Work in a Foraging Society*. Cambridge: Cambridge University Press.

Lewis, Henry T.,
   1982, "Fire Technology and Resource Management in Aboriginal North America and Australia." In *Resource Managers: North American and Australian Hunter-Gatherers* (ed. N. M. Williams and E. S. Hunn). Boulder: Westview Press, pp. 45–67.
   1989, "Ecological and Technological Knowledge of Fire: Aborigines Versus Park Rangers in Northern Australia." *American Anthropologist* 91: 940–961.

Lévi-Strauss, C.,
   1962, *The Savage Mind*. London: Weidenfeld and Nicholson.

Libby, Ronald T.,
   1989, *Hawke's Law: The Politics of Mining and Aboriginal Land Rights in Australia*. Perth: University of Western Australia Press.

Lourandos, Harry,
   1985, "Intensification and Australian Prehistory." In *Prehistoric Hunters and Gatherers: The Emergence of Social and Cultural Complexity* (ed. T. Price and J. Brown). New York: Academic Press, pp. 385–423.
   1987, "Swamp Managers of Southwestern Victoria." In *Australia to 1788* (ed. D. J. Mulvaney and J. P. White). Sydney: Fairfax, Weldon and Syme Associates, pp. 293–307.

McBryde, I.,
   1987, "Goods from Another Country: Exchange Networks and the People of The Lake Eyre Basin." In *Australia to 1788* (ed. D. J. Mulvaney and J. P. White). Sydney: Fairfax, Weldon and Syme Associates, pp. 253–273.

Maddock, Kenneth,
   1969, "The Jabuduruwa." Unpublished doctoral dissertation, University of Sydney.
   1980, *Anthropology, Law and the Definition of Australian Aboriginal Rights to Land*. Njimegen: The Catholic University.
   1982, *The Australian Aborigines: A Portrait of Their Society*. 2nd ed. Melbourne: Penguin.

1983a, *Your Land is Our Land*. Melbourne: Penguin.

1983b, "'Owners,' 'Managers' and the Choice of Statutory Traditional Owners by Anthropologists and Lawyers." In *Aborigines, Land and Land Rights* (ed. N. Peterson and M. Langton). Canberra: Australian Institute of Aboriginal Studies Press, pp. 211–225.

Marsh, J.,

1969, "Mantjiltjara Phonology." *Oceanic Linguistics* 8(2): 131–151.

1984, *Preliminary Dictionary of Martu Wangka*, 2 vols. Punmu: Punmu Community School Board.

Meehan, Betty,

1977, "Man Does Not Live by Calories Alone: The Role of Shell-fish in a Coastal Cuisine." In *Sunda and Sahul* (ed. J. Allen, J. Golson and R. Jones). New York: Academic Press, pp. 493–531.

1982, *Shell Bed to Shell Midden*. Canberra: Australian Institute of Aboriginal Studies.

Meggitt, M. J.,

1962, *Desert People*. Sydney: Angus and Robertson.

1966, "Gadjari among the Walbiri Aborigines of Central Australia." *Oceania Monographs*, 14. Sydney.

Merlan, Francesca,

1988, "Gender in Aboriginal Social Life: A Review." In *Social Anthropology and Australian Aboriginal Studies* (ed. R. M. Berndt and R. Tonkinson). Canberra: Aboriginal Studies Press, pp. 15–76.

Montagu, Ashley,

1974, *Coming into Being among the Australian Aborigines*. Revised ed. Boston: Routledge.

Morphy, Howard

1988, "The Resurrection of the Hydra: Twenty-five Years of Research on Aboriginal Religion." In *Social Anthropology and Australian Aboriginal Studies* (ed. R. M. Berndt and R. Tonkinson). Canberra: Aboriginal Studies Press, pp. 241–266.

Mountford, Charles P.

1981, *Aboriginal Conception Beliefs*. Melbourne: Hyland House.

Mountford, C. P., and R. Tonkinson,

1969, "Carved and Engraved Human Figures from North Western Australia." *Anthropological Forum* 2(3): 371–390.

Mulvaney, D. J.,

1975, *The Prehistory of Australia*. Revised ed. Baltimore: Penguin.

1976, "The Chain of Connection." In *Tribes and Boundaries in Australia* (ed. N. Peterson). Canberra: Australian Institute of Aboriginal Studies, pp. 72–94.

1987, "The End of the Beginning: 6000 Years Ago to 1788." In *Australians to 1788* (ed. D. J. Mulvaney and J. P. White). Sydney: Fairfax, Syme and Weldon Associates, pp. 75–112.

1989, *Encounters in Place: Outsiders and Aboriginal Australians 1606-1985*. St Lucia: University of Queensland Press.

Mulvaney, D.J. and J. Peter White, eds.,

1987, *Australians to 1788*. Sydney: Fairfax, Syme and Weldon Associates.

Munn, Nancy, D.,
   1970, "The Transformation of Subjects into Objects in Walbiri and Pitjantjatjara Myth." In
   Australian Aboriginal Anthropology (ed. R. M. Berndt). Perth: University of
   Western Australia Press, pp. 141–156.
   1973, *Walbiri Iconography. Graphic Representation and Cultural Symbolism in a Central
   Australian Society*. Ithaca, N.Y.: Cornell University Press.

Myers, F. R.,
   1976, "To Have and to Hold: A Study of Persistence and Change in Pintupi Social Life."
   Unpublished doctoral dissertation, Bryn Mawr University.
   1982, Ideology and Experience: The Cultural Basis of Politics in Pintupi Life." In
   Aboriginal Power in Australian Society (ed. M. C. Howard) St Lucia: University of
   Queensland Press, pp. 79–114.
   1986, *Pintupi Country, Pintupi Self*. Washington, D.C.: Smithsonian Institution Press.

Neate, Graeme,
   1989, *Aboriginal Lands Rights Law in the Northern Territory*. Vol 1. Sydney: Alternative
   Publishing Cooperative.

O'Connell, J. R.,
   1976, "Report of Investigations of Alyawara Land Claims." Department of Prehistory,
   Research School of Pacific Studies, Australian National University, Canberra.
   (Mimeo., 27 pp.)

Parsons, P. A. and N. G. White,
   1973, "Genetic Differentiation Among Australian Aborigines With Special Reference to
   Dermatoglyphics and other Anthropometric Traits." In *The Human Biology of
   Aborigines in Cape York* (ed. R. L. Kirk). Canberra: Australian Institute of Aboriginal Studies, pp. 81–94.

Peterson, Nicolas,
   1972, "Totemism Yesterday: Sentiment and Local Organisation Among the Australian
   Aborigines." *Man* 7(1): 12-32.
   1975, "Hunter-Gatherer Territoriality: The Perspective From Australia." *American Anthropologist* 77: 53–68.
   1976a, "Introduction." In *Tribes and Boundaries in Australia* (ed. N. Peterson). Canberra:
   Australian Institute of Aboriginal Studies, pp. 1–11.
   1976b, "The Natural and Cultural Areas of Aboriginal Australia: A Preliminary Analysis
   of Population Groupings with Adaptive Significance." In *Tribes and Boundaries in
   Australia* (ed. N. Peterson). Canberra: Australian Institute of Aboriginal Studies,
   pp. 50–71.
   1977, "Aboriginal Uses of Australian Solanaceae." In *The Biology and Taxonomy of the
   Solanaceae* (ed. J. G. Hawkes, R. N. Lester, A. D. Skelding). New York: Academic Press, pp. 171–189.
   1986, (In collaboration with Jeremy Long). "Australian Territorial Organization." *Oceania
   Monograph* 30.

Peterson, Nicolas and Marcia Langton, eds.,
   1983, *Aborigines, Land and Land Rights*. Canberra: Australian Institute of Aboriginal
   Studies.

Roheim, G.,
   1945, *The Eternal Ones of the Dream*. New York: International Universities Press.

Rowley, C. D.,
1972, *The Remote Aborigines*. London: Pelican.

Rumsey, Alan,
1989, "Language Groups in Australian Aboriginal Land Claims." *Anthropological Forum* 6(1): 69–79.

Sackett, Lee,
1975, "Exogamy or Endogamy: Kinship and Marriage at Wiluna, Western Australia." *Anthropological Forum* 4(1): 44–55.
1976, "Indirect Exchange in a Symmetrical System: Marriage Alliance in the Western Desert of Australia." *Ethnology* 15(2): 135–149.

Sahlins, M.,
1972, *Stone Age Economics*. Chicago: Aldine Atherton.

Service, E. R.,
1960, "Sociocentric Relationship Terms and the Australian Class System." In *Essays in the Science of Culture in Honor of Leslie A. White* (ed. G. E. Dole and R. L. Carneiro). New York: Cornell, pp. 416–436.

Shapiro, W.,
1979, *Social Organization in Aboriginal Australia*. New York: St Martin's Press.

Simmons, R. T.,
1976, "The Biological Origin of Australian Aborigines." In *The Origin of the Australians* (ed. R. L. Kirk and A. G. Thorne). Canberra: Australian Institute of Aboriginal Studies, pp. 307–328.

Smith, M. A.,
1986, "The Antiquity of Seedgrinding in Arid Australia." *Archaeology in Oceania* 21: 29–39.
1988, "The Pattern and Timing of Prehistoric Settlement in Central Australia." Unpublished Ph.D dissertation, University of New England.

Spencer, B., and F. J. Gillen,
1899, *The Native Tribes of Central Australia*. London: Macmillan.

Stanner, W. E. H.,
1958, "The Dreaming." In *Reader in Comparative Religion* (ed. W. A. Lessa and E. Z. Vogt) New York: Harper & Row, pp. 513–525. [*Reprinted in* White Man Got No Dreaming; Essays 1938–1973, *by W. E. H. Stanner. 1979. Canberra: Australian National University Press.*]
1965a, "Religion, Totemism and Symbolism." In *Aboriginal Man in Australia* (ed. R. M. and C. H. Berndt) Sydney: Angus and Robertson, pp. 207–237. [*Reprinted in* White Man Got No Dreaming; Essays 1938–1973, *by W. E. H. Stanner. 1979. Canberra: Australian National University Press.*]
1965b, "Aboriginal Territorial Organization: Estate, Range, Domain and Regime." *Oceania* 36(1): 1–26.
1966, "On Aboriginal Religion." *Oceania Monographs,* 11. Sydney. [*Reprinted 1989 as* Oceania Monograph 36, *with an Appreciation and Introduction.*]

Strehlow, T. G. H.,
1947, *Aranda Traditions*. Melbourne: Melbourne University Press.
1965, "Culture, Social Structure and Environment in Aboriginal Central Australia." In

Aboriginal Man in Australia (ed. R. M. and C. H. Berndt). Sydney: Angus and Robertson, pp. 121-145.

Sutton, Peter,
1978, "Wik: Aboriginal Society, Territory and Language at Cape Keerweer, Cape York Peninsula." Unpublished Ph.D dissertation, University of Queensland.

Sutton, Peter and Bruce Rigsby,
1982, "People with "Politicks": Management of Land and Personnel on Australia's Cape York Peninsula." In *Resource Managers: North American and Australian Hunter-Gatherers* (ed. N. M. Williams and E. S. Hunn). Boulder: Westview Press, pp. 155–171.

Thorne, Alan and Robert Raymond,
1989, *Man on the Rim: The Peopling of the Pacific*. Sydney: Angus and Robertson.

Tindale, N. B.,
1974, *Aboriginal Tribes of Australia*. Berkeley: University of California Press.

Tonkinson, Robert,
1970, "Aboriginal Dream-Spirit Beliefs in a Contact Situation: Jigalong, Western Australia." In *Australian Aboriginal Anthropology* (ed. R. M. Berndt). Perth: University of Western Australia Press, pp. 272-291.
1974, *The Jigalong Mob: Aboriginal Victors of the Desert Crusade*. Menlo Park: Cummings.
1977, "Aboriginal Self-Regulation and the New Regime: Jigalong, Western Australia." In *Aborigines and Change: Australia in the '70s* (ed. R. M. Berndt). Canberra: Australian Institute of Aboriginal Studies, pp. 65–73.
1978a, "Aboriginal Community Autonomy: Myth and Reality." In *"Whitefella Business": Aborigines in Australian Politics* (ed. M. C. Howard). Philadelphia: Institute for the Study of Human Issues, pp. 93–103.
1978b, "Semen Versus Spirit-Child in Western Desert Culture." In *Australian Aboriginal Concepts,* (ed. L. R. Hiatt). Canberra: Australian Institute of Aboriginal Studies, pp. 81–92. [*Revised version appears in* Religion in Aboriginal Australia, 1984 (*ed. M. Charlesworth, H. Morphy, D. Bell and K. Maddock). St Lucia: University of Queensland Press, pp. 107–123.*]
1979, "The Desert Experience." In *Aborigines of the West: Their Past and Present* (ed. R. M. Berndt and C. H. Berndt). Perth: University of Western Australia Press, pp. 140–150.
1982, "Outside the Power of the Dreaming: Paternalism and Permissiveness in an Aboriginal Settlement." In *Aboriginal Power in Australian Society* (ed. M. C. Howard). St Lucia: University of Queensland Press, pp. 115–130.
1987, "Mardudjara Kinship." In *Australians to 1788* (ed. D. J. Mulvaney and J. P. White). Sydney: Fairfax, Syme and Weldon Associates, pp. 197-217.
1988a, "Reflections on a Failed Crusade." In *Aboriginal Australians and Christian Missions* (ed. T. Swain and D. B. Rose). Adelaide: Australian Association for the Study of Religions, pp. 60–73.
1988b, "One Community, Two Laws: Aspects of Conflict and Convergence in a Western Desert Aboriginal Settlement." In *Indigenous Law and the State* (ed. B. Morse and G. Woodman). Dordrecht: Foris, pp. 395–411.
1988c, "Egalitarianism and Inequality in a Western Desert Culture." *Anthropological Forum* 5(4): 545–558.

1988d, "'Ideology and Domination' in Aboriginal Australia: A Western Desert Test Case." In *Hunters and Gatherers 2: Property, Power and Ideology* (ed. Tim Ingold, David Riches and James Woodburn). Oxford: Berg, pp. 150–164.

1990, "The Changing Status of Aboriginal Women: 'Free Agents' at Jigalong." In *Going It Alone? Prospects for Aboriginal Autonomy: Essays in Honour of Ronald and Catherine Berndt* (ed. R. Tonkinson and M. C. Howard). Canberra: Aboriginal Studies Press, pp. 125–147.

Tonkinson, R. and M. C. Howard, eds.,

1990, *Going It Alone? Prospects for Aboriginal Autonomy: Essays in Honour of Ronald and Catherine Berndt* Canberra: Aboriginal Studies Press.

Trigger, D. S.,

1981, "Blackfellows, Whitefellows and Head Lice." *Australian Institute of Aboriginal Studies Newsletter* 15:63–72.

1987, "Languages, Linguistic Groups and Status Relations at Doomadgee, an Aboriginal Settlement in Northwest Queensland." *Oceania* 57(3): 217–238.

Turner, D. H.,

1980, *Australian Aboriginal Social Organization*. Atlantic Highlands: Humanities Press.

Veth, P. M.,

1987, "Martujarra Prehistory: Variation in Arid Zone Adaptations." *Australian Archaeology* 25: 102–111.

1989a, "Islands in the Interior: a Model for the Colonization of Australia's Arid Zone." *Archaeology in Oceania* 24: 81–92.

1989b, "The Prehistory of the Sandy Deserts: Spatial and Temporal Variation in Settlement and Subsistence Behaviour Within the Arid Zone of Australia." Unpublished Ph.D dissertation, University of Western Australia.

Veth, Peter and Giles Hamm,

1989, "The Archaeological Significance of the Lower Cooper Creek." Report Prepared for the South Australian Museum.

Veth, P. M. and F. J. Walsh,

1988, "The Concept of 'Staple' Plant foods in the Western Desert of Western Australia." *Australian Aboriginal Studies* 1988/2: 19–25.

von Sturmer, J. R.,

1978, "The Wik Region: Economy, Territoriality and Totemism in Western Cape York Peninsula, North Queensland." Unpublished Ph.D dissertation, University of Queensland.

Walsh, F. J.,

1990, "An Ecological Study of Traditional Aboriginal Use of 'country': Martu in the Great and Little Sandy Deserts, Western Australia." *Proceedings of the Ecological Society of Australia* 16: 23–37.

Warburton, P. E.,

1875, *Journey Across the Western Interior of Australia*. London: Low, Marston, Low and Searle.

Warner, W. L.,

1937, *A Black Civilization: A Study of an Australian Tribe*. New York: Harper and Row.

White, J. Peter and Ronald Lampert,

1987, "Creation and Discovery." In *Australians to 1788* (ed. D. J. Mulvaney and J. P. White). Sydney: Fairfax, Syme and Weldon Associates, pp. 2–23.

White, J. Peter and D. J. Mulvaney,
  1987, "How Many People?" In *Australians to 1788* (ed. D. J. Mulvaney and J. P. White). Sydney: Fairfax, Syme and Weldon Associates, pp. 115–117.

White, J. Peter and J. O'Connell,
  1982, *A Prehistory of Australia, New Guinea and Sahul*. Sydney: Academic Press.

White, N. G.,
  1989, "Cultural Influences on the Biology of Aboriginal People: Examples from Arnhem Land." In *The Growing Scope of Human Biology* (ed. L. H. Schmidt, L. Freedman and N. W. Bruce). Perth: Australian Society for Human Biology, pp. 171–178.

Williams, N. M.,
  1986, *The Yolngu and Their Land*. Stanford: Stanford University Press.
  1987, *Two Laws: Managing Disputes in a Contemporary Aboriginal Community*. Canberra: Australian Institute of Aboriginal Studies.
  1988, "Studies in Australian Aboriginal Law 1961–1986." In *Social Anthropology and Australian Aboriginal Studies* (ed. R. M. Berndt and R. Tonkinson). Canberra: Aboriginal Studies Press, pp. 191–237.

Wilson, John,
  1979, "The Pilbara Aboriginal Social Movement: An Outline of its Background and Significance." In *Aborigines of the West: Their Past and Present* (ed. R. M. Berndt and C. H. Berndt). Perth: University of Western Australia Press, pp. 151–168.

Wolf, Eric R.,
  1982, *Europe and The People Without History*. Berkeley: University of California Press.

Woodburn, James,
  1980, "Hunters and Gatherers Today and Reconstruction of the Past." In *Soviet and Western Anthropology* (ed. E. Gellner). London: Duckworth, pp. 795–815.
  1982, "Egalitarian Societies." *Man* 17: 431–451.

Glossary

Activists-Mourners (*jinjanungu-garnku*): a dual division of considerable importance in certain Mardu activities, particularly male initiation, death, and burial. Mourners, who include all a person's close kin and most members of the first ascending and first descending generation, play a passive role in the proceedings.

Affinal Kin: relatives by marriage; usually contrasted with consanguineal kin, who are relatives by birth, although it is possible for affinal kin to also be consanguines.

Ancestral Totem (*jugurr*): the ancestral Dreaming being(s) from whom a person is "descended" by virtue of having been left behind by them as life-essence which becomes a spirit-child.

Band (also known as the Horde): the land-occupying group, consisting of one or more families, whose male heads are more often than not related patrilineally. Flexible in size and composition, the band is the basic residential and economic unit in Aboriginal society.

Bardunjarri **(Dream-Spirit):** the spirit that assumes a bird-like form and sometimes leaves the body during sleep.

Big Meeting (*jabal*): the large assembly of Aboriginal groups from widely separated areas that takes place once or twice a year; a time of great ritual and social intensification and the high point of the Aboriginal year.

Conception Totem (*jarrin/nyuga*): the plant, animal, or mineral form assumed by a spirit-child (which derives from the life essence left by Dreaming beings) before entering its human mother.

Cosmic Order: the totality of a people's conceived universe, including the physical environment, flora and fauna, human society, spiritual or extrahuman presences, and any other true or conceived realms that are assumed to exist.

Cross-Cousins: the children of a sister and brother are cross-cousins to one another; Parallel Cousins are the children of a woman and her sister and of a man and his brother (among the Mardu, they are classed as siblings).

Dream-Spirit (see *Bardunjarri*)

Dreaming (*manguny/jugurr*): a complex concept of fundamental importance to Aboriginal culture, embracing the creative era long past (when ancestral beings instituted Aboriginal society) as well as the present and the future.

Estate: the heartland of a local group and the locus of its members' attachment to territory; its sites are of considerable mythological and totemic significance to group members, and it includes at least one storehouse of sacred boards.

Featherfeet (*jinagarrbil*): groups of men who wear special moccasins to disguise their footprints while en route to kill somebody; their alleged presence in an area causes desert Aborigines great concern.

Garnku (**Mourners**): (**see Activists-Mourners**)

Increase rite: a ritual that is performed each year at an increase center (*jabiya*) with the intention of causing the spirits of the animal or plant species associated with that spot to emerge and be plentiful.

Jabiya (**see Increase Rites**)

Jijigarrgaly (**see Spirit-Children**)

Jinjanungu (**see Activist-Mourners**)

Law (*Yulubirdi*): the Dreaming legacy of social institutions, norms, and behaviors that provide a blueprint or life design for the Aborigines to follow.

Language-(or Dialect-) named Unit: comprises all those groups whose primary identification is with the territory named for the dialect that most will speak as their first language. The people termed "Mardu" in this study are in fact members of several different but neighboring dialect-named units.

Mabarn: this term refers both to the "diviner-curer" and to the magical objects that are essential to his craft.

Manggalyi: "surgeons;" the two, three, or four men who perform the initiatory operations of circumcision or subincision.

Manguny (**see Dreaming**)

Men's Country: areas that are temporarily or permanently taboo to women and children; the venue of men's secret-sacred ritual and locations of storehouses of sacred objects, or mythologically validated sacred sites.

Merged Alternate Generation Levels: egocentrically defined dual division of considerable ritual importance; an Ego's "own side" is his or her own generation level plus those of grandparents and grandchildren, and "opposite side" comprises members of first ascending and first descending levels (for example, parents, children).

Penis-holding Rite: a rite that identifies men as subincised and therefore eligible to participate in men's secret rituals; also used as a right of entry into other groups' territories and in dispute settlements.

Range: the area over which a band normally hunts and gathers in the course of its yearly travels. It will overlap with the ranges of neighboring bands and normally includes the estate.

Sections: division of a society into four named categories which indicate intermarrying divisions (but do not regulate marriage) and are useful mainly as labeling devices.

Siblings: one's brothers and sisters.

Sociocentric Terms: objectively applied labels usable by all members of a society; contrasts with egocentric terms which are defined only from the viewpoint of the individual, for example, "my group" and "other group."

Spirit-Child: a very small, humanoid being that magically enters a woman and is later born as a human. They are called *jijigarrgaly,* a term which is also used for spirit-beings that act as intermediaries between the spiritual and human realms.

Subincision: the slitting open of the underside of the penis, which exposes the urethra; a ritual operation that is performed some time following circumcision and is an essential stage in Western Desert male initiation.

Thread-Cross: a class of sacred objects, secret to men, consisting of a wooden base (spears or sacred carved wooden boards) and crosspieces on which is threaded twine; must be dismantled after a single use; used in dancing; some are very similar to the "gods-eye" type crosses of the Huichol Indians of Mexico.

Yulubirdi (**see Law**)

Films on Western Desert Aborigines

In 1965 and 1967, two series of films were shot in the Western Desert; they were produced and directed by Ian Dunlop of the Australian Commonwealth Film Unit (now Film Australia) for the Australian Institute of Aboriginal Studies. The films were shot in 35mm black-and-white film, without synchronized sound; each has spoken commentary. They are listed as follows:

PEOPLES OF THE AUSTRALIAN WESTERN DESERT

PARTS 1–10 (1965)

Part	Subtitle	Time minutes
1	Seedcake Making and General Activity in the Camping Area.	21
2	Gum Preparation (Spinifex Resin). Stone-flaking. Djagamara Leaves Badjar.	19
3	Sacred Boards and an Ancestral Site (Restricted).	8
4	A Family Moves Camp and Gathers Food.	48
5	Old Campsites at Tikatika. Mending a Cracked Dish. Medicinal Use of Quandong	11
6	Spearmaking. Boys' Spear Fight.	9
7	Spearthrower Making, including Stone-flaking and Gum (Spinifex Resin) Preparation	34
8	Fire Making	7
9	Spinning Hair-string. Getting Water from a Well. Binding Girl's Hair.	12
10	Cooking Kangaroo.	17

PARTS 11–19 (1967)

Part	Subtitle	Time minutes
11	Water Snake Story and Stone Quarry at Partantja	11
12	At Partantja Clay Pan (Restricted)	55
13	Stone and Gum Working	25
14	Making a Wira	9
15	Mamu	8
16	Headache	5
17	Feather Boots and Manguri	11
18	Quandong Cake	9
19	Kangaroo Cooking at Kunapurul (In color)	19

DESERT PEOPLE

This 51-minute film was made from material contained in Parts 1, 2, 4, and part of 9 above. It depicts a day in the life of two desert families. In editing this film, the actual sequence of filming was ignored; that is, the events as depicted did not necessarily happen in the order presented. A few activities were filmed as they actually occurred; most were initiated at our request—the Aborigines were then left undirected, except for stopping and restarting actions to fit in with film and lens changes, and such. Since the people being filmed were those whose contact with whites prior to that time had been minimal (although they possessed some metal tools), we believe that the activities filmed were carried out much as they would have been in precontact days. (I acted as scientific advisor for the 1965 filming.)

The main film in the 1967 series is Part 12, *At Partantja Clay Pan,* which also provides a general account of daily life. Parts 3 and 12 are not available for general screening because they contain material that is secret-sacred.

There are some important points to keep in mind when viewing these films. Because they lack synchronized sound, they convey no impression of the liveliness and chatter that accompany much of the everyday activity of the desert people. Also, the films focus mainly on one facet of the culture: subsistence activities—and then only a narrow range of the total possible (for example, the complexities of hunting are hardly touched upon). Given the small number of Aborigines involved, it was impossible to portray adequately the functioning of kinship, the organization of activities when a band is involved, or aspects of the ceremonial life. What is thus missing is much that the Aborigines themselves would regard as of primary significance to their culture.

What the films do convey very well, however, is a feeling for the physical environment of the Western Desert and for the routines of daily life among the people. Since this way of life is now gone forever, these films stand as a poignant, even poetic, record of a traditional existence, relatively free of European influences.

Film Availability   Anyone interested in seeing the films described above should contact Film Australia Pty Ltd, Eton Road, Lindfield, NSW 2070, Australia.

Index

Aborigines, Australian
  biological diversity-homogeneity, 5–6, 6n,
    10
  cultural diversity-homogeneity, 6–9
  demography, 2, 3, 3n, 4, 6, 7n
  languages, 7–8, 9n, 66n, 67
  Macassan and Papuan contacts, 4–5
  origins and peopling of Australia, 1–4, 5,
    6
  physical characteristics, 5–6, 14
  See also Western Desert
Activists-Mourners *(Jinjanungu-Garnku)*, 76–
    78, 77n, 87–92, 93, 94–98, 102–105
  See also Ritual
Alcohol, 166, 169, 170, 172, 178, 179
Allen, J. J., 2n
Alliances, 53, 64n, 65, 98, 99, 145, 149
Altman, J. C., 56n
Anderson, C., 56n
Anger, 55, 62, 102, 151, 153
Avoidance Behaviors, 11, 59, 62, 63, 65, 71,
    74, 89, 156

Band, 9, 11, 37, 40, 42, 43, 45, 50, 53, 66,
    67, 68, 69, 70–71, 73, 77, 83, 86, 100,
    102, 119, 135, 139, 144, 150, 153, 156,
    164
Barker, G., 65n
Bern, J., 9n, 25, 65n, 101, 107, 108, 139,
    139n, 140n
Berndt, C. H., 35n, 58n, 65n, 72n, 128, 137
Berndt, R. M., 9n, 23, 24, 35n, 58n, 65n,
    66n, 68n, 72n, 79n, 111, 124, 126, 127,
    128, 136, 137, 139n
Big Meetings *(Jabal)*, 40, 40n, 53, 67, 72,
    75, 104, 107, 118, 119, 127, 134, 137,
    141, 149, 165, 166, 173
Birdsell, J. H., 2n, 5, 65n
Birth, 82
Boundaries
  maintenance, 8, 9, 66, 139, 142, 146, 149,
    160, 166, 180
  permeability, 10, 35, 55, 70, 139, 141,
    142n, 149, 160
  territorial, 35n, 65n, 67
Bowdler, S., 2, 3, 4

Bowler, J. M., 2n
Burbank, V., 170
Burridge, K. O. L., 72, 78, 137, 158

Cane, S., 10, 44, 47n
Carnegie, D., 34
Ceremonies, *see* Rituals
Charlesworth, M., 25
Chase, A. K., 9n, 139
Children, 14, 36, 43, 47, 48, 54, 68, 69,
    103, 138, 151, 163, 165, 166, 168, 178,
    179
  childhood, 82–86, 150
  kinship and, 59, 60, 62, 65, 101, 150
  ritual and, 108, 119, 120, 123, 145, 148
  section membership, 73, 74, 75
  sex, 84, 86, 99
Christianity, 163, 166, 172–173, 180, 181
  See also Missionaries
Clans, 67, 81, 82, 139, 139n
Clarke, P., 10
Compassion, 82, 149, 150
Conflict
  intergroup, 5, 98, 140, 146, 147, 148,
    149, 169
  interpersonal, 64, 100, 132, 148, 150, 152,
    153, 154, 155, 156–157
  management of, 144, 148–149, 153, 154,
    155, 156–157, 165, 169
  post-contact, 162, 163, 169, 170, 170n,
    171, 174
  violence, 83, 99n, 100, 132, 149, 151,
    153, 155, 156, 161, 162, 163, 163n,
    168, 170, 178
  warfare, 147, 158
Conformity, 20, 22, 25, 57, 59–60, 78, 106,
    135, 143–144, 146, 150, 165, 169
Coombs, H. C., 175n
Cowlishaw, G., 82n
Creative (Ancestral, Dreaming) Beings, 19,
    20–25, 36, 57, 79, 90, 92, 97–98,
    104, 106, 113, 117, 120, 121, 126, 132,
    136, 137, 140
  Dingari, 68, 68n, 135
  Garlaya, 95, 109
  Marlu, 22, 87, 88, 89n

Creative (Ancestral, Dreaming) Beings (*continued*)
  Minyiburru, 68, 81, 107, 109
  Ngayunangalgu, 27, 27n, 81, 109, 114–115, 129
  Wadi Gujarra, 81, 93, 94, 110–111, 112, 118
  Wirnba (Garbadi), 125
  See also Dreaming beings; Spirit-beings
Creativity
  ancestral, 36, 57, 106, 109
  human, denial of, 20, 20n, 57, 133, 135, 158

Dance, 35, 60, 89, 90, 92, 93, 94, 95, 107, 111, 120, 121, 123, 126, 131, 137, 138
Death, 9, 11, 79, 79n, 82n, 102–105, 125, 131, 140, 151, 170
  infanticide, 82, 82n, 99
  mortuary rituals, 76, 103–105, 119, 124
  myth concerning, 79, 105
  sorcery and, 77, 130, 133, 147, 165
Dexter, B. G., 175n
Dialect-Named Units, *see* Language-Named Units
Diffusion, Cultural, 3, 7, 8, 35, 40, 110, 134, 135, 142n, 145, 166
Dingo, 3, 15, 22, 24, 45, 45n, 48, 50, 68, 69, 70, 79, 103, 104, 110, 146, 152, 162n
Dispute-Settlement, 92, 132, 145, 147, 148, 156
  See also Conflict
Division of Labor, *see* Sex Roles
Dixon, R. M. W., 8, 66n
Douglas, W. H., 35n, 104n
Dreaming (Dreamtime), 20–25, 20n, 36, 42, 57, 97, 104, 105, 106, 107, 109, 126, 133, 135, 143, 144, 149, 158, 160
  See also Creative Beings; Spirit-Beings; Spiritual Realm
Dreams, 21–22, 22n, 23, 105, 115, 123, 130–131, 135
  See also Spirit-Beings
Dual Organization
  dual kin terms, 61
  dualism, 72, 75, 76, 77, 87, 140n
Dunlop, I., 32, 199
Durkheim, E., 25, 72n
Dynamism, Religious, 133–135, 137, 138

Ecological Conditions, 6–7, 11, 26–30, 34–35, 37, 38, 42, 55–56, 139, 140, 141
Economy, *see* Hunter-Gatherer Adaptation; Western Desert
Egalitarianism (Equality), 9, 9n, 23, 57, 61, 100, 101, 135, 138, 139, 139n, 140, 141, 168
Eggleston, E., 170
Elkin, A. P., 9, 60n, 81, 81n, 128
Elopement, 84, 99, 146, 147

Elphinstone, J. J., 54
Endicott, K. L., 100
Estate, 66, 67–70, 71, 90, 97, 102, 107, 117, 119, 137, 141, 147, 150
Estate Group, 66, 67–70, 70n, 73, 96, 97, 98, 107, 117, 127, 138, 139, 140, 165
Etiquette, *see* Host-Visitor Statuses; Kinship (interpersonal behavior)
Ethnocentrism (parochialism), 66, 133, 139, 140, 140n, 141, 142, 146, 149, 165
Exchange
  affinal, 65, 95
  ceremonial, 4, 8, 75, 86, 93, 107, 125, 134, 141, 144, 145, 148, 156
  gift-, 4, 49, 53, 95, 104, 127, 144, 162
  sister-, 64
  See also Reciprocity
Explorers, 26, 31–34, 161

Family, 50, 53, 71n, 71–72, 86, 95, 97, 98, 99, 101
Fear, 27, 51, 133, 146, 155, 156, 158, 161, 161n
Feasts, Ritual, 46, 88, 94, 96–97, 105, 108, 119, 120, 138, 148
Featherfeet Ritual Killers, 35n, 120, 123, 129, 129n, 131, 132, 146
  See also Revenge Expeditions
Fertility, 83n, 95, 117, 118, 158
  rites, 9, 124
  See also Increase Rites
Feuding, 140, 147
  See also Conflict
Fire
  burns from, 54
  cooking, use in, 9, 45, 48, 53
  for warmth, 43, 50
  -making, 49, 50
  -sticks, 51, 52, 89, 93, 121, 123
  tool-making, use in, 48, 49n
  vegetation management by, 3, 4, 29, 51, 51n
Flexibility
  group size, in, 35, 71, 133
  movement, of, 36, 37, 71
  social-cultural, 16, 35n, 41, 62, 65, 104n, 134, 136, 137, 139n, 141
Flood, J., 1n
Food
  exchange/sharing/gifts, 48, 53, 71, 76, 87, 95, 97, 98, 103, 111, 130, 143, 144, 150, 162
  preparation, 45–47, 49, 96, 99, 100, 105, 108
  rations, 162, 163, 164
  resources, 2, 10, 11, 30–31, 31n, 32, 37, 38, 38n, 39, 40, 41, 43, 47, 47n, 49, 51, 53, 54, 70, 141, 161
  storage, 9, 12, 37, 50
  See also Gathering; Hunting; Taboos
Forrest, J., 33

Gathering, 31, 40, 42–43, 45, 47, 51–52, 53, 81, 86, 98, 99, 108, 162, 175
  See also Hunter-Gatherer Adaptation; Western Desert, Economy
Geertz, C., 143
Giles, E., 33–34
Gillen, F. J., 35, 81n
Glass, A., 35n
Golson, J., 2n
Goodale, J. C., 9n
Gould, R. A., 1n, 10, 40, 43, 45n, 48, 49n, 51n, 65n, 88, 141
Government Policies, 162, 163–164, 165, 166–167, 167n, 168, 169, 174, 177, 178, 179
Grief, 77, 102, 103, 108, 151
Grievances, 145, 152, 153, 155
  See also Dispute-Settlement

Hackett, D., 35n
Hallam, S. J., 2n, 3
Hamilton, A., 9n, 35n, 65n, 71n, 82n, 83n, 118, 143, 144, 150n
Hamm, G., 4
Hansen, K. C., 35n
Hansen, L. E., 35n
Health/Illness, 54–55, 93, 105, 107, 128, 129–130, 132, 151, 170, 176
Hercus, L., 10n
Hiatt, L. R., 9n, 65n, 94n, 101, 139n, 140n, 175n
Hierarchy/Inequality, 9, 23, 118, 139, 163
  age-based, 23, 57, 64, 98, 103, 149–150
  kin-based, 57, 58, 60, 62, 101, 118, 140, 145, 149, 157
  ritual, 138, 140–141, 146, 151
  sex-based, 23, 57, 86, 100, 100n, 101, 107–108, 139n, 140, 141, 158, 162, 162n, 170
  See also Egalitarianism
Hiscock, P., 10n
Horton, D. R., 2
Host-Visitor Relationships/Statuses, 73, 90, 92, 137, 141, 144–145, 148, 165
Howard, M. C., 167n
Hunn, E. S., 51
Hunter-Gatherer Adaptation, 2, 3, 4, 5, 9, 10, 22, 25, 26, 42–43, 51, 53, 55, 56n, 118, 139
Hunting
  dingoes, use of, in, 24, 45
  game, 14, 27, 28, 30, 31, 38, 41, 44, 45, 46, 47, 110, 118
  kinship obligations, 69, 71, 86, 95, 154
  ritual obligations, 86, 94, 96, 97, 98, 138
  strategies, 12, 14, 29, 37, 40, 42, 45, 55n, 70, 157, 166
  See also Hunter-Gatherer Adaptation; Western Desert, Economy

Ideology
  cultural, 57, 141, 158
  immutability of, 20, 133, 136
  male, 101, 107, 108
Individuality, 20, 22n, 58, 59, 62, 70, 78, 81, 103, 110, 127, 135, 139n, 140, 141, 143, 147, 149, 158
Initiation, male, 9, 24, 64, 76, 77, 86–98, 121, 124, 145, 150, 166, 171
  initiated men, 25, 50, 83, 93, 107, 108, 109, 118, 120, 127, 138, 141, 145, 170
  initiator ("surgeon"), 90, 92, 93, 95, 156
  initiates (novices), 70, 71, 77, 86–98, 119, 121, 123, 138, 141, 145, 145n
  See also Ritual; Rituals
Interdependence, 8, 108, 118, 140, 144, 171

Jealousy, 64, 83, 99, 108, 123, 130, 151, 153, 158
Jigalong, 160, 160n, 161, 162–175, 167n, 172n, 177–180
Joking Relationships/Humor, 60, 62, 63, 76, 121
Jones, R., 2n, 51n
Jones, T. A., 125

Keats, B., 10
Keen, I., 65n, 139, 140n
Kendon, A., 35
Kimber, R. G., 51n
Kinship
  classificatory, 9, 17, 58, 58n, 59, 59n, 65, 75, 101–102, 154
  consanguineal, 58, 58n, 59n, 65, 69, 76, 77
  incorporative nature of, 17, 58, 142, 158, 160
  interpersonal behavior and, 22, 50, 58–60, 62–64, 67, 71, 73, 76, 101, 144, 145, 149, 150, 154–155, 156, 171
  Obligations, 53, 60, 101–102, 118n
  significance of, 19, 56, 57, 57n, 58, 58n, 65, 70, 71, 73, 77, 140, 142, 143, 144, 145, 149, 150, 156, 157, 166
  systems, 35, 59, 60, 60n, 61–62, 64n, 101, 166
  terminology, 57–58, 60, 61
  See also Avoidance Behaviors; Joking Relationships/Humor
Kirk, R. L., 6
Knowledge
  mundane, 25, 30, 31, 34, 36, 37, 45, 55, 60, 110, 124, 134, 137, 149, 179
  origins of, 22, 113, 123, 136, 158
  religious, 37, 90, 101, 108, 110, 111, 119, 123, 125, 127, 134–135, 136, 137, 145, 145n, 150, 164
Kolig, E., 48

Lampert, R., 1, 2n, 19
Lance, K., 162
Land
  attachment/attitudes to, 8, 16, 29, 36, 40–
    42, 66–71, 70n, 102, 110, 139n,
    149, 163, 175
  Council (Western Desert), 174, 175, 176,
    177, 178
  landforms, creation of, 20–21, 25, 109,
    110, 117, 126
  human impact on, 14, 36, 51
  ownership, 66, 67–70, 71, 139, 140, 165,
    174, 175
  See also Boundaries
  religious significance of, 21, 25, 42, 70,
    98, 106, 109, 126, 139
  rights/claims, 140n, 174, 174n, 175
  topography, 26–29, 33, 34, 35
Langton, M., 174n
Language/Dialect-Named Units, 13 (map),
    35n, 66–67, 66n
  Budijarra, 12
  Gardujarra, 12, 60, 64, 66, 90, 148, 165,
    180
  Gurajarra, 12
  Manyjilyjarra, 12, 64, 67, 68, 70, 89, 148,
    161n, 165, 174, 175, 180
  Nyiyabarli, 162, 165
  Warnman, 64, 89, 175, 177
  See also Tribes
Larbalestier, J., 140n
Latz, P. K., 38n, 51, 51n
Law (Yulubirdi), 22, 22n, 23, 24, 25, 57, 89,
    96, 97, 106, 111, 113, 121, 123, 124,
    126, 133, 141, 143, 144, 146, 148, 150,
    151, 154, 157, 158, 163, 164, 165, 166,
    167, 168, 170, 171, 172, 173, 178, 179,
    180, 181
Lawrence, P., 22
Lawrence, R., 174n
Leadership, 9, 69, 101, 108, 119, 121, 129,
    136, 138, 139, 140, 145, 151, 152, 172,
    173
Lee, R. B., 118
Lévi-Strauss, C., 72
Lewis, H. T., 51n
Libby, R. T., 175n
Life Essence/Force, 21, 68, 79, 98, 113, 126
  See also Power
Linguistic Unit, see Language-Named Unit
Local Organization, 62–75, 164–165
  See also Band; Family; Estate Group; Land
Lourandos, H., 4

Mabarn (Diviner-Curer), 27, 97, 105, 116,
    128–132, 128n, 129n, 146, 149
McBryde, I., 4
Maddock, K., 20n, 23, 77, 134, 140n, 145,
    174n

Magic, 21, 27, 35n, 79, 80, 82, 93, 116,
    127, 128–131, 132
  See also Sorcery
Marriage
  arrangement of (betrothal), 64, 98, 134,
    145, 146, 171
  polygyny, 71–72, 99, 163, 171
  practices, 72, 82, 86, 97, 98, 99, 100,
    105, 145, 153, 150, 165, 171
  reciprocity and, 65, 70, 76, 142, 165
  residence and, 69, 71, 107
  rules, 35, 57, 64, 64n, 65, 72, 74, 143,
    171, 173
  wrong/alternate, 65, 161n, 171
Marsh, J., x, 35n
Meehan, B., 7
Meggitt, M. J., 43, 65n, 71n, 73
Merlan, F., 100n
Mining, 160, 173, 174, 174n, 175, 175n,
    177, 181
Missionaries, 163–168, 170, 172n, 173
  See also Christianity
Mobility, Spatial, 3, 7, 12, 16, 37, 40, 41,
    102, 127, 134, 144, 162, 164, 165, 169
Moieties, see Social Categories
Montagu, A., 80
Morality, 23–24, 57, 86, 160
Morphy, F., 140n
Morphy, H., 135, 140n
Mountford, C. P., 27n, 80, 111n
Mulvaney, D. J., 1n, 4, 4n, 5, 7n, 56n
Munn, N. D., 77, 106n
Myers, F. R., 35n, 65n, 68n, 70n, 168
Mythology, 2, 5, 25, 66, 79, 96, 97, 117,
    133, 135
  characters in, 27, 68, 81, 107, 110, 121,
    136
  categorization of myths, 109–110
  religious element, as, 106, 109–111, 125–
    127, 134–137

Neate, G., 140n, 174n
Nose Piercing, 87–88
  See also Initiation, Male
Nurturance, 59, 69, 71, 80, 101, 107, 168

Ochre, 4, 14, 16, 19, 49, 50, 53, 54, 70, 89,
    90, 94, 96, 104, 116, 121, 127, 138
O'Connell, J. R., 1n, 67
O'Connor, S., 3, 3n
Outstations, 174, 175, 175n, 176 (map),
    177–181, 179n

Paraphernalia, Religious, 5, 21, 24, 36, 70,
    83, 89, 93, 95, 104, 106, 119, 151
  boards, sacred, 96–98, 109, 121, 127,
    129, 132, 133, 138, 138n, 148, 156
  stones, sacred, 109, 125, 126, 127, 136,
    137
  thread-crosses, 121, 121n, 123, 127, 134

Parsons, P. A., 5, 6n
Peterson, N., 7n, 54, 65n, 67, 102, 174n
Politics, 9, 9n, 55, 65n, 136, 137, 138–140,
    147, 163, 164, 173, 174, 174n
Polygyny, *see* Marriage
Power, 86, 89, 110, 116, 138–142
    domains of, in contact-situation, 160, 161,
        164, 167–168, 170, 172–173, 174,
        181, 182
    objects/sites, possessing, 79, 89, 96, 97,
        106, 107, 136
    religious/spiritual, 16, 20, 21–25, 36,
        37, 51, 57, 69, 80, 81, 93, 97, 108,
        111, 113, 124, 126–127, 135, 139,
        140, 145, 146, 148, 156, 160, 172,
        173
    See also Life Essence
    secular, 101, 141, 163, 165, 167, 170
    See also Politics

Range, 66, 70, 71, 139n, 146
    See also Local Organization; Estate
Raymond, R., 2n, 6
Reciprocity/Sharing, 20, 22, 23, 25, 53–54,
    98, 111, 113, 144, 158
    See also Exchange
Revenge Expeditions, 51, 105, 132, 146,
    156, 161
    See also Featherfeet Ritual Killers
Rigsby, B., 9n, 139, 139n
Ritual
    diffusion of, 119, 134, 141, 145, 164
    functions of, 21, 23, 25, 51, 70, 106, 111,
        113, 124, 126, 158
    relationship to other religious elements, 24,
        111, 124, 125–126, 136
    role allocation in, 76, 108, 138, 145
    technology, as, 3, 36, 37, 51
    types of, *see* Rituals
    See also Dance; Feasts; Featherfeet; Para-
        phernalia; Status
Rituals
    collective, 113, 118–123
    commemorative, 68n, 69, 120–121
    Dreaming, from the (Mangunyjanu), 123
    dream-spirits, from (Bardunjarrijanu), 119,
        123, 123n, 124, 135
    increase, 37, 117n, 117–118
    individual, 113, 116–117
    initiation, male, 62, 70, 87–98
    love-magic, 131
    mortuary, 103–105
Roheim, G., 128
Rowley, C. D., 181
Rumsey, A., 66

Sackett, L., 64n, 65
Sacred
    realm, *see* Spiritual

(secret)-activities, 66, 69, 88, 89, 93, 96,
    100, 102, 107, 119, 120, 123, 148,
    155, 156
(secret)-areas/sites, 24, 66, 69, 83, 83n,
    124
(secret)-objects, *see* Paraphernalia
Sahlins, M., 3, 42, 43, 55
Sanctions, 24, 101, 107, 108, 121, 150, 163,
    171
Service, E. R., 72n
Sex Roles, 9, 9n, 43–46, 48–50, 53, 57,
    59, 86, 90, 92, 94, 96, 99, 100, 101,
    107–109, 119, 120, 121, 123, 127,
    138–141, 139n, 144, 145, 148,
    148n, 149, 150, 151, 153, 154, 155,
    156, 158, 162, 162n, 164, 167, 170–
    171
    See also Status; Status Distinctions
Sexuality, 59, 62, 64, 65, 68, 76, 82, 84,
    86, 99, 121, 131, 131n, 147, 151, 153,
    158, 170, 171, 178
Shame (Embarrassment), 22, 60, 62, 63, 121,
    150, 154, 155, 156
Shapiro, W., 65n, 70n
Sign Language, 35, 93
Simmons, R. T., 6
Sites
    archeological, 2, 10
    campsites, 50, 146
    religious/sacred, 40, 66, 70, 79, 107, 109,
        117, 126, 137
Smith, M. A., 2n, 10
Social Categories, 9n, 72–78
    Generation Level Groupings, 60, 74–76,
        78, 87, 141
    Moieties, 72, 75, 76, 77, 93
    Sections, 72–76
    Subsections, 35, 72, 73, 77
    See also Activists-Mourners
Social Control, 51, 169, 170
    See also Conformity
Socialization, 24, 59, 71, 83–86, 150, 150n,
    164
Song (Songlines), 25, 35n, 106, 109, 119,
    123, 124–126, 134, 136–137
    See also Ritual
Sorcery, 117n, 128, 131–133, 138n, 146,
    147, 148, 156, 165
    See also Featherfeet, Magic
Spencer, B., 3, 81n
Spirit-Beings
    animal/plant, 73, 117, 118, 129
    dream-spirits, 117, 119, 123–124, 123n,
        129, 130, 135, 141, 175
    evil, 48, 82, 94, 104, 105, 116, 129, 130,
        132, 132n, 146
    intermediaries, 23, 113, 123, 135, 137
    spirit-children, 21, 68, 79–81, 80n, 105,
        113n, 146, 151
    spirit-familiars, 105, 128, 129

Spirit-Beings (*continued*)
  spirit, bodily, 9, 16, 69, 79, 92, 102–105,
    130
Spiritual
  basis for life, 20, 134
  imperatives, 19–20, 22, 25, 106, 143,
    144, 158, 172
  See also Law
  realm, 21, 22, 23, 25, 69, 79, 106, 109,
    111, 113, 116–117, 126, 128, 140,
    158, 160
Stanner, W. E. H., 20, 21, 22, 22n, 23, 24,
    65n, 66, 133, 134, 136, 137n
Status
  individual, 53, 57, 69, 108, 130, 135, 141,
    149, 158
  intergroup, 141, 144
  ritual, of females, 96, 101, 107, 108, 138
  ritual, of males, 95, 96, 98, 101, 107,
    136, 137, 138, 145–146, 151
  See also Egalitarianism; Hierarchy/
    Inequality
Stories, *see* Mythology
Strangers, 24, 48, 58, 73, 78, 80, 104, 105,
    138, 144, 146, 160
Strehlow, T. G. H., 68, 81n, 133, 142n
Subincision, 89n, 95–96, 148, 171
  See also Initiation, Male
Subsistence, *see* Food; Gathering; Hunting
Sutton, P., 9n, 66n, 139, 139n
Symbols
  Dreaming as key symbol, 143
  objects as, 89, 90n, 95, 118, 127, 164
  re-birth, 86, 94, 94n
  symbolic death, 65, 86, 88, 93, 104, 108,
    129

Taboos, 11, 69, 81, 82, 83, 96, 102, 104,
    148n
Thorne, A., 2n, 6
Tindale, N. B., 65n
Tonkinson, M., 108
Tonkinson, R., 9n, 27n, 35n, 60n, 80n,
    100n, 101, 110n, 111n, 118, 120, 123n,
    139n, 140, 160n, 162n, 163n, 164,
    167n, 172n, 175, 181
Tools, 2, 3, 4, 10, 10n, 14, 30, 39, 48–50,
    162
Totemism, 8, 9, 22, 25, 66, 68, 69, 110,
    119, 127, 146, 158
  ancestral, 27, 68, 69, 81, 81n, 110, 118,
    130, 132, 140
  conception, 68n, 79–82, 81n, 110
  personal, 68
  See also Spirit-Beings
  social, 81n, 139, 140

Tooth Evulsion, 87
  See also Initiation, Male
Trade, 3, 4, 5, 6, 53–54, 162n
  See also Exchange, Reciprocity
Tribes, 65n, 66n, 142n
  See also Language-Named Units
Trigger, D. S., 54n, 66n
Turner, D. H., 65n

Values, 4, 8, 23–24, 70, 108, 141, 143,
    144, 150, 157, 163, 164, 166, 177, 179,
    180
  See also Worldview
Veth, P. M., 2n, 4, 10, 10n, 31n, 53, 54
Violence, *see* Conflict
von Sturmer, J. R., 9n, 139, 141

Walsh, F. J., 30, 31n, 35n, 37, 38, 38n, 40,
    41, 51, 51n, 53, 54, 55
Warburton, P. E., 33
Warfare, *see* Conflict
Warner, W. L., 140
Weapons, 27, 48, 49, 85, 89, 104, 110, 120,
    147, 148, 151, 152, 153, 154–155, 156
Western Desert
  climate, 10, 11, 15, 16, 28, 29, 30, 31,
    35, 37, 38, 40, 41, 65, 141
  cultural homogeneity, 11, 35, 35n, 101,
    117, 139, 139n, 143, 146
  demography, 10, 11, 12, 37, 67, 119, 139,
    144, 165, 166, 178
  ecological diversity-homogeneity, 11, 26–
    30, 34–35, 37, 38, 42, 55–56, 139,
    140, 141
  economy, 10, 13, 22, 26, 42–43, 51, 53,
    57, 65, 66, 66n
  economic change, 161–162, 166, 167, 175
  frontier, 49, 160–163, 171, 177
  language, 12, 12n, 35, 35n, 66, 67, 104n
  location, 26
  maps, frontispiece, 13, 113, 176
  migration, settlements, to, 12, 12n, 35n,
    67, 159, 160, 161–163, 179, 180
  seasonality, 11, 28, 34, 37, 40, 41
  vegetation, 28, 34, 51
White, J. P., 1, 1n, 2, 7n, 19, 56n
White, N. G., 5, 6n, 7n, 10
Williams, N. M., 51, 65n, 139, 139n, 170n
Wilson, J., 173n
Wolf, E. R., 57n
Woodburn, J., 101, 139n
Worldview, 1, 19, 20, 25, 106, 110, 138,
    142n, 157, 158
  See also Values